Surviving repression

Manchester University Press

IDENTITIES AND GEOPOLITICS IN THE MIDDLE EAST

After the Arab Uprisings and the ensuing fragmentation of regime–society relations across the Middle East, identities and geopolitics have become increasingly contested, with serious implications for the ordering of political life at domestic, regional and international levels, best seen in conflicts in Syria and Yemen. The Middle East is the most militarised region in the world where geopolitical factors remain the predominant factor in shaping political dynamics. Another common feature of the regional landscape is the continued degeneration of communal relations as societal actors retreat into sub-state identities, whilst difference becomes increasingly violent, spilling out beyond state borders. The power of religion – and trans-state nature of religious views and linkages – thus provides the means for regional actors (such as Saudi Arabia and Iran) to exert influence over a number of groups across the region and beyond. This series provides space for the engagement with these ideas and the broader political, legal and theological factors to create space for an intellectual re-imagining of socio-political life in the Middle East.

Originating from the SEPAD project (www.sepad.org.uk), this series facilitates the re-imagining of political ideas, identities and organisation across the Middle East, moving beyond the exclusionary and binary forms of identity to reveal the contingent factors that shape and order life across the region.

Previously published titles

Houses built on sand: Violence, sectarianism and revolution in the Middle East
Simon Mabon

Transitional justice in process: Plans and politics in Tunisia
Mariam Salehi

Surviving repression

The Egyptian Muslim Brotherhood after the 2013 coup

Lucia Ardovini

MANCHESTER UNIVERSITY PRESS

Copyright © Lucia Ardovini 2022

The right of Lucia Ardovini to be identified as the author of this work has been asserted by them in accordance with the Copyright, Designs and Patents Act 1988.

Published by Manchester University Press
Oxford Road, Manchester M13 9PL

www.manchesteruniversitypress.co.uk

British Library Cataloguing-in-Publication Data
A catalogue record for this book is available from the British Library

ISBN   978 1 5261 4929 9   hardback
ISBN   978 1 5261 9570 8   paperback

First published 2022
Paperback published 2026

The publisher has no responsibility for the persistence or accuracy of URLs for any external or third-party internet websites referred to in this book, and does not guarantee that any content on such websites is, or will remain, accurate or appropriate.

EU authorised representative for GPSR:
Easy Access System Europe – Mustamäe tee 50,
10621 Tallinn, Estonia
gpsr.requests@easproject.com

Typeset
by New Best-set Typesetters Ltd

*For all the strong women in my life.
This book would not have been possible without your continuous
love and support.*

Contents

Acknowledgements	*page* viii
Introduction	1
1 The Freedom and Justice Party in power: Islam is (not) the solution?	19
2 The fall from grace	49
3 The *tanzim*, shattered	69
4 Lessons learnt? Stagnation vs adaptation	96
5 Divided, together	117
Conclusion	140
Glossary	146
Bibliography	148
Index	156

Acknowledgements

This book has been long in the making, and now that it is ready to see the light, I need to take the time to thank the many wonderful individuals who I met throughout the years and to whom I owe my deepest gratitude.

First of all, I am grateful to those whose voices are at the centre of this book, as without them I would not have been able to navigate the many research and logistical challenges of the past few years. I started researching the Brotherhood as a PhD student in 2013, just a month after the coup, and from the very beginning I was struck by how welcoming, open and sincere those belonging to this notoriously secretive organisation are. They made the time to talk to me, a complete stranger, as they were going through a series of incredibly traumatic events, and for that I will always be grateful. Throughout the years I met more current and former Brothers than I can count, and I am thankful to each and every one of them. We had conversations in the corridors of crowded conference halls, over Skype, WhatsApp and Facebook, in offices, restaurants, on public trams in Istanbul and in coffee shops all over London. More than once we were kicked out by staff closing down the premises after we had been talking for hours. Many welcomed me into their own homes and others showed incredible patience with my follow-up questions, text messages and requests to meet over and over again. Each and every one of them let me, an outsider, into a deeply traumatic part of their lives and shared memories that were painful to re-live. To all of you, thank you for letting me into your world. Many of my interlocutors cannot be named for security reasons, but I want to especially thank Mohammed Sudan, Mohammed Affan, Osama al-Sayyad and Amr Darrag.

I want to say a deep, heartfelt thank-you to Erika Biagini, who since 2018 has been the best collaborator, friend and supporter that I could have ever asked for. Thank you for welcoming me into your home, for all the hours spent on Skype, for always pushing me to dig deeper, for the endless conversations, and for all of our projects – those we have completed and those that are still in the making. I am also very grateful to all the other colleagues and friends who supported me throughout the process of researching and writing the book, be it by reading endless drafts, debating key concepts, sitting in cold libraries, providing feedback, or simply being there to remind me that it was all worthwhile. They are, in no particular order, Serena C. Perfumi, Mustafa Menshawy, Simon Mabon, Paola Rivetti, Victor Willi, Khalil al-Anani, Francesco Cavatorta, Nathan Brown, Janine Clark, Anna Hammarstedt, Dylan O'Driscoll, Nina C. Krickel-Choi, and all of my colleagues at the Swedish Institute of International Affairs. I also want to thank the Institute for funding my postdoctoral post and supporting my research project.

I am also grateful to Manchester University Press for its support of this project, to my editor Robert Byron, and to the anonymous reviewers for their constructive feedback.

I want to say the most genuine thank-you to my parents, for supporting me throughout this journey since the day I left home at 18 to pursue my University studies in a country far away from home. This book would have not been possible without their endless love and belief in me. Last, but not least, I need to thank Zane, for helping me navigate through moments of self-doubt, for giving up his home office to allow me to work through the final stages of the book in the midst of the COVID-19 pandemic, and for keeping me sane during the worst of lockdown.

Introduction

> I believe that 2013 is the biggest crisis we have ever had facing us, but if you think that we are done, that is not true. Because the Ikhwan is just a thought, and we will rebuild.[1]

The day of 14 August 2013 might have appeared like any other sunny day in Cairo's summer heat. Instead, it witnessed the worst mass killings in Egyptian modern history, which posed an unofficial end to both the dreams at the heart of the Arab uprisings and to the Muslim Brotherhood's (*al-Ikhwān al-Muslimīn* or 'Brotherhood') short spell in power. Mohammed Morsi's rise to presidency through the ballot box in June 2012 was a deeply symbolic moment not only for the Brotherhood, but also for Islamist movements across the region more widely. It embodied the end of decades of illegality and celebrated the fact that, for the first time since the Brotherhood's creation in 1928, the Islamist project finally seemed to be within reach. Morsi was also Egypt's first freely elected president after 60 years of authoritarianism, and the first president without a military affiliation or background. However, just over one year after his election and six mere weeks after the military coup that paved the way for President Abdel Fattah Al Sisi's seizure of power, nearly 1,000 lives were lost in Raba'a to intentional and systematic state-sponsored brutality.[2]

As the dust settled over the square, the Brotherhood entered one of the harshest periods of repression and persecution in its troubled history and fell into a deep state of stagnation. Proscribed as a terrorist organisation by Egypt's newly installed military regime and its allies in the Gulf, the movement and its members were systematically targeted, as al Sisi showed his willingness to go to any length necessary to suppress the support for the deposed Islamist government.[3] Those who escaped persecution found themselves having to flee the country, being forced from power into exile almost overnight. The deeply traumatic experiences of repression and displacement came with a complex set of challenges and with fundamental questions of identity and belonging, together with the monumental task of rebuilding a fragmented organisation. Over seven years on, there are still so many that are stuck in the grips of the blood spilled in Raba'a. This goes beyond the number of victims, and includes the thousands that have since been imprisoned, killed, tortured, and have had to flee the country or go into hiding. Because of its far-reaching implications, the massacre in Raba'a and the ensuing persecution of the Brotherhood are about much more than just the movement itself. Just like Morsi's election as Egypt's first Islamist president held a great amount of symbolism, so did his brutal toppling at the hands of the armed forces. Being one of the oldest and most influential Islamist organisations across the region, for decades the Brotherhood had been a prime example of the ever-changing relationship between Islam, political activism and state institutions. Its rise to power through the ballot box led many to fear the regional takeover of previously semi-legal religious opposition movements, but its violent removal caused the resurfacing of old questions about the compatibility of Islam and democratic institutions.

Morsi's destitution also marked the beginning of a new phase for the organisation, meaning that its political skills and credibility as an Islamist movement are now under scrutiny. With most of its leadership either in jail or scattered abroad, mostly between Turkey, Qatar, Malaysia and the UK, the Brotherhood now faces the monumental task of having to reunite while in exile. In turn, this new dimension is leading to the resurfacing of previously suppressed questions and debates. Overall, there are two main points of contention dividing the movement in the post-2013 context: the interpretation of what went wrong with the political experience and the lessons that should be learnt from it; and what strategy should be implemented to face the current crisis and move forward. These fundamental questions, combined with the unprecedented brutality of repression, are creating deep schisms within the Brotherhood, as individual responses openly clash with the movement's official narrative, further widening the disconnect between those at the top of the organisation and the rank-and-file members. There are growing tensions between calls for the movement to adapt to its changed circumstances and the refusal to implement internal reforms, indicating that another major issue which needs to be renegotiated is that of the changing relationship between the Brotherhood and its members.

Away from the Egyptian context, members now have the opportunity to reflect upon what it means to be a Brother and to question the structures and collective identity that they have been socialised into. In doing so, many are rethinking the terms of their belonging to the movement as well as the core principles and values upon which the Brotherhood historically rests. As new fragmentations and factions emerge, the challenges posed by growing calls for internal reforms go hand in hand with those of having to adapt the Brotherhood's ideology and strategy to its changed circumstances. This shows that while there is a collective commitment to the Brotherhood's survival, there is a marked difference between those who aspire to just that and those who instead want to see the movement thrive despite the ongoing repression. Yet, despite its status as a repressed and divided group, the Brotherhood remains a significant and symbolic movement. Therefore, the study of its evolution since 2013 sheds light on the changing nature of Islamist politics in the region after the Arab uprisings. More importantly, it also helps us to better understand how individual experiences, perspectives and emotions shape responses to repression and, in turn, the responses of the movements they belong to.

Despite the multiplicity of internal and external challenges that it faces in the aftermath of the coup, the Brotherhood has proven to be highly resilient and there are signs of internal renewal starting to appear. This book traces the movement's restructuring and transformation after 2013 in light of its perceived failure and ongoing repression. It focuses on the Brotherhood and on its members within the dimension of forced exile, identifying the challenges that come with having to rebuild a fragmented organisation abroad. Emphasis is placed on individual members' experiences, perspectives and emotions to better understand how their responses to repression are affecting the movement as a whole. In order to do so, the book unpacks the debates that are driving the Brotherhood's engagement with longstanding questions related to ideology, strategy and identity, and aims to give a platform to the voices of the individual members whose initiatives and experiences are at the core of the movement's ongoing transformation. Drawing on several years of ethnographic fieldwork I show that the main forces driving the movement's restructuring are questions about organisational identity and, even more importantly, the emergence of its members' increased agency and subjectivities, which openly challenge the Brotherhood's hierarchical structures, principles and collective identity.

2013 as the 'moment of change'

The levels of state-sponsored repression currently confronting the Brotherhood are unmatched in its history, but this is not the first time that the organisation has had to reinvent itself to avoid annihilation. Repression at the hands of the regime is not new to the movement, which has a history of what Alison Pargeter defines as 'patience and persecution'.[4] Morsi's violent removal after a short spell in power is therefore symptomatic of the Brotherhood's historically complicated relationship with the modern authoritarian state. Since its inception as a grassroots social movement in 1928, the Brotherhood has been at the centre of an alternating cycle of repression and semi-toleration, but nevertheless has managed to flourish into one of Egypt's most influential opposition groups and civil society actors.[5] Throughout the decades the movement not only continued to operate despite its illegal status, but also successfully filled the vacuum left by the state, thanks to its strong organisational structure and commitment to *da'wa* (preaching) and charitable activities. The popular support and services that the Brotherhood dispensed, to an extent unmatchable by the various regimes it operated under, allowed it to effectively become a 'state within a state' and to develop a strong popular base.[6] Faithful to its origins as a socio-religious movement the Brotherhood was devoted to the gradual institution of an Islamic society, in line with the belief that reforming the individual first is key for then reforming society as a whole. This gradualist approach remained central to the movement, even when it inevitably politicised and grew to become one of the country's most powerful opposition actors. Its famous slogan 'participation not domination' became characteristic during its involvement in the 2011 uprisings and, despite the Brotherhood's contradictory behaviour, its historical nature as an evolutionary rather than revolutionary group is fundamental to understand its political behaviour.[7]

These historical experiences are significant as, throughout eight decades of illegality, the Brotherhood developed a very specific set of tools of resistance that allowed it to keep operating inside Egypt and to not only survive, but indeed thrive, despite several waves of repression. Its members' participation in elections as independents in the 1990s meant that the Brotherhood developed a political identity alongside its grassroots one, while the movement's charitable initiatives made it an irreplaceable civil society actor. While the Brotherhood remained effectively banned, it managed to turn this permanent state of repression into a defining element of its own collective identity and narrative.[8] Repression therefore became 'the glue that binds us [the Brotherhood] together and reflects that we are on the right path'[9] and directly related to *mihna* (ordeal/tribulation) as both a call for patience and a test of the persistence of true believers in the pursuit of justice and truth.[10] *Mihna* therefore contributed to the construction of a collective organisational identity and narrative based on persistence in the face of authoritarianism, and is still a key driver of the call for organisational unity in the aftermath of 2013. These historical tools of resistance meant that, despite existing under illegality for most of its history, the Brotherhood nonetheless succeeded in becoming inherently entrenched in the Egyptian socio-political system.

However, these survival strategies have been drastically impaired in the aftermath of the 2013 coup. This is the case as the Brotherhood suddenly found itself not only uprooted from power, but also in deeply unfamiliar territory. There are four dimensions of the 2013 crackdown that set it apart from the organisation's historical experiences. First, repression has been indiscriminate, not only targeting the Brotherhood leadership but also its ranks and files and supporters.¹¹ It therefore affected members across the organisational and generational spectrums who were unfamiliar with such levels of regime brutality, making the current crisis somewhat 'new' to the movement. Second, the crackdown took place just after the Brotherhood governed Egypt for the first time, a test that exposed the ineptitude and lack of political vision of its leadership.¹² Since then, members have been questioning the scope and viability of the political project, as well as the effectiveness of the old schemes, rules and principles over which the organisation historically rested. From this, the third element that marks novelty is the increased agency of individual members, who are reclaiming the space for internal debates and developing their own strategies to confront repression. Openly challenging official narratives, they are also questioning traditional commandments such as 'listen and obey' and vocally asking for the introduction of new values, focused on enhancing pluralism, representation and dialogue. Last, but not least, is the dimension of forced exile and the ensuing internal fragmentation. The partial disintegration of established lines of command and the Historical Leadership's loss of legitimacy (i.e. those who sit in the Guidance Bureau or Guidance Office, *Maktab al-Irshad*, the highest rank below the General Guide, *murshid*), has weakened the movement's internal structures and hierarchies, leading to competition and fragmentation at both leadership and membership levels. While these processes are still in flux, they nevertheless add important dimensions to the current phase of repression and set the 2013 coup as a watershed moment in the history of the Brotherhood, from which the movement has the potential to emerge considerably changed.

Removed from the Egyptian context from the first time since its creation, the Brotherhood is now unable to rely on its historical resistance techniques, while also facing one of the harshest crackdowns of its history so far. In order to re-group while in exile and develop a coherent strategy vis-à-vis the regime, the movement needs to develop new ways of practising resistance. However, doing this goes beyond addressing ideological and strategic issues, as such a process raises questions about the movement's own identity in the post-2013 context and about the relationship between the Brotherhood and its members. The choice between restructuring itself as purely a social movement, and remaining dormant until domestic conditions radically shift, presents two very different paths ahead. Regardless of the one it chooses, the Brotherhood's future trajectory is bound to have drastic implications not only for the organisation, but also for understandings and practices of political Islam across the region.

The novelty of these circumstances and the subsequent invalidation of the Brotherhood's historical experiences call for a renewed analysis of how the movement and its members react to repression and illegality. This is because the literature on the topic has historically studied groups like the Brotherhood in light of their position vis-à-vis the state. Yet, the movement finds itself in previously unchartered waters. This is also the case for the investigation of the Brotherhood's internal schisms over matters of strategy and ideology, which have been significantly altered by both the creation of the Freedom and Justice Party (FJP) and its premature removal. From this, the Brotherhood's current attempts at restructuring are significant in many ways, as in the aftermath of the 2013 military coup the movement entered a state of ideological and strategic stagnation that it is currently struggling to break out of.

Although not without historical precedence, exceptional levels of repression have led to the emergence of new factions and debates. Fieldwork shows that there are two main points of contention currently dividing the movement, these being: the interpretation of what went wrong with the political experience and the lessons that should be learnt from it; and what strategy should be implemented to face the current crisis and move forward. The investigation of how different factions within the Brotherhood perceive the termination of its political venture is therefore key to understanding what factors are shaping its current restructuring, and the internal obstacles it faces. There are rising tensions between the desire to let processes of self-reflection drive the transformation on the one hand, and the unwillingness to stray from the organisation's traditional ideology and strategy on the other. The difference in approaches put forward by these different factions goes beyond the traditional clashes between the movement (*tanzim*) and the party (*hizb*), and the classical but disputed generational struggle between the 'Conservatives' and the 'Reformists' which used to characterise the Brotherhood prior to 2013. Rather, they highlight the extent to which the Brotherhood is tackling fundamental questions about its future directions, while individual perspectives and experiences increasingly challenge its old structures, principles and organisational identity.

Values change and the need for a new lens

This book tackles these issues by examining the internal and external challenges that the Brotherhood faces in attempting to rebuild in the post-2013 context. The analysis runs from 2013 up to 2019, looking at these crucial years as a new chapter in the history of the movement that is still largely unexplored. A number of conversations with Brotherhood leaders and rank-and-file members reveal that, while the Guidance Office and Supreme Guide remain the organisation's symbolic centres of command, the Brotherhood has had to adapt to its changing circumstances and has transferred executive decision-making to trusted members in exile. The very fact that the Brotherhood's current leadership is now primarily scattered between Istanbul and London also imposes different and context-specific restraints on how its members are able to operate, and the emergence of competing Guidance Offices also makes it considerably harder to track patterns of loyalty and legitimacy. This, in turn, feeds into tensions between growing individual agency and the Brotherhood's organisational structures, which I argue have become one of the defining forces of the post-2013 period. Among obvious ideological and strategic questions, further internal fragmentation and growing discontent towards the movement's hierarchical structure signal the emerging potential for change and internal renewal.

From this, a central argument of the book is that it is necessary to move away from the study of the organisation as a monolithic unit, and rather focus on the individual level. By doing so, it is possible to look beyond the official narrative endorsed by the Historical Leadership and gain a real insight into the internal struggles that the movement faces as it tries to react to the state of stagnation it has fallen into after 2013. This is not an easy task as, due to matters of access, the studies on Islamist movements have often relied on the analysis of the strategies and opinions of elite actors. However, to fully understand what is shaping the behaviour of the Brotherhood after 2013, it is necessary to supplement that approach with a reflection of what interactions are happening across and within it. This is a necessary exercise, especially as several rounds of ethnographic fieldwork reveal that there is a considerable part of the membership demanding and implementing internal renewal.

There is a substantial body of literature that deals with how social movements respond to repression and addresses the struggle between agency and structure, especially the assumption that membership-based organisations will almost inevitably come to be dominated by their leadership.[13] Different approaches rooted in Social Movement Theory have unpacked the implications of such processes at length, identifying co-optation, conservative goal transformation and oligarchy as the most common scenarios.[14] Some have argued that repression silences social movements;[15] others find that it enhances political participation and mobilisation;[16] while another trend focuses on the curvilinear effect of repression and claims that it can lead to alternative forms of expressing political discontent.[17] Yet, these studies do not usually account for the wide variation of responses to repression that emerge within the same movement or political community. While there is an increasing emphasis on the necessity to acknowledge this, most of the existing debates still focus on reactions to repression from the perspective of movements and parties as a whole, therefore failing to account for how individuals respond to the same circumstances. Hence the need to refocus the analysis on the individual level or, as Ali Honari puts it 'repression studies neglect the fact that individuals, even though embedded within similar networks and structural contexts, perceive and interpret repression differently: different options are available to each person, and thus each responds differently to repression. Equally importantly, individuals are strategic actors and have agency, so they can act independently of repression. Thus, the outcome of repression largely depends on how people respond to it.'[18] Overall, as individuals have the capability to act independently despite repression, agency should be taken into account when investigating the effects of repression on a particular social movement.

Indeed, given certain contingencies, the social structures, culture and socialisation techniques of these organisations can be contested and somewhat transformed by its own members.[19] The case of the Brotherhood's current internal conflicts speaks directly to this literature, albeit the organisation does not fit within the conventional understanding of a social movement or organisation. Because of this, both Noha Mellor and Carrie Rosefsky Wickham point out that New Social Movement's theoretical tools, and particularly those focusing on movements' socialisation processes and the creation of collective identities as mechanisms of control, seems to come closer to trace the internal workings of the organisation, but nevertheless still fail to capture it fully.[20] Similarly, other approaches, like the inclusion-moderation thesis and repression-dissent nexus, are also successfully used to analyse certain Brotherhood behaviours, but cannot account for others.[21] Therefore, the movement's hybrid identity, and its lack of linear development over the years, call for the need to move away from attempts to study it as a monolithic entity. Rather, focusing the analysis on the individual level allows for a clearer understanding of the forces at play within the movement's restructuring process.

In order to get a more objective picture of the various forces and dynamics at play after 2013 one needs to shift the analysis to the level of individual members, seen as actors with the agency to develop their own strategies in response to repression. Most importantly, one also needs to account for the role that emotions, individual experiences and trauma play in shaping these individual responses to repression. In line with the affective turn in social and political sciences, this trend is gaining increasing traction and the study of the Brotherhood's current trajectories speak directly to this literature, drawing on insights of how individual perceptions of repression shape tactical changes and political activities.[22] Therefore, echoing emerging scholarship on the Brotherhood, this book focuses the analysis on the level of the individual member to trace processes of internal change within the movement after 2013.[23] It builds on a developing analytical framework based on recent works by Erika Biagini, Mustafa Menshawy, Victor Willi and Khalil al Anani, among others, as well as drawing on seminal works on the Brotherhood pre-2011 by Carrie Rosefsky Wickham and Hazem Kandil.[24] What these contributions have in common is the analysis of the Brotherhood from the perspective of individual experiences, allowing for the study of how internal and external forces are influencing processes of change within the movement in the post-coup era. I believe that such an approach is most suited to capture the debates and dynamics that, at this particular point in time, are at the forefront of internal change within the organisation and that are being driven by the novelty of exile.

Aiming to display this, the research at the core of this book is informed by a long-term qualitative study of the Brotherhood's organisation and ideology, drawing on data gained through several rounds of ethnographic work and over fifty conversations, encounters and semi-structured interviews conducted in Turkey and the UK between 2013 and 2019 with current and former Brotherhood members. The sample of participants cuts across the Brotherhood's organisational and generational spectrums and therefore goes beyond the usual voices that inform several studies on the movement. Interviews were conducted primarily in English and, when a translator was employed, they were suggested by the interviewees themselves to make sure that they felt safe and comfortable. The most recent round of fieldwork also included conversations with Egyptian secular activists in exile, members of the Muslim Sisterhood and religious clerics close to the movement and its leadership. This was done to build the analysis on a comprehensive and inclusive sample of participants, reflecting the various factions at play in the Brotherhood's current restructuring. I also incorporate the analysis of written material and literature produced by the Brotherhood and some of its current and former members. All interviews have been anonymised and pseudonyms are used to avoid regime retaliation.

Throughout the fieldwork I engaged with some of the participants multiple times to investigate whether or not their perceptions had changed over time, which appears to be overwhelmingly the case. This indicates that, while the Brotherhood largely remains in a state of immobility, there are processes of self–reflection and internal renewal that are emerging. Overall, I was struck by how many participants explained just how drastically their worldviews have changed since 2013. The organisational immobility that followed 2013 has given some of these members the chance to reflect upon what it means to be a Brother for the first time in their lives, leading them to question their positions and those of the organisation itself. The sudden direction that their life experience has taken is leading many of them to significantly rethink their values and commitments, and to question their individual identity as opposed to the overarching one imposed by the Brotherhood.

These emerging processes of self-reflection highlight the value of studying the role of the individual within a given movement, as a way to overcome sweeping generalisations and attempt to better understand the internal dynamics driving evolution and transformation. In the case of the Brotherhood, while these processes are somehow still limited they nonetheless reveal that there are instances of internal renewal and reformation happening within the movement. They also indicate that now more than ever, while forcibly outside of the Egyptian context, some of its members are willing to openly challenge the historical hierarchal structure of the organisation. This is a further indication that a new chapter has definitely begun for the movement, which has the potential to drive a significant metamorphosis moving forward. In the summer of 2018, while in Istanbul, one of the Brothers belonging to this 'reformist' – or more accurately, 'adaptive' – trend told me that 'The time of following blindly is no more'.[25] This is noteworthy, especially in the light of the unprecedented struggle for survival that the Brotherhood faces. As of now there are no indications that the higher ranks of the Brotherhood intended to initiate, or even condone, review or reformation processes. However, the book shows that there are emerging challenges against the organisation's rigid internal structure, and that it is fundamental to track and understand these new internal dynamics in order to make sense of the movement's ongoing restructuring. Once again, as this fragmentation process advances, it calls for a new analytical approach from which to study the current trajectory of the Brotherhood not as a monolithic unit, but rather as an organisation composed of increasingly independent individuals.

Arab Springs vs Islamist winters

Understanding how the Brotherhood is attempting to survive its renewed state of repression also contributes to the analysis of Islamism in the region after the Arab uprisings. The Brotherhood was not the only movement to experience a quick politicisation and rise to power following the 2011 popular protests.[26] Decades-old social movements with an impressive popular base and a history of oppositional politics quickly succeeded in the first round of democratic elections that followed the removal of autocrats and dictators, but soon clashed with the harsh challenges of transitional politics. These events drastically altered the status quo and political contexts in which different Islamist movements developed and thrived, consequently demanding new approaches to study how they are reacting to their new circumstances. The scholarship on Islamist movements that emerged after the uprisings highlights the need to take stock of various aspects of Islamist movements' change, ranging from their ideological transformation, political strategies, institutional and organisational renewal and, most importantly, the political arenas these movements now operate within.[27] Overall, there is a growing consensus that Islamist movements should not be studied as solitary actors, but rather as different moving parts of a broader Islamist field that benefits from analyses that go beyond established theoretical categories.[28]

Many saw the Brotherhood's destitution as deeply symbolic, as Morsi's election was widely perceived as the peak of an 'Islamic wave' that was quickly spreading across the region in the wake of the removal of long-standing dictators. This is not because the Brotherhood had any sort of monopoly over Islamist movements in the region, but as one of the oldest and most influential ones, its rise to power through the ballot box carried a great amount of symbolism. Nevertheless, a similar all-encompassing approach also characterised a significant portion of the international reactions to Morsi's violent toppling. The coup saw popular discontent towards the Brotherhood's rule paving the way for the Egyptian armed forces to seize power once again, while many questioned what led to such a premature end of their term in power. From this, advocates of post-Islamism such as Asef Bayat and Olivier Roy look at the Brotherhood's destitution as the expression of a broader existential crisis encapsulating the end of political Islam at large.[29] Others, such as Jocelyn Cesari, note that Islamism has its roots first and foremost in social movements, rather than political parties.[30] Hence, religious notions and civil society networks are much harder to erase than a president. Muqtedar Khan also clarifies that the Brotherhood's inability to unite Egyptian society under a common purpose does not directly imply that political Islam and governance are incompatible or that its perceived failure is also the failure of Islamic values.[31] Therefore, the popular protests that escalated in the coup did not mark the rejection of Islamism or democracy at large, but were simply a refusal of the Brotherhood's rule. Recent works by Alison Pargeter and Barbara Zollner also further support this perspective, noting that there are other Islamist actors that have filled the gap left by the Brotherhood[32] and that the underlying socio-political conditions which gave birth to political Islam are still very much present across the region.[33]

Nevertheless, the rapid rise and fall of several Islamist movements in the aftermath of the Arab uprisings has significantly altered their historical patterns of interaction with the state. In light of this, the book investigates how the Brotherhood is dealing with its perceived failure in relation to both the Egyptian regime and the structures of the organisation themselves, particularly focusing on the relationship between the movement and its members. The academic literature on this topic has so far mostly focused on the conditions that led to its fall, while the ramifications and consequences of July 2013 for the organisation's ideology and composition remain largely unexplored. The book therefore focuses on the latter, but an understanding of what circumstances contributed to Morsi's removal is still a necessary starting point. Works by Ashraf El-Sherif, Carrie Wickham and Khalil al-Anani lead to a consensus that the misunderstanding of the political circumstances the Brotherhood operated in played a central role in its destitution.[34] Alison Pargeter adds that aside from the challenges posed by the Brotherhood's quick politicisation, the movement's 'failings were also a reflection of a deeper internal crisis'.[35]

Overall, what all these different contributions point to is the fact that the Brotherhood's rise to power, in the perceived regional wake of 'reformist' political Islam, came with obvious internal complications, but most of all it was ideologically and historically paradoxical. This is mostly because the Brotherhood had always been an evolutionary rather than revolutionary movement, making this a point of contention that comes up routinely throughout the book. While excellent, most of these analyses stop a few years after the Raba'a massacre, therefore leaving a gap in the observation of how the Brotherhood is fairing in the deeply unfamiliar context it finds itself in. The book addresses these questions, focusing particularly on how individual members see the movement going forward. In doing so, it investigates what the Brotherhood's destitution meant not only for its pre-existing strategic and ideological issues, but, ultimately, for its future trajectory.

Because of this, the research at the core of this book fits within emerging debates calling for a renewed analysis and approach to the study of Islamist actors.[36] What is needed is a fresh analytical approach that looks at the Brotherhood within the new, unfamiliar context it finds itself in, rather than situating its study solely within the established literature on Islamist political participation. Up until 2011, the movement and its behaviour had been investigated in regards to its position vis-à-vis the state. However, such approaches need to be revised in the light of the Brotherhood having to re-unite while in exile, which led to the emergence of challenges the movement does not have historical experience in dealing with. This book contributes to an emerging, but still very limited field, analysing the ways in which the Brotherhood is reacting to a set of external and internal circumstances that depart from its past experiences. It is worth nothing that the movement's removal from power and ensuing persecution come with several far-reaching implications, which are not solely limited to how these groups interact with regimes and with other political actors. Scholars like Jillian Schwelder and Stacey Philbrick Yadav note that a lot has also changed from the perspective of the researcher, as approaching the study of political Islam today is drastically different from what it was before the 2011 uprising.[37] Before the Arab uprisings we, as scholars and researchers, had largely become accustomed to studying these movements focusing on the civil society activities, electoral strategies, and alliances of semi-tolerated Islamist opposition parties.[38] This landscape has now vastly changed, and while a decade ago Islamist groups were mostly constrained by domestic policies and were highly organised, nowadays their functions and circumstances have considerably diversified. In turn, this makes it noticeably harder to analyse the ever-evolving relationship between Islamists and the state, and between a given movement and its members. Therefore, in the aftermath of 2011 this particular scholarship also needs to undergo some transformations. Several Islamist movements have gone from opposition, to power, to repression, to a new identity quest in very short period of time, meaning that the adjustment process is still very much in flux. Hence, there is a lot to learn from examining how these groups are reacting to their experiences. Just as the Brotherhood arguably needs to adapt to its changed circumstances, so does the scholarship that approaches the study of its current restructuring and behaviour.

The organisation of the book

Chapter 1 outlines the early history of the Brotherhood, from its founding by Hassan al Banna in 1928 to the outbreak of the 2011 Arab uprisings. This provides a necessary background to the movement's quick politicisation process that followed Hosni Mubarak's removal, and sets the bases for the analysis of its political behaviour. The chapter offers an account of the Brotherhood's participation in the uprisings and examines the implication for the movement's internal debates, identifying the schisms that emerged over the founding of the FJP and members' grievances that resurfaced. It shows that the Brotherhood was already deeply divided before going into the political experience, as would be reflected in the running of the FJP. The chapter then examines the FJP's time in government, highlighting the contradictory political choices that fuelled popular discontent against the Brotherhood's rule and revealed the lack of a concrete political project. It concludes by identifying four main factors that contributed to Morsi's untimely demise. These are: the lack of a coherent vision of an 'Islamist project'; the fact that the Brotherhood severely miscalculated the amount of support and legitimacy that it actually had; its refusal to adapt to the changing circumstances, which then accelerated internal discontent; and the failure to successfully address the permanence of the deep state across state institutions.

Chapter 2 builds on this background to examine the Brotherhood's fall from power, reporting first-hand account of the quick turn of events that unfolded in July 2013. It relies on members' personal experiences to tell the story of the brutality that followed Morsi's removal and begins to outline the Brotherhood's descent into deeply unchartered territory. The chapter traces the movement's scattering abroad and outlines the unprecedented challenges that come with the dimension of forced exile, showing how the disintegration of established lines of command led to the emergence of individual responses to repression. It takes a close look at the relationship between the Brotherhood and its members, focusing on the resurfacing of old grievances and the emergence of new ones. Throughout, the chapter shows how the traumatic experience of renewed repression and exile accentuated the pre-existing divisions between the movement and its members, further aggravated by the lack of a cohesive response to repression. It concludes by showing how the challenges posed by reuniting in exile allowed members the unprecedented opportunity to reconsider their terms of belonging to the movement, outlining how their individual experiences of repression began to dismantle the collective identity that the Brotherhood historically relied on.

Chapter 3 builds on these emerging processes of self-reflection to show how, in the post-2013 context, the battle between members' individual agency and the Brotherhood's organisational structure has taken centre stage. It outlines the reconfiguration of the movement's leadership ranks in the aftermath of the coup, showing that open competition over leadership and the emergence of warring Guidance Offices reveal yet another layer of internal fragmentation. Throughout, the chapter traces the sources and development of various dynamics of dissent in order to outline the different ways in which individual members experience repression and forced displacement. These experiences directly shape their relationship with the movement and inform their strategies to counter repression, which often clash with the Brotherhood's official narrative. The chapter considers the disintegration of the *tanzim* and identifies the processes that guide the challenging of the movement's collective identity in favour of agency and individualism. In doing so, it shows that the main grievances behind these processes have their roots in the pre-revolutionary period and were therefore brought back to the fore by the perceived failure of the political experience. The chapter concludes by arguing that in the dimension of forced exile the biggest challenges the movement has to face are those posed by its own members, and by the growing calls for internal reforms.

Chapter 4 expands on the internal challenges and debates dividing the movement to focus on the ongoing polarisation around different responses to repression and on competing strategies to move past the current crisis. It shows that a significant novelty of the post-2013 context is represented by the fact that dissenting members, along with those who do not align with the Brotherhood's official narrative, remain an active part of the movement. These behaviours were punished with expulsion prior to 2011, but the necessity to maintain unity and safety in numbers after the coup mean that the Brotherhood is characterised by an unprecedented diversity of voices and opinions. The chapter traces the development of two main trends to fight against repression, these being stagnation and adaptation strategies. It shows that the Historical Leadership and those who remain faithful to them take a generally passive approach, treating the current crisis as yet another time of hardship and calling for patience and unity in the face of oppression. This faction remains faithful to the Brotherhood's historical tools of repression and refuses to answer the call for internal reforms and changes that would allow the movement to better adapt to the circumstances of exile. On the contrary, the adaptation trend encompasses a wide diversity of voices and competing strategies that argue for a more proactive response to the current crisis. These are informed by members' increased agency and by the development of independent thinking against the Brotherhood's official stance. By providing examples and first-hand accounts of what these adaptation strategies look like, the chapter begins to outline what the main future directions for the movement might be.

Chapter 5 looks at the main demands that members are advancing in the post-2013 era and looks at the current divisions dividing the Brotherhood. It shows that, while there is a collective commitment to the movement's survival, there is a growing disconnect between those who aspire to just that and those who instead want the movement to thrive despite the current circumstances. The chapter considers ongoing debates over what kind of organisation the Brotherhood should be moving forward, showing that questions regarding the balance of political and preaching activities have once again taken centre stage. It then looks at how individual responses to repression can help us begin to trace the ongoing fragmentation that divides the Brotherhood. Focusing on individual demands, grievances and desire for change is key to identifying the main points of contention driving internal debates, which will eventually need to be addressed by the Brotherhood's leaders. By doing so the chapter offers an initial assessment of the current factions that have formed within the movement in exile. While these are not fixed categories, they can indeed help us to gain an understanding of what the future directions of the movement might be. Overall, the chapter shows that while the Historical Leadership remains in control of the movement, the vocal demands for new inclusive and democratic values are definitely growing among members in exile. While it is too early to speculate on whether or not real ideological and structural changes will be achieved, some degree of internal change is already underway.

Finally, the Conclusion presents a summary of the main points covered in the book, emphasising what is presented as the defining characteristics of the post-2013 context. These are the fact that the Brotherhood has grown increasingly fragmented along strategic, ideological and organisational lines. The movement faces several challenges while trying to rebuild in exile, yet some of the main questions it needs to address are what kind of organisation it wants to be moving forward, and whether or not its leaders are willing to renegotiate the relationship between the movement and its members in order to maximise survival and resilience.

Notes

1. Author Interview with a senior leader. London, 2019.
2. 'Rabaa: the massacre that ended the Arab Spring', *Middle East Eye* (14 August 2018) www.middleeasteye.net/news/what-is-rabaa-egypt-massacre-ended-arab-spring-1041665049 (accessed 03 March 2020).
3. May Darwich, 'Creating the enemy, constructing the threat: the diffusion of repression against the Muslim Brotherhood in the Middle East', *Democratization*, 24:7 (2017), 1289–1306, 1290–1291.
4. Alison Pargeter, *Return to the Shadows: The Muslim Brotherhood and An-Nahda since the Arab Spring* (London: Saqi Books, 2016), 1.
5. Lucia Ardovini, 'The politicisation of sectarianism in Egypt: "creating an enemy" the state vs. the Ikhwan', *Global Discourse*, 6:4 (2016), 585–595.
6. Denis Sullivan, Sana Abed-Kotob, *Islam in Contemporary Egypt: Civil Society vs. the State* (Boulder: Lynne Rienner Publishers, 1999), 20.
7. Eric Trager, 'Think again: the Muslim Brotherhood', *Foreign Policy* (2013) http://foreignpolicy.com/2013/01/28/think-again-the-muslim-brotherhood/ (accessed 03 March 2020).
8. Hazem Kandil, *Inside the Brotherhood* (Cambridge: Polity Press, 2015).
9. Khalil Al-Anani, *Inside the Muslim Brotherhood: Religion, Identity, and Politics* (Oxford: Oxford University Press, 2016), 142–143.
10. Barbara Zollner, 'Surviving repression: how Egypt's Muslim Brotherhood has carried on', *Carnegie Papers* (2019) https://carnegie-mec.org/2019/03/11/surviving-repression-how-egypt-s-muslim-brotherhood-has-carried-on-pub-78552 (accessed 03 March 2020).
11. Nathan Brown, Michelle Dunne, 'Unprecedented pressures, uncharted course for Egypt's Muslim Brotherhood', *Carnegie* (2015) https://carnegieendowment.org/2015/07/29/unprecedented-pressures-uncharted-course-for-egypt-s-muslim-brotherhood-pub-60875 (accessed 03 March 2020).
12. Ibid.
13. See for example: Robert Michel, *Political Parties: A Sociological Study of the Oligarchical Tendencies of Modern Democracy* (New York: Collier Books, 1962); Doug McAdam, John McCarthy and Mayer Zald (eds.) *Comparative Perspectives on Social Movements* (New York: Cambridge University Press, 1996), 12.
14. Elisabeth Clemens, 'Organizational repertoires and institutional change: women's groups and the transformation of U.S. politics, 1890–1920', *American Journal of Sociology*, 98 (1993), 755–798.
15. Elisabeth Jean Wood, 'The emotional benefits of insurgency in El Salvador', in Jeff Goodwin, James Jasper and Francesca Polletta (eds.) *Passionate Politics:*

Emotions and Social Movements (Chicago: University of Chicago Press, 2001), 267–281; Jules Boykoff, *The Suppression of Dissent: How the State and Mass Media Squelch US American Social Movements* (Abingdon: Routledge, 2006); Charles Brockett, 'A protest-cycle resolution of the repression/popular-protest paradox', *Social Science History*, 17:3 (1993), 457–484.

16 Paul Almeida, 'Multi-sectoral coalitions and popular movement participation', *Research in Social Movements, Conflicts and Change*, 26 (2005), 65–99; Doug McAdam, *Freedom Summer* (New York: Oxford University Press, 1990).

17 Ronald Francisco, 'The dictator's dilemma', in Christian Davenport, Hank Johnston and Carol Mueller (eds.) *Repression and Mobilization* (Minneapolis: University of Minnesota Press, 2005), 58–81; Mark Irving Lichbach, 'Deterrence or escalation? The puzzle of aggregate studies of repression and dissent', *Journal of Conflict Resolution*, 31:2 (1987), 266–297; Will Moore, 'Repression and dissent: substitution, context, and timing', *American Journal of Political Science*, 42:3 (1998), 851–873; Kevin O'Brien, Yanhua Deng, 'Repression backfires: tactical radicalization and protest spectacle in rural China', *Journal of Contemporary China*, 24:93 (2014), 457–470.

18 Ali Honari, 'From "the effect of repression" toward "the response to repression"', *Current Sociology*, 66:6 (2018), 950–972.

19 See for example: Paul Osterman, 'Overcoming oligarchy: culture and agency in social movement organizations', *Administrative Science Quarterly*, 51:4 (2006), 622–649; Mustafa Emirbayer, Ann Mische 'What is agency?' *American Journal of Sociology*, 103 (1998), 962–1023.

20 Noha Mellor, *Voice of the Muslim Brotherhood* (London: Routledge, 2016); Carry Rosefsky Wickham, *The Muslim Brotherhood: Evolution of an Islamist Movement* (Princeton: Princeton University Press, 2013).

21 Khalil Al-Anani, 'Rethinking the repression-dissent nexus: assessing Egypt's Muslim Brotherhood's response to repression since the coup of 2013', *Democratization*, 26:8 (2019), 1329–1341.

22 Marcus George, 'Emotions in politics', *Annual Review of Political Science*, 3:1 (2000), 221–250; Jeff Goodwin, James Jasper and Francesca Polletta, 'The return of the repressed: the fall and rise of emotions in Social Movement Theory', *Mobilization* 5:1 (2000), 65–84; James Jasper, 'Emotions and social movements: twenty years of theory and research', *Annual Review of Sociology*, 37 (2011), 285–303.

23 Al-Anani, 'Rethinking the repression-dissent nexus'.

24 Ibid.; Erika Biagini, 'Islamist women's feminist subjectivities in (r)evolution: the Egyptian Muslim Sisterhood in the aftermath of the Arab uprisings', *International Feminist Journal of Politics*, 22:3 (2020) 382–402; Mustafa Menshawy, *Leaving the Brotherhood: Self, Society and the* State (London: Palgrave Macmillan, 2020); Lucia Ardovini, 'Stagnation vs adaptation: tracking the Muslim Brotherhood trajectories after the 2013 *coup*', *British Journal of Middle Eastern Studies* (2020), www.tandfonline.com/doi/abs/10.1080/13530194.2020.1778443?needAccess=true&journalCode=cbjm20 (accessed 19 August 2021); Wickham, *The Muslim Brotherhood*; Kandil, *Inside the Brotherhood*; Lucia Ardovini, Erika Biagini (eds.) 'Assessing the Egyptian Muslim Brotherhood after the 2013 *coup*: tracing

trajectories of continuity and change', *Middle East Law and Governance* 13 (2021), 125–129.
25 Author Interview. Istanbul, August 2018.
26 Another one worthy of mention being the Tunisia al-Nahda. For a detailed study of their political behaviour since 2011 see: Rory McCarthy, *Inside Tunisia's al-Nahda: Between Politics and Preaching* (Cambridge: Cambridge University Press, 2018).
27 Among others, see Marc Lynch, Jillian Schwedler, 'Introduction to the special issue on Islamist politics after the Arab uprisings', *Middle East Law and Governance*, 12:1 (2020), 3–13; Hendrik Kraetzschmar, Paola Rivetti (eds.) *Islamists and the Politics of the Arab Uprisings: Governance, Pluralization and Contention* (Edinburgh: Edinburgh University Press, 2018).
28 Jillian Schwedler, 'Conclusions: new directions in the study of Islamist politics', in Kraetzschmar, Rivetti, *Islamists and the Politics of the Arab Uprisings*, 367.
29 Asef Bayat, *Post-Islamism: The Changing Faces of Political Islam* (New York: Oxford University Press, 2013); Olivier Roy, 'Political Islam after the Arab Spring', *Foreign Affairs* (2017) www.foreignaffairs.com/reviews/review-essay/2017-10-16/political-islam-after-arab-spring (accessed 03 March 2020).
30 Jocelyn Cesari, *What is Political Islam?* (Boulder: Lynne Rienner Publishers, 2018), 3–6.
31 Muqtedar Khan, 'Islam, democracy and Islamism after the counterrevolution in Egypt', *Middle East Policy*, 21:1 (2014), 75–86.
32 Barbara Zollner, 'Does participation lead to moderation? Understanding changes in the Egyptian Islamist parties post-Arab Spring', in Kraetzschmar, Rivetti, *Islamists and the Politics of the Arab Uprisings*, 149–166.
33 Pargeter, *Return to the Shadows*.
34 Ashraf El-Sherif, 'The Egyptian Muslim Brotherhood's failures', *Carnegie Papers* (2014) https://carnegieendowment.org/2014/07/01/egyptian-muslim-brotherhood-s-failures-pub-56046 (accessed 03 March 2020); Khalil Al-Anani, 'Upended path: the rise and fall of Egypt's Muslim Brotherhood', *The Middle East Journal*, 69:4 (2015), 527–543; Wickham, *The Muslim Brotherhood*.
35 Pargeter, *Return to the Shadows*, 6.
36 Kraetzschmar, Rivetti, *Islamists and the Politics of the Arab Uprisings*.
37 Stacey Philbrick Yadav, 'Roundtable: future of political Islam in the MENA under the changing regional order', *Maydan* (2018) www.themaydan.com/2018/08/roundtable-future-political-islam-mena-changing-regional-order/#journal2 (accessed 03 March 2020).
38 Ibid.

1

The Freedom and Justice Party in power: Islam is (not) the solution?

The popular uprisings that spread through Egypt on 25 January 2011 temporarily disrupted the status quo to an extent that no one would have expected. The removal of long-standing dictator Hosni Mubarak was followed by a power vacuum that opened up unprecedented political opportunities, taking by surprise even those who had filled the country's streets. Yet, the protesters struggled to translate their revolutionary demands into actual reforms, and the uprisings effectively resulted in a 'change of regime' rather than a 'regime change'. This was mostly due to the fact that the so-called revolution failed to restructure the existing state institutions and to challenge political elites, meaning that Egypt remained under the control both of the military forces and the deep state. Nevertheless, it is undeniable that the brief opening up of the political space that followed Mubarak's removal allowed some actors, the Brotherhood first and foremost, to quickly shift from the periphery to the centre of the Egyptian political landscape.

Despite its leaders' initial reluctance to join the popular protests, the Brotherhood quickly became one of its main protagonists, eventually emerging as one of the most powerful civil actors of the Egyptian uprisings. Two of its representatives[1] sat in the Constitutional Committee overseen by the Supreme Council of the Armed Forces (SCAF) from the very beginning, and in April 2011 the organisation was given permission to form its own political party for the first time in its history.[2] However, the Brotherhood's rapid politicisation came with a unique set of challenges, which were very different from those that the movement had faced historically. While the opening up of unprecedented political space and opportunity allowed the movement to pursue a more direct involvement in politics, this soon revealed the internal lack of members' consensus on how to proceed without compromising the balance between preaching and political activities. Moreover, Brotherhood leaders also had to move carefully to avoid being accused, by both external actors and the organisations' own members, of hijacking the revolution for their own means. Indeed, the biggest obstacle that the movement had to face came from its own ranks, this being the growing calls for internal reforms and for the restructuring of its strong hierarchical structures. This is a grievance that would come to characterise the Brotherhood's time in power, and is also central to its current restructuring.

The political opportunities brought about by the uprisings were seen by many as a remarkable moment of change in the history of the Brotherhood. After spending most of its existence as an illegal movement, the organisation quickly rose to power following Egypt's first free and democratic election. However, a closer look at the organisation's history and internal dynamics, as well as conversations with former and current members, reveal that very little changed internally as a consequence of the uprisings. Rather, the events of 2011, and the quick politicisation that followed, ignited internal grievances and tensions that had started to develop in the previous decade, but had always been dismissed by its leaders. First and foremost, tensions between members' individual agency and the organisation's strict hierarchical structure were drastically exacerbated by the creation of the Freedom and Justice Party (FJP) in April 2011. Because of this, while the Brotherhood struggled to project a united front, the internal tensions that had been simmering for years led to the defection and expulsion of a considerable part of the membership, mostly associated with its politically oriented factions such as the Reformists and the Youth. The departure of many of its pragmatic members affected the Brotherhood's ability to perform politically, also contributing to its demonstrated exclusionary character. But what exactly went wrong along the way?

Let us analyse more closely how the Brotherhood's unwillingness to adapt to change, among other factors, influenced its performance in government, and the other circumstances that led to its rapid rise and even hastier fall. It is worth nothing that the history of what happened as a direct consequence of the 2011 uprisings is inseparable from the main challenges that the Brotherhood faces now, so I will routinely come back to key events and developments throughout the book. Nevertheless, I aim to give a basic understanding of how the speed and novelty of the events that followed Mubarak's ousting shaped the behaviour of the Brotherhood, affected its members, and what that meant for its organisational cohesion and unity.

The Brotherhood and Egypt: between repression and toleration

The Brotherhood was one of Egypt's most powerful opposition forces at the outbreak of the 2011 popular protests, drawing its legitimacy from both its civil society network and decades of political engagement. This meant that, a few months down the line, in comparison to other parties that emerged during the transitional period, the movement could rely on an already established popular base and a renowned ability to mobilise the masses. While exact numbers are hard to obtain, it is estimated that just before 25 January the organisation had approximately 600,000 to 1 million active members, and a support base of approximately 2 million Egyptians.[3] Whereas its rapid politicisation and electoral successes were, therefore, not at all surprising, Morsi's rise to presidency arguably was. His candidature directly contradicted the Brotherhood's gradualist approach to politics, and revealed the lack of a coherent political agenda. Looking back at the political frenzy that characterised the post-Mubarak period, it becomes clear that the founding of the FJP was a problematic process from the very start, bringing back historical internal tensions that consequently affected its political behaviour. Yet, the question of what factors led to the FJP's premature end, and of what lessons can be learnt from that experience, still remain unanswered.

The Brotherhood's politicisation process had been at the core of the organisation's internal debates for most of its history. The struggle between the movement's *da'wa* (preaching) and political mission goes back to the question of what the very nature of the organisation is. Founded in 1928 as a grassroots religious movement aimed at combating colonialism and a perceived moral decadence, the movement was always characterised by a somewhat dual nature. Under the guidance of its founder, Hassan al Banna, the Brotherhood was built on a comprehensive ideology and understanding of Islamic values as core pillars of society – hence its slogan 'Islam is the solution'.[4] It was not long before its activities expanded into Egypt's political arena, with a religious message incorporating themes of resistance and identity politics and an open condemnation of the British occupation.[5] Yet, one key consideration that needs to be taken into account here is that the Brotherhood was never a revolutionary movement, neither ideologically nor politically. Al Banna was committed to the Islamisation of society through a gradualist bottom-up approach, according to which the movement had to operate within 'the existing constitutional parliamentary framework in Egypt [that], if reformed, would satisfy the political requirements of Islam for a Muslim state'.[6] Therefore, the Brotherhood was always evolutionary rather than revolutionary in nature, an aspect that would drive not only its political behaviour after the 2011 uprisings, but now also elicits strong critiques by some of its former members.

Because of this multi-layered identity, the question of the extent to which the Brotherhood should engage in politics – if at all – is historically at the core of the organisation's internal divisions. As I will show later, it is also one of the main ideological struggles that is dividing the movement today. Al Banna was openly against a party-system, but recognised that direct involvement in politics would strengthen the organisation's scope and aims without diminishing its ideological profile. The clear shift from a purely socio-religious movement to a political one was marked during the Brotherhood's 5th Conference in Cairo in 1939, during which al Banna stated 'we need to become political'.[7] The subsequent decision to enter parliamentary elections for the first time in 1941 came at the peak of the organisation's popular success, which included approximately 150,000 supporters and more than 300 branches spread across the country.[8] However, the Brotherhood's official debut into politics caused both internal and external issues.

Firstly, it meant that the movement inevitably clashed with the regime. After being banned by the monarchy in 1948, the Brotherhood entered a complicated relationship with the Egyptian state, characterised by brief periods of toleration and violent crackdowns. The movement and its expanding popular base were simultaneously a source of legitimacy and an existential threat to the regime, which saw cycles of political cooperation alternating with repression and mass arrests. The Nasserist era in particular was one of the most violent times in the Brotherhood's history.[9] Following its dissolution at the hands of the regime in 1954, its members were subjected to mass executions and concentration camps-like prisons.[10] Brutal repression lasted until the presidency of Anwar Sadat in the 1970s, who saw the movement as a useful political resource against his opponents.[11] The Mubarak regime was also marked by routine repression against the Brotherhood, which remained an illegal movement until 2011. Yet, the brutality of regime-enforced crackdowns it faced under Nasser remained unmatched until the coming of al Sisi and the recent wave of repression against the organisation. While still outlawed and subjected to routine crackdowns, the Brotherhood entered an era of so-called 'Islamic revivalism', during which it recruited new members from within universities and workers' associations, who breathed new life into the movement and went on to become today's leadership.[12]

Most importantly, the Brotherhood managed to turn this permanent state of repression into a defining element of its own identity and narrative, thriving despite the recurrent crackdowns rather than just surviving. Repression therefore became 'the glue that binds us [the Brotherhood] together and reflects that we are on the right path'[13] and directly related to *mihna* (ordeal/tribulation) as both a call for patience and a test of the persistence of true believers in the pursuit of justice and truth. *Mihna* therefore contributed to the construction of a collective identity and narrative based on persistence in the face of authoritarianism, which is being revived in the aftermath of 2013 as a reaffirmation of the need for internal unity. Notions such as that of a collective identity that binds its members into emotional, biological and ideological ties and of core values such as 'listen and obey' were key to the movement's survival throughout decades of repression, but are also only sustainable as long as members themselves fully subscribe to them.

Tensions between individual agency, subjectivities and desires have always been present within the Brotherhood, especially from the late 1980s' debut into formal politics, but were routinely suppressed in favour of a top-down collective sense of identity and purpose. Nevertheless, these older grievances against the organisation's strict hierarchical structures and lack of space for debates and individualism would be highly exacerbated by the creation of the FJP, and are now at the centre of current reformation trends. I will unpack these tensions in more details later on; for now, it is enough to keep in mind that these historical tools of resistance meant that despite existing under illegality for most of its history, the Brotherhood nonetheless succeeded in maintaining a presence in politics and a sizeable grassroots following by becoming inherently entrenched in the Egyptian system, and by relying on its secretive, but often praised, hierarchal organisational structure.

A 'state within a state'

The Brotherhood was an established opposition force by the time Mubarak became president in 1981. Nevertheless, its relationship with the regime remained marked by alternating cycles of toleration and repression, which put the movement in a rather unique and incongruous position. True to its slogan 'participation, not domination', the Brotherhood steadily grew more political during Mubarak's rule. In particular, the years between the late 1990s and the 2005 parliamentary elections witnessed the reinforcement of the movement's political agenda and identity as an opposition actor.[14] While still existing under illegality the Brotherhood skilfully expanded its social provision schemes, to the point of effectively becoming a 'state within a state'. This was made possible by Egypt's turn towards liberalism that had left a wide-open gap in social services, which the Brotherhood skilfully filled. To put things into perspective, it is estimated that in 2006 alone 20% of about 5,000 legally registered non-governmental organisations in Egypt were Brotherhood-run or affiliated,[15] along with 22 hospitals and at least one school in each of Egypt's governorates, hospitality and care centres for orphans and widows, and training programmes for the unemployed.[16]

The Brotherhood's social provision programmes, and the special attention paid to the more deprived parts of the population, allowed it to firmly embed itself within Egyptian society and build the popular base that allowed it to succeed in the post-2011 context. These activities also demonstrate its great capability to survive repression and develop dynamic tools of resistance. Despite existing under illegality for most of its history, the Brotherhood nevertheless managed to become an integral part of the Egyptian social fabric, adapting to rapidly changing situations and remaining anchored within the country's socio-political life. This is why today's forced exile and wave of repression is deeply unfamiliar for the Brotherhood, which, after the 2013 coup, entered a state of stagnation it is struggling to break free from. Having been removed from the Egyptian context, the movement has lost more than just its political power. The most recent wave of repression saw its social provision networks and assets seized by the regime, which therefore also removed one of the movement's main strategies for survival and a source of popular support. This means that the organisation's historical tools of resistance are now largely ineffective, which, coupled with the novelty of exile, leaves the Brotherhood in deeply unchartered waters.[17] In order to move forward, the movement needs to develop new ways to react against the unprecedented situation it finds itself in, but it is struggling to do so. Together with external factors, the growing tensions between its members' individual agency, demands for internal reforms, and the organisation's strict hierarchical structure exacerbated by the events of 2011 represent a major obstacle in the Brotherhood's post-coup trajectory.

A history of internal divisions

Later in the book it will become clear that internal fragmentation is one of the biggest obstacles that the Brotherhood faces in the post-2013 context, especially as it tries to reunite while in exile. Recent conversations with both current and former members show that these tensions mostly centre around strategic debates on how the Brotherhood should move forward to effectively re-group after the coup, and are driven by the growing discontent with the organisation's immobility and refusal to reform. Abdullah, a former member in his forties, always aligned with the conservative wing of the organisation and was in Raba'a when the regime's crackdown was unleashed on the Brotherhood and his followers. He managed to escape arrest and has since relocated to the UK with his family. After the coup he grew increasingly disillusioned with the way in which the leadership was handling the crisis, and eventually left the organisation in 2017. While walking through a park in London, he recalls the chaos of the weeks that followed the Raba'a massacre: 'everyone was running around, we were just trying to survive. Leaders were being arrested, others were running away, but they did not say anything! We needed directions, but everyone was talking over each other and everyone was saying different things! This is not our way. We should have been better prepared.'[18]

This sentiment is echoed by Tamer, a Youth member who eagerly participated in the uprisings from the very beginning. He is the only Brotherhood member in his family and left his parents behind to flee to Turkey when it became clear that the regime was targeting anyone affiliated to the movement. He recalls his frustration with the way in which the crisis was handled and says that, since the coup, the higher ranks of the movement are still stuck debating fundamental questions that should have been addressed long ago.

> So after the coup there were internal discussions about what went wrong and why did this happen. One of the reasons was of course that the leaders were not qualified to handle this kind of phase, a transitional period, they are good at having the patience to endure hardships, prison and so on, but people started saying 'are we stuck with being in prison again?' We need to break this circle and these people are not qualified to handle the pre-coup and the post-coup phases. The leaders are getting very old, they are not allowing young people to be part of the decision-making process, a lot of young people are very active but they are excluded from the strategic planning. Women as well are very active within the Ikhwan, but excluded from any decisional process.[19]

Yet, while the current internal struggles reflect the Brotherhood's new circumstances, the organisation has a history of internal divisions concerning ideological and tactical matters that are also feeding into its contemporary issues. Disagreements over how the Brotherhood should have responded to recurrent regime crackdowns first came to the fore during Nasser's persecution of the movement, and escalated in 1973 after the appointment of the third General Guide, Umar al-Tilmisani. At the time, the Brotherhood started to polarise into two main groups. The first one was composed of those following Tilmisani, mostly university students in the 1970s, who envisioned the movement as an 'open society' willing to welcome anyone committed to the Islamic project.[20] They argued that the Brotherhood should fully engage in formal politics and thought that progression through its internal ranks should be based on democratic decision-making procedures.[21] They were opposed by a group of hardliners whose experiences had been shaped by hardship and imprisonment under Nasser. Those belonging to this cohort were distrustful of outsiders, saw their suffering as a rightful claim to leadership and maintained that the Brotherhood should focus on religious and educational activities rather than political ones.[22] These schisms grew to be characteristic of the Mubarak era, and were further ignited by the organisation's rapid politicisation following the events of 2011. For example, conversation with dissidents and former members confirmed that discontent towards the Brotherhood's strict hierarchical structure indeed dates back to the late 1970s, and has now returned to the fore following the FJP's destitution. This is why understanding the Brotherhood's internal divisions on the eve of the 2011 uprisings is fundamental to make sense of its trajectories after Mubarak's removal.

By the end of 2010, the Brotherhood encompassed a wide range of interests, activities and experiences. This resulted in the organisation's division into a number of factions, which are generally thought of in terms of generational groups. Khalil al-Anani and Carrie Rosefsky Wickham have studied these divisions in depth and identified four main trends: the Old Guard or Da'wa faction, the pragmatic conservatives, the reformists and the youth. Although biological age is not necessarily a key component of these divisions, it is undeniable that at the end of the Mubarak era those belonging to a specific group shared common experiences that, in turn, influenced their intellectual stance. In the case of the Da'wa faction, its members consisted of those who had survived Nasser's persecution and derived their authority from both old age and respect for the personal sacrifices they made on the movement's behalf. They controlled the distribution of resources and shared the view of the Brotherhood as an encompassing organisation, therefore opposing its transformation into a legal party that would subject it to state control.[23] The pragmatic conservatives brought together those who came to the organisation in the 1970s from both student associations and other Islamist groups, with some of them showcasing Salafi tendencies. Khairat al-Shater, Mohammed Morsi and Saad el-Katatni were all leaders in this faction, and played a key role in the creation and running of the FJP.[24] Those belonging to this group had a more political inclination, and headed the Brotherhood's bloc in parliament under Mubarak.

The reformist group also included members who came to the Brotherhood in the late 1970s or early 1980s and shared a general background as student activists, therefore being more open to outsiders, and willing to engage in dialogue and political activities with external actors. Abu el-Fotouh was a key figure among the reformists, whose views were generally in clear opposition with those of the Brotherhood's Conservative members. In particular, one of the main points of departure was the Reformists' push for a greater engagement with secular actors and more openness towards the West.[25] Finally, the youth section represented the new generation of activists in the Brotherhood at the time of the 2011 uprisings. Male and female activists in their twenties and thirties were politically and intellectually engaged, and pushed for internal reforms and greater openness towards other political groups. A defining characteristic of this faction is its members' open criticism of the Brotherhood's ideological rigidity, lack of internal transparency and opportunities, and the strict containment of members' individual initiatives.[26] Even before the divisions that came to the fore over the creation of the FJP, the youth contested the Brotherhood's traditionalist values that put emphasis on gradualism, hierarchy and 'listening and obeying'.[27] Most importantly, they were known for cooperating with secular activist groups in the decade before the 2011 uprisings, which would shape the key role that they played during the protests.[28]

All in all, the generational categorisation offered by al-Anani and Wickham successfully captures the broad internal divisions that characterised the Brotherhood even before the events of 2011, despite its efforts to portray a united front. However, the data shows that this 'classic' way to look at the Brotherhood's composition fails to fully reflect the internal dynamics of the movement, and the range of points of contention that would eventually be catalysed by Mubarak's removal. The categorisation of different factions based on biological age also does not offer any insights into how intellectual currents lead to interaction between and outside of these group that, as we will see, are key in the post-2013 context. Nevertheless, what needs to be kept in mind to understand the movement's trajectory after 25 January is the fact that tensions between the organisation's traditional values and its members' individual agency were already characteristic of the pre-2011 period, as evidenced by the Wasat Party split in 1996.[29] Conversations with both current and former members reveal that the creation of the FJP in itself was not the genesis of new internal schisms, but rather acted as catalysis for discontent and grievances that had been present for at least two decades, but were routinely dismissed by the leadership. This finding is highly significant as organisational fragmentation represents a key challenge for the Brotherhood after 2013, as will become clear later. Most importantly, the factions that emerged in the post-2013 context – or were reinforced by it – are largely cross-generational in nature and mostly reflect different approaches to organisational strategy and reforms.

What captured my attention during several rounds of fieldwork is the fact that, when talking to former members and dissidents, they are always keen to emphasise the centrality of internal schisms in the pre-2011 period. This is an aspect that I have discussed at length with Mohammad, a Brotherhood youth leader and co-founder of *Hezb Al-Tayyar Al-Masry* (the Egyptian Current Party), who left the organisation in September 2011 after a long series of disputes with the Historical Leadership. Now based in Istanbul, he too identifies the creation of the FJP as the moment in which old tensions came back to the fore. In particular, Mohammad contends that the younger members of the Brotherhood, along with some more senior ones who aligned with their intellectual position, had already started pushing for more individual autonomy by the end of the 1990s. He argues that the very issues that would later be emphasised by the FJP's political performance, namely the lack of accountability and professionalism, had already been identified as core concerns by some members at least 10 years prior: 'I discovered that we as Ikhwan lacked a very important thing: professionality'.[30] In particular, he recalls that this issue started to become clear to members not involved in the movement's political committees when Mohammed Mahdi Akef became the General Guide in 2004. One of al Banna's original followers, Akef partially dismantled the layers of secrecy that shielded the members of the Guidance Bureau and the organisation's leaders from the general membership, exposing their activities and saying 'I turned on the lights and I put them [the Guidance Bureau] on the stage'.[31] By doing so he drastically reduced the gap between the leadership and the rest of the organisation, beginning to challenge their sense of 'untouchability' and questioning the blind respect owed to them up until that point in the process.

As a consequence, Mohammad recalls, that 'In the early 2000s, we started looking more closely at the leaders and at their behaviours, and we started criticising them [...] it was impossible not to! We realised that the leaders are very average people. There was obedience [to the ideology of the Brotherhood] but not performance'.[32] This root of discontent is directly linked to bigger issues of accountability and the difficulty to progress within the Brotherhood because of its heavily hierarchical structure. Mohammad talks about members who, like himself, repeatedly asked for more space to pursue political activities, education and dialogue with other activists, but were routinely shut down by those in higher positions within the movement:

> Accountability as a concept came up two or three years before the revolution. We challenged this, [the Brotherhood's highly hierarchical structure] we said we need to introduce accountability in our way of managing things. The problem was, accountability within the Ikhwan was about obedience, not performance. [...] People who are obedient, keep a low profile, who have no personality, they can proceed [in the ranks] while the people who are challenging and have different ideas are cast aside.[33]

Trained as a medical doctor, Mohammad recalls that when his requests to go back to university to pursue a course in political sciences were rejected by his Brotherhood superior, he and some friends eventually went to enrol without seeking permission first. Once they got to the university, they were surprised to recognise other Brotherhood members who were also there to enrol in the same course, unbeknown to the movement. Just like Mohammad, others also confirm that instances of individual agency had started developing before the outbreak of the 2011 revolutions, and therefore found an avenue in the opening of the political space that followed Mubarak's removal. This shows that the tensions dividing the Brotherhood today are not necessarily a new phenomenon, but rather embody the evolution of long-standing, cross-generational grievances between the rank-and-file members and the Historical Leadership. It follows that the creation of the FJP also catapulted this lack of internal unity and cohesion to the public eye, gravely affecting the Brotherhood's credibility. Several secular activists agree that '[before 2011] people definitely viewed the Brotherhood as one monolithic block [...] when Fotouh left, that's when the divisions became public'.[34]

Unwilling revolutionaries

The Brotherhood's engagement with the uprisings clearly reflected its lack of internal cohesion. Despite its wide popular base, the Brotherhood leadership was definitely reluctant when it came to joining or even just endorsing the protests. This was partly due to the lack of clarity as to what was actually happening, but mostly led by a self-preservation instinct. Having had to survive through routine crackdowns and under illegality for so many decades, the Brotherhood knew that the regime would target the organisation as soon as it joined, and was unwilling to risk what little freedom it had. Its gradual approach also played a big part in delaying official participation, as joining a revolution did not align with the movement's evolutionary strategy. Yet, many of the Brotherhood's rank-and-file members and especially the Youth divisions were involved in the protests from the very start, and expressed frustration at the leadership's unwillingness to endorse their participation.

When Egyptians took to the streets on 25 January 2011, it was impossible to predict the turn that such an event would take. Decades of worsening economic conditions, restriction of political space and gross abuses of human rights under the Mubarak regime had left Egyptians – literally – hungry for change. Protesters on the streets did not just call for the fall of the regime; a demand louder than all others was for 'bread, freedom, and [human] dignity'.[35] Given the Brotherhood's history of activism and its status as one of the most powerful opposition groups, many expected its members to endorse the protests and take part in the uprisings straight away. Yet, it was only its Youth activist wing that did so, having also played a part in organising the protests in cooperation with their secular counterparts.[36] Anchored in its mutually defining forced coexistence with the regime, the leadership was torn between seizing the opportunity for change and fearing even harsher persecutions if the protests failed.

The position that the Brotherhood took throughout the 2011 uprisings therefore reflected the long running internal divide between its Reformist and Conservative wings. While the senior leadership was sceptical towards the outcome of the protests and feared repercussions, the Brotherhood's activist Youth were more eager to participate in anti-regime protests and to tackle Mubarak's deep state head on. This created immense internal frustration, especially when the Guidance Bureau denied the Youth's plea to let them participate in the protests.[37] A former member recalls these times of rising tensions: 'We contacted them [the Guidance Bureau] and told them: "there is a revolution in the street! Let us participate!"'[38] The only concession made was that the Youth could indeed take part in the protests, but not under the Brotherhood's name, as clearly reflected in Secretary General Mahmoud

Izzat's words: 'go and be with the people in the square. If they stay in the square stay with them and if they leave, then leave too'.[39]

Yet, as the protests spread and gained momentum, the leadership started to realise the significance of what was happening. They found themselves facing two inherently opposite choices: extreme provocation of the regime, or detachment from the broader nationalist movement.[40] Ultimately, they decided to seize the unique opportunity presented to them, and issued a statement announcing that they would take part in the 'Friday of Rage'. Mohammed Sudan, the FJP's Foreign Relations Secretary and a Brotherhood member for over 30 years, identifies Friday 28 as the day the 'real revolution' started. He recalls 'From the 27th at night, we got an order from the Guidance Bureau saying that everyone had to go and join the revolution. We got the plan, the agenda, and a breakdown of who was doing what at which time [...] it was not random, everything was planned. We took 3 million people with us'.[41]

The Brothers were in their element once they joined the uprisings. They brought their historical experience of successfully managing protests to the streets, taking on the role of organisers and protectors of those stationed in squares across the country. There is a shared consensus among secular activists that along with manpower, the Brotherhood's organisational capabilities were key to the uprisings' success. During our conversation, many of them joke that they are not happy to admit it. They come from secular families and activist backgrounds and, most of all, they feel betrayed by the Brotherhood's behaviour and by the political choices of the FJP. Yet, recalling those weeks of revolution on the streets, they are forced to recognise the key role played by the movement: 'they [Brotherhood members] led many of the protests, organising where they would be starting from, where they were going to go, but also providing the cars, and the microphones, and the flags, all of this was really organised by the Brotherhood'.[42] Others also praise the courage of the Brotherhood's cadres, saying 'they were at the forefront. They defended us all, this is a fact'.[43]

Joining the uprisings therefore awakened the Brotherhood from the stagnation it had fallen into under Mubarak's regime. Along with the constraints imposed by authoritarian rule, internal disagreements had locked the movement into a state of pseudo-stability, its desire for change almost forgotten. Therefore, the popular protests shook the Brotherhood awake, producing a real opportunity for change for the first time in decades. However, they also presented its leadership with two key challenges: fighting perceptions that the Brotherhood was hijacking the revolutions for its own gains, and managing the growing internal calls to reform the organisation's hierarchical structure. The Guidance Bureau quickly stressed that its members had joined the protests as Egyptians and not Islamists, stating 'we come with no special agenda of our own – our agenda is that of the Egyptian people. We aim to achieve reform and rights for all: not just for the Brotherhood, not just for Muslims, but for all Egyptians'.[44] Nevertheless, the widening internal divide over the role the Brotherhood should play in the post-Mubarak era was much harder to disguise, and would have considerable implications for the organisation's trajectory.

A marriage of convenience

The Brotherhood was treading a very thin line in the days leading up to Mubarak's deposition on 11 February 2011. In accordance with its slogan 'participation, not domination', the movement historically strived to demonstrate its willingness to work within the existing structures and institutions of the state, rather than disrupting them. However, the unprecedented opportunity ahead of them made it hard to stick to its evolutionary rather than revolutionary approach. Therefore, when the Supreme Council of the Armed Forces (SCAF) took control of the transitional process, the Brotherhood saw it as an opening rather than as a return of the *fulul* (old regime). Its leaders were aware that military support was necessary to install a new regime and political order, and unsurprisingly chose appeasement over transformation, beginning to cooperate with the armed forces straight away. Retrospectively, this stance further fragmented the Brotherhood and planted the seed for its downfall.

It is important to note here that the bases for this cooperation had been established even before Mubarak was toppled, unbeknown to the Youth leaders who would have condemned such actions. In one of the most iconic moments of the uprisings, on 2 February, protesters in Tahrir square were viciously attacked by regime-hired thugs. The so-called 'Battle of the Camels' ultimately delegitimised Mubarak's regime, and saw the Brotherhood Youth fighting side by side with the activists in the square. Rumours of the Guidance Bureau ordering its members to withdraw from Tahrir were dismissed, yet they revealed the struggle for power that was taking place behind the scenes. Unbeknown to most, as the Brotherhood Youth fought against the regime, the leadership had already initiated negotiations for a post-revolutionary settlement. Mohammed Morsi and Saad el-Katatni met with Vice-President Omar Sulayman and asked for the release of Conservative leader and businessman Khairat al-Shater from prison, in exchange for ordering its members to leave the square. They also agree that any post-revolutionary government would maintain the SCAF's economic privileges, and that in return the military would 'cement the road' for the Brotherhood to obtain power democratically.[45] These deals mark the very moment in which the

Brotherhood leaders betrayed the revolution and, in the process, a significant part of their own membership.

These negotiations were facilitated by the fact that both the SCAF and the Brotherhood had a lot to gain from cooperating with each other. The SCAF was set to hold onto their economic and political privileges, while knowing that the Brotherhood's lack of direct political experience would make it an easily controllable partner. On the other hand, the Brotherhood leaders knew that dialogue with the military was necessary to ensure a place in the post-revolutionary order, and were determined to turn the uprisings into political gains. From then onwards its leaders unofficially sided with the *fulul*, while portraying themselves as 'the people's voice' in their public speeches and gestures. However, just a few days into the transition, the Brotherhood's internal disagreements quickly resurfaced.

The proportion of these internal tensions when it came to decision-making was embodied by the scandal that erupted when it transpired that Morsi and el-Katatni had already secretly negotiated with the SCAF. The Youth and Reformist wings felt that their leaders had betrayed not only themselves, but the credibility of the movement and of the revolution as a whole. El-Fotouh angrily addressed the General Guide during a Shura Council meeting in February 2011, saying 'There was a first meeting, Badi'? Have you ever heard something like this in the history of this Society? Shame on you!'[46] Insubordinations like this also characterised confrontations between the Youth activists and the leadership. As talks of electoral politics started to emerge, Youth members and those who took a more active part in the protests realised that their interpretation of the uprisings had little in common with that of the Guidance Bureau. This act of betrayal would tear the Brotherhood apart, and make the foundation of the FJP deeply problematic from the very start.

The Brotherhood's political trajectory as it entered the transition period would therefore be defined by the widening gap between the Guidance Bureau and the more Reformist wings of the organisation. The military quickly took control of the country's institutions, with the SCAF suspending the Constitution and vowing to oversee a 'just and democratic transition to an elected government'.[47] Parliamentary elections were set to take place in September 2011, and representatives from the main groups that took part in the uprisings were invited to participate in a national dialogue. All the while, the Brotherhood was immediately a step ahead of the other players around the table, at least from the outside. The smaller political groups that were behind the uprisings' success lacked leadership, structure and political experience, while the Brotherhood boasted decades of familiarity with the inner workings of Egyptian politics. Its consistent availability of funding, outreach capacity and popular support contributed to its apparently advantageous position.

Nevertheless, internal divisions became apparent once again when the SCAF announced that a Constitutional Referendum would take place on 18 March. This was meant to pave the way towards the September 2011 parliamentary elections, amending articles from the 1971 Constitution that severely limited political participation.[48] Despite this, the majority of the country's opposition groups were concerned that an election held too soon would inevitably favour long-established movements, such as the Brotherhood, over the newly formed revolutionary ones.[49] This concern was shared by a large portion of the Brotherhood's own ranks, who feared that by endorsing the referendum the Brotherhood would lose the support of the population. This was not limited to those belonging to the Youth or more Reformist members, but was shared by some Conservatives and hardliners. A senior member who at the time was very close to al-Shater also recalls that he was angered and confused by the way in which the leadership was handling the transitional period:

> I met the *murshid* [Supreme Guide] soon after Mubarak resigned. And I told him 'this is not the way we work. You educated us to change step by step in society, why are we sharing with the secular revolutionaries, whose strategies we don't agree with?' And he said that we share because now doing this was the best for society, so now I can understand why [from his perspective] we changed and went directly into the revolution, then into elections and supported SCAF in the referendum. We made the people we shared Tahrir square with into enemies and I think the army knew us. They knew our ideology and they manipulated us, they tried to use us as a threat to the secular groups. So the military used the Islamists as a tool, which is not the first time in the history of the country.[50]

Dismissing growing internal concerns, the Guidance Office campaigned in favour of the referendum, fearing that siding against the SCAF would take away its privileges. The beginning of the transition process was therefore marked by competing narratives coming out of the Brotherhood, as internal divisions started to become apparent. Despite calls to boycott, more than 18 million Egyptians voted in the referendum, which passed with 77% of the vote, therefore paving the way to parliamentary elections.[51] With these results in mind, the Brotherhood set out to establish the first official political party in the history of the organisation.

The Freedom and Justice Party

The FJP (*hizb al-hurriya wa al- 'adala*) was founded on 30 April 2011, officially marking the Brotherhood's break from illegality and setting a milestone in its history. The party represented more than just the movement's means to compete in the upcoming parliamentary elections and embodied the peak of its troubled politicisation process that had begun in 1939. After decades of operating at the fringes of Egyptian politics, it appeared that the Brotherhood had managed to make the long-sought shift to centre stage. However, the FJP did not have a smooth ride ahead. The founding of the party was problematic from the very start, as years of internal struggles and rivalries were encapsulated in its creation. Because of its divisive foundation process, the FJP was weakened by significant internal difficulties. The movement's organisational structure and pre-existing schisms greatly limited its development and political trajectory and, rather than representing the progression into its new political role, the FJP became a mirror of the movement's lack of unity and cohesiveness.

Nevertheless, its creation was highly symbolic, as it also embodied Egypt's newly found political openness. Eleven individuals 'known for their religious commitment and discipline' were handpicked to form the party's executive board.[52] Mohammed Morsi was appointed as president, and Essam al-Arian as vice-president, while the position of Secretary General went to Saad el-Katatni. From the very beginning the FJP sought to appeal to the Egyptian masses and was put forward as a *hizb madani* (civil party) 'with an Islamic frame of reference', with inclusiveness as one of its strong points.[53] Its founding statement also declared its faithfulness to the aims of the revolution, claiming:

> We are working to rebuild state institutions on the basis of a strong and sound commitment to the will of the free Egyptian people [...] to enhance the unity of the national fabric and induce a united coherent and solid fusion within the community. We aspire to get everyone in the nation working as part of a team, seeking to achieve the hopes and goals of Egypt in the battle of renaissance and construction.[54]

Inclusiveness was also reflected in its membership, as the party leaders stated that they were 'willing to form an alliance with the political forces that agree to our principles, whether they are socialists, liberals, or other Islamist forces and all forces concerned about this homeland'.[55] Reportedly, only 35% of its 500,000 members came from the Brotherhood, women held full membership,[56] and the chairman was Rafiq Habib, a well-known Cristian Copt.[57] This diversity was also meant to symbolise the FJP's apparent independence from the Brotherhood, an aspect that was central to Supreme Guide Mohamed Badie's message stating that the movement 'sought to participate, not to dominate' and aimed at advancing the interests of the nation as a whole.[58] However, this portrayed autonomy was far from reality.

Behind the scenes, there was no doubt that the Brotherhood envisioned the FJP to be its political arm from the very start. The FJP's official founding statement itself reads 'we are [...] a civil party with an Islamic frame of reference, *founded by the Muslim Brotherhood*, for all Egyptians'.[59] Similarly, the party programme and platform drew considerably from the 2007 Brotherhood's manifesto, stating that 'the party is dedicated to peaceful and gradual reform along Islamic lines', which includes 'the reform of the individual, the family, the society, the government, and the institutions of the state'.[60] To anyone familiar with the Brotherhood's history it becomes immediately clear that these were the organisation's aims, rather than those of the revolution. Therefore, from the very start, the FJP had a double nature and objective: achieving the demands of the uprisings as well as implementing the organisation's mission.[61] This duality would of course bring about some considerable inconsistencies between strategy and ideology, but the movement's internal discontent represented a much bigger challenge.

The creation of the FJP was treated as a formality by the Brotherhood's leadership, who did not engage the wider membership in any process of reflection or discussion.[62] Khairat al-Shater, now out of prison, was one of the driving forces behind the FJP's trajectory. The businessman saw the FJP as an 'instrument to engage in political conflict' and to facilitate the Brotherhood's rise to power. He was also behind the move forbidding its members to join any party other than the FJP. The Youth leaders who had argued in favour of the creation of a political party for years, such as Mohammad, felt completely alienated from the entire process and internal disagreements reached an all-time high. They felt that the creation of the FJP went against the aims of the revolution, and that the leadership was manipulating the transitional process for its own gains. In an unprecedented move, hundreds of members came together against the organisation's Supreme Guide, asking for 'better representation [...] in the group's higher power structures and the full independence of the Brotherhood's nascent FJP from all proselytizing bodies'.[63] Some of them angrily defeated and created their own parties, such as the *Hizb al-Nahda* (Renaissance Party) and the *Hizb al-Tayyar al-Masry* (Egyptian Current Party). One of its founders recalls the reasons that led him to leave the organisation: 'We told them [the Guidance Bureau] 'You cannot go by yourself, create a party, you'll get burned. Wait 3 or 4 years, and *then* create a party. [...] You need to take a step back and let [the people] fight. But they did not listen to us'.[64] Upon the Brotherhood refusal to listen to the demands of its Reformist wings the movement was marred by a high number of defections from its members, while others were purged by the Conservative leadership themselves. Ultimately, this projected the movement's internal schisms and lack of a cohesive message and political manifesto into the public realm, dealing a heavy blow to its credibility and legitimacy.

Further fragmentation and the road to the presidency

Despite its internal chaos, the FJP performed remarkably well in the September 2011 parliamentary elections. It ran with the Democratic Alliance, which won a staggering 10,138,134 votes, over a third of the total, meaning that the FJP emerged as the largest bloc in parliament, holding 47% of the available seats.[65] This victory solidified the fact that, over the course of a few months, the Brotherhood transformed from an illegal movement into a powerful political actor – a metamorphosis that came with both internal and external challenges. First of all, the organisation's popularity was not lost on the SCAF, which also did not intend to relinquish power. According to Mohamed Sudan, the realisation that the deep state essentially continued to run Egypt was a major factor behind the Brotherhood's decision to field a presidential candidate. The organisation had stated several times that they did not wish to do so, as they professed no desire to become a complete ruling majority.[66] However, after a meeting between el-Katatni and the SCAF, it became clear that 'is a façade, we are not a democracy but a military state, we are just actors fighting SCAF and the deep state at the same time, we cannot change anything, we have no real power [...] We did not like it [filing a presidential candidate], but we had to do it'.[67] Despite internal calls against doing so the final decision was left to the Brotherhood's Shura Council, where the motion passed with a narrow margin of 56 to 52 votes. It is clear that this was far from a unanimous decision, with even Mohammed Morsi himself stating 'We have chosen the path of the presidency not because we are greedy for power, but because we have a majority in parliament which is unable to fulfil its duties'.[68]

Regardless of the real reasoning behind it, the decision to compete in the presidential elections was the final straw that irremediably broke the organisation apart. The Youth and other dissidents vehemently opposed it, rightly arguing that it would tarnish the Brotherhood's credibility. The decades-long struggle for power between Fotouh and al-Shater also reached its peak, with the former announcing that he would then run for the presidency as an independent.[69] This act of rebellion would result in such animosity that Fotouh eventually left the organisation, whose internal struggle had by then become evident to the public. A former member who also left the Brotherhood over these very issues told me:

> It was all al-Shater's idea, as he was one of the most influential leaders in the Brotherhood. [...] During the transition, we spoke to them and said 'you have to wait 3–4 years', if in 4 years, we have equality, justice, freedom, and free elections, the Brotherhood would naturally come to power. [...] We have to make sure not to overstretch ourselves, we need to make sure that people do not think that this is going to be an Islamic state. But al-Shater wanted a

president. They just wanted to take over. They kept saying 'this is our time, after 80 years, we must take over'. They waited 80 years, could they not have waited 4 more?[70]

Another former member reinforced these rumours, explaining that al-Shater had been allegedly grooming 'his people' for years, with Morsi being one of them, ready to place them in positions of power: 'He [al-Shater] restructured the Brotherhood in such a way that it will always be in his favour. He created people in the past twenty years to put them in key positions. He can be in control behind the curtains. People like Morsi'.[71]

From then on, everything happened at augmented speed. With Fotouh now out of the picture, al-Shater was put forward as the presidential candidate by the Shura Council. Being one of the four deputies of Supreme Guide Mohamed Badie, al-Shater's influence went way beyond that role: the multimillionaire was one of the Brotherhood's main financers, and because of the position of power he held in the past, the senior leader would give the group a strong grip on both the country's legislative and executive branches.[72] However, his candidacy was short lived, as it was rejected by the Presidential Election Commission in April 2012.[73] With the presidential elections only a few months away, the Brotherhood had to file another presidential candidate in order to make use of the unprecedented opportunity ahead of them. Its back-up candidate was Mohammed Morsi, head of the FJP, Guidance Bureau's former member, head of the Brotherhood's parliamentary bloc in 2000–2005, and one of al-Shater's closest pupils.[74]

Despite his developed political career, Morsi's association to the more conservative wing of the Brotherhood and his lack of charisma when compared to al-Shater arguably limited his appeal. When asked about Morsi's candidacy, a former member commented: 'Morsi was not even the second choice, he was the third one. [He was chosen because] he was a student in the class of al-Shater, so obviously he trusted him'.[75] As it was the case with the foundation of the FJP, this particular appointment was also made on the basis of loyalty over expertise. Arguably, this is one of the main internal factors that led to the premature fall of the FJP.

The Islamists' takeover

Despite the less than favourable circumstances, Morsi ended up being referred to as 'the candidate of the revolution'. This was mostly due to the fact that, during the second and last round of presidential elections, his only opponent was Mubarak-affiliated ex-Prime Minister Ahmad Shafiq. These particular circumstances meant that Egyptians essentially had to choose between the blatant continuation of the Mubarak regime, or take a leap of faith and endorse the Brotherhood. Several secular activists indeed recall reluctantly voting for Morsi because of the real lack of alternatives. This also led to them being labelled as 'lemon-squeezers', a nickname that refers to the Egyptian custom of squeezing lemon over food on the verge of going off in order to mask its flavour. This alone indicates that, from the very beginning, the Brotherhood did not enjoy the high levels of popular support that they claimed – and thought – they did.

Morsi won with 13.2 million votes or 51.7% of the ballot, against Shafiq's 12.3 million votes or 48.3%.[76] He was sworn in on 30 June 2012 as Egypt's first democratically elected president, first without an affiliation to the military forces, and as a representative of one of the very few Islamist organisations to gain power in the region through a democratic process. These conditions made it clear from the start that the president-elect was set to tackle unprecedented expectations and challenges, some of the main ones being the task of guiding Egypt through a post-revolutionary democratic transition while facing the remnants of Mubarak's deep state. In addition to this was the Brotherhood's lack of unity and internal cohesion, which saw large numbers of dissatisfied members either leaving the organisation or being expelled. Nevertheless, Morsi's rise to the presidency through the ballot box was a deeply symbolic moment not only for the Brotherhood, but also for Islamist movements across the region more widely. It signified the end of decades of illegality and celebrated the fact that, for the first time since the Brotherhood's creation in 1928, the Islamist project finally seemed to be within reach. However, this elation was short-lived, as it would all come crashing down just over one year later.

A complete breakdown and analysis of the FJP's political performance in government is beyond the scope of this book. The aim here is to clearly trace the existence of internal tensions and splinters within the Brotherhood before and after the 2011 uprisings, in order to understand what is behind the fragmentation it experienced following the 2013 coup d'état. Indeed, there are many compelling works that have closely examined the FJP's time in government, such as those by Carrie Rosefsky Wickham, Hazem Kandil and Alison Pargeter.[77] Nevertheless, a brief discussion of the circumstances that led to the rapid decline of the Brotherhood's popular support and to the military coup is necessary, to then analyse how different factions within the organisation are reflecting upon them after their violent removal.

Morsi's election undeniably constituted an unprecedented breakthrough for an organisation that had spent most of its existence under illegality and state repression. Yet, despite decades in opposition the Brotherhood lacked any real experience in governing a country, especially one on the road to a democratic transition. In addition, Morsi had to do so while trying not to trigger a major backlash from the deep state, and without simultaneously alienating either the Brotherhood's secular supporters or its own members. The fact that a large portion of the Brotherhood membership felt increasingly disillusioned with the political project further exacerbated these already challenging circumstances. This was mostly because both the Brotherhood and the FJP were controlled by the same small handful of individuals, among whom al-Shater was the undiscussed leader, whose conservative stance alienated the majority of those members who actively participated in the uprisings. Therefore, when it was faced with the task of forming a government, the Brotherhood was neither united nor had a coherent overarching agenda.

Any external observer might speculate that, given the precariousness of these circumstances, the easiest choice for the Brotherhood would have been entering into some sort of cooperation with its secular counterparts that played a key role in the uprisings. Yet, those in charge of the Brotherhood mostly belonged to its conservative wing and were therefore deeply suspicious of outsiders. There was also a sense that, after waiting to rule for over 80 years, Brotherhood leaders did not want to share such a milestone achievement with any other political force. Regardless of the reasoning behind it, this isolationist stance played a considerable part in the Brotherhood's demise and is still affecting its regrouping process today.

The FJP's party formed a cabinet composed mostly of technocrats who were once again chosen largely according to personal loyalty rather than technical competency – a practice that is now referred to as the 'Ikhwanization' of the state. This speaks directly to the issue of the lack of professionalism that certain Brotherhood members had already identified in the decade preceding the 2011 uprisings, who now also accuse the FJP of not having been humble enough to realise that the movement could not have ruled by itself. As demonstrated further on, a desire to go back into education to tackle this professionalism gap is something that characterises a vast portion of the movement's membership today. For now, this also shows that the Brotherhood's performance while in government is indeed inseparable from the party's troublesome foundation process, and that Morsi's rule further exacerbated pre-existing internal divisions rather than restoring organisational unity.

Once elected into government, the Brotherhood faced an unprecedented existential question, concerning how to maintain ideological legitimacy while also fulfilling the goals of the revolution. One of the major obstacles during this process was that, while Brotherhood leaders all shared a commitment to reforms within 'an Islamic frame of reference', they also lacked a blueprint of what an Islamic state would look like. A point of contention that comes up repeatedly during my conversations with former and current members is indeed this lack of a common vision, and the different values held by factions within the Brotherhood. For example, while many senior figures in the Guidance Bureau subscribed to a very conservative version of Islam, the more Reformist and Youth wings shared a vision that emphasised the importance of pluralism, human rights and gender equality.[78] It follows that any attempt from the FJP to appease either side would result in the other one feeling betrayed, without even taking into account the perceptions of the population.

Amr Darrag, who served as Egypt's Minister of Planning and International Cooperation under the FJP, also blames the FJP's chaotic political behaviour on the organisation's lack of a coherent ideological and political vision:

> This is what I really mean when I said that we, as the Ikhwan, failed because we were not revolutionary enough. We had to continue on that [revolutionary] path while the transitional period was allowing us to set the structures in place to eventually lead to major change. Nobody thought that the revolution was going to happen, so nobody had any plans for the transitional period, or the expertise and plans necessary to rule a country. We had a lot of knowledgeable and expert people in the Ikhwan who participated in political life throughout Mubarak's time, but we lacked an overall strategy and agenda.[79]

This lack of a clear political vision was openly reflected in the FJP's political trajectory, and embodied by the so-called 'Brotherhood Constitution' of November 2012. From the beginning, the process of forming a Constitutional Committee was an incredibly troublesome one, with secular groups such as the Kefaya (Enough) movement calling for a boycott and accusing the Brotherhood of having betrayed the goals of the revolution.[80] The actual text that was produced epitomised both the country's lack of political consensus and the Brotherhood's ideological confusion. For example, controversial articles included in the Constitution confirmed Sha'ria Law as the main source of jurisprudence, but failed to kick-start institutional reforms, openly protect human rights, or enforce freedom of expression and religion.[81] The wave of popular discontent that characterised the entire process, coupled with confusion of the Brotherhood's Nahda (Renaissance) Project to tackle the worsening economic crisis, eventually escalated in the bloody clashes now known as the 'battle of Itthihadiya'.

Back to square one

The battles that took place outside the presidential palace in the week of 5 December 2012 saw anti-Brotherhood protesters clashing with both police forces and Brotherhood supporters. The armed forces quickly capitalised on the high levels of brutality from all sides and released a statement in which they withdrew their alleged support for the government, saying: 'The Armed Forces realise their responsibility to preserve the higher interests of the country and to secure and protect vital targets, public institutions and the interests of innocent citizens'.[82] The withdrawal of what little military support Morsi could count on marked the beginning of the end of the Brotherhood government, as in the following months the presidency's authority was eroded little by little, eventually culminating in the 3 July 2013 coup d'état.

Soon after the approval of the Constitution, it became clear that the Brotherhood's lack of a strong political vision and its internal crisis were taking their toll on its ability to stay in power, as the FJP consistently alienated secular and revolutionary groups and refused to take part in dialogue. In the months that followed the battle of the Itthihadiya, popular protests and violent clashes continued as Morsi scrambled to maintain power. Popular discontent escalated steadily and on 30 June 2013, the day marking the one-year anniversary of Morsi's presidential inauguration, millions of Egyptians gathered in squares across the country chanting 'the people want the fall of the regime'.[83] The ominous echo of the cry that became symbolic of the 2011 uprisings effectively signalled the end of the Brotherhood government. Driven by the Tamarod (Rebellion) movement, a grassroots Youth group formed in April 2013, demonstrators accused the Brotherhood of having hijacked the revolution for its own means and asked for early presidential elections.[84] This was the opening that the armed forces had been waiting for.

After a series of failed ultimatums al Sisi led the military coup against Morsi on 3 July 2013. The armed forces arrested Morsi and other prominent Brotherhood leaders, suspended the 2012 Constitution, and declared Adly Mansour, the SCAF's Chief Justice, as interim president of Egypt.[85] In the months following the events of 3 July, the Brotherhood entered the harshest repression of its troubled history so far, and fell into a deep state of stagnation, which it is still struggling to get out of. From this, in order to fully understand the main challenges that the Brotherhood now faces in the aftermath of the coup, it is necessary to briefly unpack the main circumstances that led to the FJP's toppling.

Assessing the Brotherhood's fall

Just over 12 months after Morsi's symbolic rise to power, the organisation found itself in the midst of the worst crisis in its history so far. The reasons behind such a rapid rise and fall have since been the subject of numerous studies, most notably by Khalil al-Anani and Ashraf El-Sherif. In the words of El-Sherif 'though it had to operate in a hostile political environment, the Brotherhood ultimately failed because of its own political, ideological, and organisational failures'.[86] Al-Anani also attributes the fall of the Islamist government to three key factors: the Brotherhood's lack of a revolutionary agenda; its organisational stagnation and inertia; and its leaders' incompetence and inexperience in government.[87] However, while the Brotherhood undeniably had a part in creating the circumstances that led to its fall, the context in which it politicised also has to be taken into account. In particular, two key external factors that considerably exacerbated the Brotherhood's own shortcomings were the deep state's unwillingness to relinquish power, and the domestic and international media's smear campaign against Islamist movements that gained power through the uprisings, and which significantly shaped perceptions and narratives. Overall, through my conversations with both current and former members I have identified four main factors that contributed to Morsi's untimely demise. In the aftermath of 2013, these have now become core points of contention that contribute to the Brotherhood's ongoing fragmentation and troublesome restructuring process.

First of all, from an ideological perspective, it is undeniable that the Brotherhood lacked a coherent vision of an 'Islamist Project' and consequently made policy decisions that were inconsistent with its ideological claims to Islamic legitimacy. In the political vacuum that followed the fall of Mubarak, the organisation chose power politics and a quick ascent over ideological integrity, pursuing direct rule rather than the gradual Islamisation of society.[88] There was also a considerable gap between its claims to Islamic legitimacy and its actual policy-making, as it was embodied by the controversial 2012 Constitution. Therefore, the lack of coherence between the Brotherhood's Islamist roots and its actual behaviour in power left many dissatisfied, and negatively impacted on its credibility.

Politically, the Brotherhood severely miscalculated the amount of support and legitimacy it actually had, failing to include secular and revolutionary groups into the decision-making processes. The combination of its inexperience and quick move towards political domination meant that the organisation failed to reform the state institutions that remained faithful to the Mubarak regime, which eventually caused its downfall. In addition, the Brotherhood Conservative leaders were deeply distrustful of outsiders, and failed to realise that forming a coalition with secular forces would have been key to successfully dismantling the deep state. As al-Anani points out, the selection of al-Shater and then Morsi as presidential candidates is an accurate reflection of what the balance of power was within the organisation at the time.[89] In the words of a former member:

> The big problem is that the Brotherhood was still controlled by the older generation, and they were fixed back in time way before 2011. I don't think they understood what happened and how big and dynamic it was; I don't think they understand it today [...] Every time it came to taking a decision that was going to either please the revolutionaries or the old guard/deep state,

they went with the deep state. They were thinking that rather than dismantling the deep state and its institutions, they thought they could use it for their benefit. That was so naïve.[90]

Another shortcoming comes from the structure of the Brotherhood organisation itself. Its hierarchical rigidity meant that the movement was incapable of adapting to its changing circumstances, which, in turn, accelerated internal mutiny rather than unity. This becomes clear when looking at the political appointments that were made within the FJP, which took place according to personal loyalty rather than expertise. This not only alienated a considerable part of the membership, but also meant that those in a position of power often lacked any real professionalism, which then translated into the FJP's political behaviour. Mohammad, who left the movement to co-found the Egyptian Current Party, says:

> One of their biggest mistakes was trying to build on loyalty rather than on competence [...] it was all about the inner circle and the clique, all the while there were excellent people from the Brotherhood and from outside who were willing to work with them in the early stages [...] there were some excellent people who were reduced to tears because of direct exclusion.[91]

Finally, the Brotherhood did not manage to successfully address the permanence of the status quo in the country, which saw the armed forces still controlling the security and judiciary apparatuses. While there were some attempts to do so, the Brotherhood's historically complicated relationship with the regime allegedly led to some of its leaders believing that they could successfully co-opt the deep state. Throughout Morsi's presidency, the FJP's political analysts failed to correctly assess the balance of power in the country, the real objectives of the deep state, the size of the opposition, and the surprising rate at which the Brotherhood's popularity was dropping. These miscalculations also led to some of the key leaders, such as al-Shater and foreign affairs secretary Mohamed Sudan, to disregards direct warnings about an upcoming coup. Despite the general consensus that the armed forces would have seized power regardless of which government was appointed, the Brotherhood's dismissal of their influence came with a harsh price to pay.

Conclusion

In conclusion, some common themes emerge from the analysis of both the Brotherhood's rapid politicisation and the circumstances that led to its fall. Namely, the lack of professionalism in its leaders, the absence of internal unity and cohesion, and the refusal to reform the organisation's rigid hierarchical structure to accommodate differences and individual initiatives. While the Brotherhood's history of repression can explain tendencies such as isolationism, distrust towards outsiders, and organisational rigidity, it nevertheless does not justify them. If anything, the Brotherhood's unwillingness to reform itself in the light of the changes brought about by the 2011 uprisings, and its inability to win over the hearts of the people and placate state institutions, ultimately made its leadership unsustainable.

More importantly, the themes that have emerged reflect grievances internal to the Brotherhood that pre-date the events of January 2011, rather than having been created by them. This also shows that 2011 did not represent a moment of real change in the history of the movement, as it is widely claimed, since the Brotherhood did not drastically alter its behaviour or trajectory once it seized the opportunity it was given. On the contrary, the premature failure of its political experiment and the wave of repression that followed have since dramatically challenged its historical experiences and patterns of behaviour.

Having a working understanding of the main factors that led to the Brotherhood's fall is crucial to understanding the challenges that the organisation faces in the aftermath of the 2013 coup. The pre-existing grievances and internal tensions identified above are playing a central role in the Brotherhood's current fragmentation, as discussed below.

Notes

1 They were Mohammed Morsi and Saad el-Katatni. Kandil, *Inside the Brotherhood*, 137.
2 Marie Vannetzel, 'The party, the *Gama'a* and the *Tanzim*: the organizational dynamics of the Egyptian Muslim Brotherhood's post-2011 failure', *British Journal of Middle Eastern Studies*, 40:2 (2017), 211–226, 213.
3 Eric Trager, 'The unbreakable Muslim Brotherhood' (Sept/Oct 2011) www.foreignaffairs.com/articles/north-africa/2011-09-01/unbreakable-muslim-brotherhood (accessed 16 April 2020).
4 Zachary Laub, 'Egypt's Muslim Brotherhood', *Council on Foreign Relations* (3 December 2012) www.cfr.org/africa/egypts-muslim-brotherhood/p23991 (accessed 16 April 2020).
5 Mohammed Ayoob, *The Many Faces of Political Islam: Religion and Politics in the Muslim World* (Ann Arbor, M.I.: University of Michigan Press, 2008), 65.
6 Richard Mitchell, *The Society of the Muslim Brothers* (New York: Oxford University Press, 1969), 235.
7 Brynjar Lia, *The Society of the Muslim Brothers in Egypt: The Rise of an Islamic Mass Movement 1928–1942* (Reading: Ithaca Press, 1999), 202.

8 Robin Wright, *Secret Rage: The Wrath of Militant Islam* (New York: Simon & Schuster, 2001), 175–179.
9 Barry Rubin, *Islamic Fundamentalism in Egyptian Politics* (New York: St. Martins Press, 1990), 10–13.
10 Ibid.
11 Raymond Hinnebusch, 'Egypt under Sadat: elites, power structure, and political change in a post-populist state', *Social Problems*, 28:4 (April 1981), 442–464, 441.
12 Abdullah al-Arian, *Answering the Call: Popular Islamic Activism in Sadat's Egypt* (New York: Oxford University Press, 2014), 17.
13 Al-Anani, *Inside the Muslim Brotherhood*, 142–143.
14 Mona El-Ghobashy, 'The metamorphosis of the Egyptian Muslim Brothers', *International Journal of Middle East Studies*, 37:3 (2005), 381–387.
15 'Egypt: social programmes bolster the appeal of Muslim Brotherhood', *IRIN* (February 2006) www.irinnews.org/report/26150/egypt-social-programmes-bolster-appeal-of-muslim-brotherhood (accessed 16 April 2020).
16 Ibid.
17 Steven Brooke, 'Egypt', in Shadi Hamid, William McCants (eds.) *Rethinking Political Islam* (Oxford: Oxford University Press, 2017), 17–32.
18 Author Interview. London, 2017.
19 Author Interview. Istanbul, 2018.
20 Ana Soage, Jorge Fuentelsaz Franganillo, 'The Muslim Brothers in Egypt', in Barry Rubin (ed.) *The Muslim Brotherhood in Focus: The Organization and Politics of a Global Islamic Movement* (London: Palgrave Macmillan, 2010), 40–43.
21 Victor Willi, *The Fourth Ordeal: A History of the Muslim Brotherhood in Egypt* (Cambridge: Cambridge University Press), 388.
22 Ibid., 389.
23 Wickham, *The Muslim Brotherhood*, 133.
24 Ibid., 134.
25 El-Ghobashy, 'The metamorphosis of the Egyptian Muslim Brothers', 374.
26 Khalil Al-Anani, 'The young Brotherhood in search of a new path', *Hudson Institute* (October 2009) www.hudson.org/research/9900-the-young-brotherhood-in-search-of-a-new-path (accessed 16 April 2020).
27 Shadi Hamid, William McCants, Rashid Dar, 'Islamism after the Arab Springs: between the Islamic State and the Nation State', *Brookings* (January 2017), 3.
28 Doha Samir, 'The Muslim Brotherhood's generational gap: politics in the post-revolutionary era', *AlMuntaqa*, 1:2 (2018), 32–52, 39.
29 Meir Hatina, 'The "other Islam": the Egyptian Wasat Party', *Critique: Critical Middle Eastern Studies*, 14:2 (2005), 171–184.
30 Author Interview. Istanbul, September 2018.
31 Author Interview. London, 2018.
32 Ibid.
33 Ibid.
34 Author Interviews with secular activists, 2014.

35 Salma El Shahed, 'Freedom, bread, dignity: has Egypt answered January 25th demands?' *Al Arabiya* (January 2015) http://english.alarabiya.net/en/perspective/ (accessed 16 April 2020).
36 Wickham, *The Muslim Brotherhood*, 155.
37 Ibid., 160.
38 Author Interview with a former Brotherhood member. London, 2016.
39 Author Interview with a former Brotherhood member. London, 2015.
40 Ibrahim El Houdaiby, 'Islamism in and after Egypt's Revolution', in Bahgat Korany, Rabab El-Mahdi (eds.) *Arab Spring in Egypt: Revolution and Beyond* (Cairo: American University of Cairo Press, 2012), 130.
41 Author Interview with Mohammed Sudan, FJP Foreign Relations Secretary. London, 2016.
42 Author Interviews with secular activists, 2016.
43 Ibid.
44 Essam El-Errian, 'What the Muslim Brotherhood wants', *The New York Times* (February 2011) www.nytimes.com/2011/02/10/opinion/10erian.html (accessed 16 April 2020).
45 Wickham, *The Muslim Brotherhood*, 169.
46 Haitham Abu Khalil, *The Reformist Brotherhood* (Cairo: Dawwin House, 2012), 231.
47 Tarek Osman, *Egypt on the Brink: From Nasser to the Muslim Brotherhood* (London: Yale University Press, 2013), 119.
48 Proposed amendments included a limitation to the presidency to at most two four-years terms, judicial supervision of elections, a requirement for the president to appoint at least one vice president, a commission to draft a new Constitution following the parliamentary election, and easier access to presidential elections by candidates (to be done by achieving 30,000 signatures from at least 15 provinces, 30 members of a chamber of the legislature, or nomination by a party holding at least one seat in the legislature). Noha El-Hennawy, 'Commission announces proposed changes to Egyptian Constitution, *Egypt Independent* (February 2011) www.egyptindependent.com/news/commission-announces-proposed-changes-egyptian-constitution (accessed 16 April 2020).
49 'Egypt to call March referendum this week: lawyer', *Reuters* (March 2011) www.reuters.com/article/us-egypt-referendum-idUSTRE71Q11620110227 (accessed 16 April 2020).
50 Author Interview. Istanbul, 2017.
51 'Egypt referendum strongly backs constitutional changes', *BBC News* (March 2011) www.bbc.co.uk/news/world-middle-east-12801125 (accessed 16 April 2020).
52 Mahmud, 'Abd al-Mun'im. Interview, quoted in Wickham, *The Muslim Brotherhood*, 175–176.
53 The Founding Statement of the Freedom and Justice Party (2011), www.fjponline.com/view.php?pid=1 (accessed 16 April 2020).
54 Ibid.

55 Mohammed Zaid, 'El Erian to political parties: win votes then discuss power', *Ikhwan Web* (June 2011) www.ikhwanweb.com/article.php?id=28713 (accessed 16 April 2020).
56 Although women were historically barred from full membership in the Brotherhood, roughly a thousand of the FJP's founding members were female.
57 Azzurra Meringolo, 'Egypt: Rafiq Habib and Muslim Brotherhood-Coptic relations', *Reset Dialogues* (August 2011) www.resetdoc.org/story/egypt-rafiq-habib-and-muslim-brotherhood-coptic-relations/ (accessed 16 April 2020).
58 'MB Chairman: we seek to participate not to dominate', *Ikhwan Web* (April 2011) www.ikhwanweb.com/article.php?id=28432 (accessed 16 April 2020).
59 Freedom and Justice Party's political platforms (2011), www.fjponline.com/articles.php?pid=80 (accessed 16 April 2020). Emphasis added.
60 Nathan Brown, 'The Muslim Brotherhood as a helicopter parent', *Carnegie* (May 2011) http://carnegieendowment.org/2011/05/27/muslim-brotherhood-as-helicopter-parent (accessed 16 April 2020).
61 Vannetzel, 'The party, the *Gama'a* and the *Tanzim*', 222.
62 Ibid., 220.
63 Mona Farag, 'Egypt's Muslim Brotherhood and the January 25 Revolution: new political party, new circumstances', *Contemporary Arab Affairs*, 5:2 (April 2012), 214–229, 219.
64 Author Interview. London, 2015.
65 'Muslim Brotherhood tops Egyptian poll result', *Al Jazeera* (January 2012) www.aljazeera.com/news/middleeast/2012/01/2012121125958580264.html (accessed 16 April 2020).
66 Farag, 'Egypt's Muslim Brotherhood', 221.
67 Author Interview with Mohammed Sudan. London, 2015.
68 As quoted in Pargeter, *Return to the Shadows*, 41.
69 Abu Khalil, *The Reformist Brotherhood*, 19.
70 Author Interview with a former Brotherhood member. Istanbul, 2015.
71 Author Interview with a former Brotherhood member. London, 2016.
72 'Muslim Brotherhood: Khairat al Shater', *Islamic Human Rights Commission* (May 2007), 10–13.
73 According to new elections rules, a candidate had to have been released from prison for six years before being allowed to run. Al Shater did not fit that requirement because he was only released in 2011. 'Egypt sets presidential elections rules', *BBC News* (January 2012) www.bbc.com/news/world-middle-east-16785829 (accessed 16 April 2020).
74 'Profile: Egypt's Mohammed Morsi', *BBC News* (April 2015) www.bbc.com/news/world-middle-east-18371427 (accessed 16 April 2020).
75 Author Interview with a former Brotherhood member. London, 2016.
76 'Muslim Brotherhood's Mursi declared Egypt's president', *BBC News* (June 2012) www.bbc.com/news/world-18571580 (accessed 16 April 2020).
77 Wickham, *The Muslim Brotherhood*; Kandil, *Inside the Brotherhood*; Pargeter, *Return to the Shadows*.

78 Wickham, *The Muslim Brotherhood*, 275.
79 Author Interview with Amr Darrag. Istanbul, August 2018.
80 Mirette Mabrouk, 'The view from a distance: Egypt's contentious new Constitution', *Brookings: Middle East Memo* (January 2013), 5.
81 'Egypt: New constitution mixed on support of rights', *Human Rights Watch* (November 2012) www.hrw.org/news/2012/11/30/egypt-new-constitution-mixed-support-rights (accessed 16 April 2020).
82 'Army warns it will not allow "dark tunnel"', *BBC News* (December 2012) www.bbc.com/news/world-middle-east-20651896 (accessed 16 April 2020).
83 'Profile: Egypt's Tamarod protest movement', *BBC News* (July 2013) www.bbc.co.uk/news/world-middle-east-23131953 (accessed 16 April 2020).
84 Adam Hellyer, 'Egypt after the Arab Spring: revolt and reaction', *Adelphi Series*, 55 (2015), 453–454, 35.
85 Mohammad Tabaar, 'Assessing in(security) after the Arab Spring: the case of Egypt', *American Political Science Association* (2013), 727–735, 731.
86 El-Sherif, 'The Egyptian Muslim Brotherhood's failures', 13.
87 Al-Anani, 'Upended path: the rise and fall of Egypt's Muslim Brotherhood'.
88 El-Sherif, 'The Egyptian Muslim Brotherhood's Failures', 13.
89 Al-Anani, 'Upended path: the rise and fall of Egypt's Muslim Brotherhood', 538.
90 Author Interview. London, 2015.
91 Author Interview. Istanbul, 2018.

2

The fall from grace

> We have a big war, but we are a peaceful movement and we want to go through it peacefully, doing the best for our people, and we will never give up, we need to save our history and our country too. We don't want power. We never wanted power, we have always looked to have a better lifestyle for our people.[1]

Many within the Brotherhood now refer to the toppling of Mohammed Morsi as a 'slow coup', which began straight after Mubarak's removal and the SCAF's seizing of the transitional process. Looking back, there are undeniably strong indications that the military forces never fully intended to relinquish power and that the deep state worked behind the scenes to stage and incite the popular protests that eventually led to the 3 July coup d'état. Nevertheless, the Brotherhood's shortcomings and role in bringing about their own downfall cannot be overlooked. As discussed later on, the interpretation of what factors led to such a premature overthrow of the movement, and the lessons that should be learnt from it, are a major point of contention dividing the Brotherhood in the post-2013 context and are therefore worthy of analysis.

Besides the permanence of the deep state and the obvious challenges posed by governing Egypt through a transitional process, the common perception among the population from the very beginning was that the Brotherhood was more interested in consolidating its own power rather than in fulfilling its ideological commitment to the establishment of an Islamic state, or in ensuring the safeguarding of Egyptian society. This is shared by Shuruq, a young activist who participated in the uprisings from the very beginning. She comes from a family of activists and recalls having to spend several hours debating with her parents to convince them to vote for Morsi. Yet, as she maintained contact with Brothers in the youth wing throughout the transitional period, she soon started having doubts about the intentions of the movement as a whole:

> The Brotherhood activists were saying 'ok we are fighting with you, but elections are the way to go'. The people started thinking that they were being

opportunistic, and if they said they were all about Islam they should be fighting together with us for *qassas* (retribution). The Brotherhood was using many buzzwords, such as 'the ballot box' and 'free elections', but I think they were trying to appease us, and to appease the West [...] they needed that acceptance. They needed to be seen as legitimate.[2]

The Brotherhood's policies and erratic political behaviour also failed to inspire trust in the population. During its one year in power the FJP rushed through a controversial Constitution, failed to include other actors in the decision-making process, and spent more time trying to re-establish organisational unity than providing good governance.[3] Indeed, two of the biggest grievances against the Morsi regime were the fact that he fell back upon the Brotherhood's infamous isolationism, actively alienating non-Islamists, and that the FJP consistently ignored the aims and goals of the revolution. While some of these behaviours can be traced back to the Brotherhood's troubled relationship with state institutions and general distrust of outsiders, it is also evident that those involved in the policy-making process quickly developed an almost idiosyncratic blind faith in democratic institutions. To many within the organisation, winning the presidential elections meant that nothing would prevent them from serving their term. Not only is such an approach in direct contrast with the movement's history as an opposition actor, but also reflects a criticism that many from within the Brotherhood commonly move against those who were in power at the time: that they were blinded by *hubris* (excessive pride, defiance). The organisation leaders' eagerness to gain and retain power after Mubarak's removal no matter what – even through striking deals with the deep state behind the scenes – further alienated those members who had already started to disengage from the movement, as well as furthering the perception that the Brotherhood was being not only 'not revolutionary enough', but also almost 'counter-revolutionary' in its ways.[4]

While these behaviours could in part be driven by the Brotherhood's lack of any direct experience in politics, many admit that in retrospect gaining power through a democratic process definitely contributed to making the organisation feel like it would be untouchable for the duration of their term, therefore feeding into the arrogance and naivety of its leaders.[5] This element is also recurrent in conversations with FJP ministers and leaders who, looking back, reveal that they were personally approached by both domestic and international figures warning them that a coup was in the making. One of the FJP's heads recalls being warned against the military's plans just a few weeks before Morsi's toppling, and now regrets not heeding that advice:

> On 21st June 2013 the American Consul called me and said she absolutely needed to see me because it was very urgent [...] She asked what Morsi was

going to do on the 30th [June]. I told her Morsi had faced lots of protests since he came to office and he always treated them softly, he would never use violence against them. She told me 'this time is different, what is he going to do?' [...] Then she stood up and asked me 'How much does Morsi trust Sisi?' and she was smiling.[6]

Throughout years of fieldwork I heard many similar variations of this story, meaning that there were several figures within the high ranks of the organisation who knew that a military coup was at least a plausible possibility. Despite their differences, they all now regret not taking such warnings seriously, even though they also point out that there was very little that the Brotherhood could have done at the time to stop it from happening. Nevertheless, such an overconfident approach also explains why the organisation did not acknowledge the real threat that popular discontent posed to their legitimacy until it was too late.

Power gained, power lost

Popular protests against the Brotherhood government routinely took place after the day of Morsi's election, and began escalating after the imposition of the controversial Brotherhood's Constitution in November 2012. The violent clashes that took place between Brotherhood supporters and protesters in December 2012, referred to as the battle of Ittihadiya,[7] were a clear warning that the movement was quickly losing what little popular support it had, but were unsurprisingly downplayed by Morsi's cabinet. The steady growth of popular discontent led to the formation of the Tamarod (rebellion) movement in April 2013, which played a key part in staging the popular uprisings that were then hijacked by the military in July. Channelling discontent against the Brotherhood from across the Egyptian population, the Tamarod gathered over 22 million signatures on a petition calling for early elections and for Morsi to step down, as an estimated 12 million Egyptians took to the streets on 30 June.[8] This came after Abdel Fattah al Sisi, then Minister of Defence, issued an ultimatum on 23 June calling for all political forces to reach an agreement, which we know never materialised.[9] However, such a statement from al Sisi was really aimed at deeply destabilising the Brotherhood's leadership, who had come to see the army general as their own man within the SCAF. Nevertheless, the FJP's newly acquired blind faith in electoral legitimacy and its desire to hold on to power marked the beginning of the end for the Brotherhood government, which refused to make compromises or enter into talks with other political forces until it was much too late. Despite growing unrest and clear warnings, the Brotherhood remained in denial until Morsi was actually put under house arrest on 3 July, the day that marked the military coup d'état which would drastically change the organisation's trajectory and from which the movement is still trying to recover.

While it did not necessarily come as a surprise to anyone familiar with the Brotherhood's history, the movement's confrontational stance and refusal to compromise until it was much too late can be explained by a combination of several key factors, such as the group's historical isolationism, distrust towards outsiders, lack of political expertise and a good dose of *hubris*. Nevertheless, such a defiant approach came with tragic consequences for the movement, as it spurred a regime crackdown that was much more brutal and bloodier than what the Brotherhood could have ever anticipated. Indiscriminate arrests, disappearances and targeted attacks against Brotherhood members and supporters began immediately after the coup and steadily escalated throughout July, eventually culminating in the Raba'a and Nah'da massacre on 14 August. Since the coup, the two squares had become the hub of nation-wide protests against the military takeover and the largest sit-in was held in Raba'a al-Adaweya Square, in the northern Cairo district of Nasr City.[10] Some 85,000 protesters from a variety of religious and political backgrounds camped there for six weeks, in a manner that much resembled the barricades in Tahrir Square during the 2011 uprisings. On 14 August, army tanks blocked all five exits to the square and security forces used snipers, bulldozers and ground forces to disperse the protesters. The bloodshed that followed killed over 1,000 people and is now considered a crime against humanity, even though the Sisi regime is still to be held accountable for it. The massacre also marked the beginning of a new, dark era in the Brotherhood's history, leaving the organisation in deeply unchartered territory.[11]

More than the coup itself, the massacres in Raba'a and Nah'da will forever scar the psyche and emotions of the Brothers who were there over those few weeks, especially during the last couple of days. In the years immediately following the bloodshed I felt like there was an unspoken agreement between me and my interviewees – we do not talk about Raba'a. Conversations would immediately shift, subjects would change, or we would refer to it as 'what happened in August', with lowered voices and averted gazes. Yet, over the past couple of years, something has drastically changed. As those who were in the square or lost a loved one begin settling into their new lives abroad and start to rethink what belonging to the Brotherhood means to them, they have also started to open up about Raba'a, unsolicited. Since then I have sat through more conversations than I can remember where the main topic was the horrors which took place that day at the hands of the military regime. I was told about siblings and relatives being killed on the spot, about people disappearing never to be found again; I saw men the age of my father weep uncontrollably in front of me. Many of my interviewees clearly display signs of deep trauma, while countless others do not have the tools or the means to properly process what they witnessed. Nevertheless, what this made me realise was that it was not the coup that shattered the hopes and dreams of those Brothers who were committed to the political process, rather, it was the Raba'a massacre that really embodied the unprecedented and unfamiliar nature of what was to follow.

The moment of change

The ousting of Mohammed Morsi and the Raba'a massacre combined left the Brotherhood in an unprecedented state of anguish and shock.[12] Having lost all control and facing a wave of repression and unprecedented brutality, the movement quickly found itself unable to rely on the historical tools of resistance that had allowed it to survive, and even thrive, under repression for most of its history. The movement lost power just as suddenly as it had gained it two years prior and, just as it was unable to govern Egypt through its transitional process, also found itself utterly unprepared to deal with the aftermath of the coup.

The chaos and lack of internal directions that followed Morsi's toppling were the first indicators that the Brotherhood was entering into deeply unchartered territory. This is particularly significant as the movement is no stranger to repression, having operated under a state of illegality since the 1950s that meant it only ever enjoyed limited freedoms and political inclusion, according to its alternating relationship with the regimes of Nasser, Sadat and Mubarak. Nevertheless, one of the Brotherhood's key resistance tools had been its ability to capitalise on its outlawed status by turning repression into a key marker of organisational identity that, combined with its famously strict hierarchical structure (*tanzim*), allowed it to survive and even thrive under an authoritarian environment. Much has been written about how the Brotherhood's organisational structure is one of its key assets, especially from the point of view of Social Movement Theory, which also points to the institution of a strong collective identity as a key factor that grants unity at times of turmoil.[13] In the case of the Brotherhood a key component of such a strong organisational identity is *mihna*, meaning ordeal or tribulation, which historically entrenched a sense of victimhood among its members and became 'the glue' that bound them together, providing a shared experience which boosted their resolve against authoritarianism and reinforced the movement's status as a legitimate opposition actor.[14] Other principles at the core of the Brotherhood's *tanzim*, such as 'listen and obey', historically allowed the leadership to control its members while at the same time putting forward a cohesive message and promoting loyalty and unity. In particular, through the imposition of a strong, top-down collective identity, loyalty and obedience to the movement's political mission were also promoted by intertwining members' ideological indoctrination to their advancement in the organisation's hierarchical system[15] and by tying members together in Brotherhood-only emotional, material and biological networks.[16] Therefore, these elements are at the core of what I refer to as the movement's historical 'tools' of resistance, which up to 2011 contributed to portraying the Brotherhood as a strong and united opposition actor.

However, the trauma and shock caused by Morsi's removal and the brutal wave of repression that followed largely invalidated these tools, leaving the Brotherhood to face an unprecedented set of challenges. Throughout numerous conversations that span over years with both former and current members, I have identified four elements that make the current repression facing the movement qualitatively different from anything it faced in the past. These are: the impact of the Brotherhood's experience in government; the scale of repression; the role of the younger generations; and the ensuing internal fragmentation.[17] While fully unpacking them here is beyond the scope of the book, it is nevertheless necessary to quickly review them in order to fully understand the dynamics and trajectories that are characteristic of the post-2013 context.

To begin with, the Brotherhood's sudden debut into electoral politics forced the movement to considerably rethink its strategy and message. The creation of the FJP brought old grievances back to the fore, with members openly condemning the organisation's lack of transparency and asking for political appointments to be made according to criteria such as professionalism, competency and pluralism, rather than loyalty or seniority.[18] Such high levels of internal discontent directly began to challenge core principles based on blind obedience and hierarchy, therefore weakening the organisation from the inside. It follows that the Brotherhood was already deeply divided by the time Morsi became president and this lack of internal unity was further aggravated by the brutality that followed his removal. The repression deployed by the Sisi regime is in fact qualitatively different from anything that the Brotherhood had experienced before. This is not only related to the unprecedented scale of brutality, which surpasses even that witnessed under Nasser; what makes this wave drastically different is the fact that repression is not only targeting the Brotherhood's leaders and senior members, but, rather, indiscriminately affects members from across the organisational spectrum, as well as supporters.[19] This dimension in particular makes the regime's crackdown somewhat new for a big portion of the Brotherhood's membership and also directly affects one of the core ways in which its leaders historically gain legitimacy, which up until 2011 was directly tied to the personal sacrifices they made for the organisation and the time they spent in prison.

The novelty of this dimension is therefore having unprecedented repercussions on the Brotherhood's younger generations, who are also one of the historically more internally marginalised groups. Their personal experience of repression up to this point was drastically different from that of the older leaders, as under Mubarak they became accustomed to taking part in electoral politics, albeit with limitations in place. In addition, their role in bringing about the 2011 uprisings and their participation alongside secular activities also means that the Youth tends to be more politically proactive than the Historical Leadership, and more open to dialogue and cooperation with outsiders. Mustafa Menshawy notes that this exposure to other political experiences partly feeds into processes of personal and ideological disengagement from the Brotherhood that pre-date the events of 2011, and that subsequently shaped the behaviour of a large part of the membership in the years that followed.[20] This disengagement means that many members now largely reject the Brotherhood's historical isolationism and are therefore unwilling to blindly follow orders, with many taking it upon themselves to develop ways to move past the current crisis. It follows that there is a large disconnect between the approaches to repressions that are being put forward by the Historical Leadership, and those faithful to them, and other factions within the movement in the aftermath of the coup. Internal fragmentation is now one of the biggest challenges that the Brotherhood has to tackle to successfully reunite and face the regime. However, in overt contrast to historical dynamics, these divisions do not only exist across the membership body but are, rather, affecting the leadership as well. The creation of rival and parallel offices, discussed later on, is therefore indicative of the Brotherhood being divided along vertical lines, which further complicates the process of rebuilding and creates greater space for competing views and initiatives to emerge.

From power to persecution

In the years that followed the coup, the movement grew increasingly fragmented along ideological, geographical and organisational lines. The rapid escalation of violence at the hands of the regime following Morsi's ousting reinforced the Brotherhood's conviction that the movement is still fighting an existential battle against the state. Indeed, al Sisi seems to be engaged in an almost personal struggle against the organisation, with another milestone being the designation of the Brotherhood as a terrorist organisation on 25 December 2013.[21] While the legality of such a designation remains disputed, it nevertheless allowed the regime to ban the FJP, seize and therefore freeze the movement's economic assets and to effectively shut down its civil society network.[22] Hit at the very source of its popular support base, this meant that almost overnight the Brotherhood's remaining historical tools of resistance were completely invalidated, leaving its leaders scrambling for alternatives.

The unfamiliarity of such a situation was further complicated by the mass arrest of the organisation's leaders and the scattering abroad of those who escaped. When the unprecedented brutality of the crackdown against the organisation became clear, a few Brotherhood leaders and FJP ministers fled to Qatar, Malaysia, Turkey and the UK to avoid being imprisoned. Soon enough, lower-ranking members realised that they were also being targeted and found themselves having to flee, often leaving their families behind. While this is hard to trace, it appears that those seeking a more ideologically compatible environment fled to Turkey, Qatar, Malaysia and Sudan, while more senior members relied on older connections and networks already established in the UK. There is also an undeniable class element that played a big part in determining who was able to flee and to where, which also still currently shapes the internal dynamics of Brotherhood diaspora groups that are in the process of settling abroad, as I have examined in the case of Turkey.[23] Nevertheless, the dimension of forced exile is not only relatively new to the Brotherhood, but is also further disrupting its strict organisational structures by bringing together members from a variety of social and economic backgrounds, as well as old leaders being dethroned in favour of new ones. By doing so, it is providing an avenue for renewed discontent against the movement's hierarchy to come to the fore, as individual members pursue greater agency, individualism and pluralism.

This new dimension and the other novelties brought about by forced exile are particularly clear in the case of Turkey, where a lot of the conversations at the core of this book took place. In the aftermath of the coup Turkey has become the hub of the Brotherhood's headquarters, hosting their media channels and mobilisation activities as well as witnessing the creation of competing leadership offices.[24] There are some clear factors that have facilitated the Brotherhood's settling in Turkey, the first and foremost being a historical relationship between the Brotherhood and Turkish Islamic figures that created an ideological welcoming context for its members.[25] Even more importantly, President Erdogan has consistently denounced the July 2013 military coup as illegitimate, launched a media campaign against al-Sisi and even openly challenged him in the United Nations' Security Council.[26] His support has gone even further, providing the Brotherhood with the legal and financial backing they needed to start building their transnational activism and advocacy networks.

However, a welcoming political and ideological environment is proving not to be enough to keep the Brotherhood united. In fact, the reality of having to settle into life in exile has considerably weakened the movement's organisational structure and therefore its ability to respond cohesively to repression.

Forced exile and the need for a new lens

The process of diasporic formation is almost entirely new for the Brotherhood. The organisation historically has a strong international network with branches spread across the world, but this transnational connotation should not be exaggerated. In fact, several studies on the Brotherhood's international presence point to an inherent disconnect between the 'mother' organisation and these international offices.[27] Moreover, with the exception of some senior figures, prior to 2013 Brotherhood members were seldom forced to leave the country en masse, as regime crackdowns on the movement historically took the form of lengthy prison sentences being imposed on its leaders.[28] With these patterns being significantly disrupted by the coup, the Brotherhood was suddenly faced with the monumental task of having to reunite while scattered abroad.

While these processes are still in flux and therefore complicated to assess fully, resettling and rebuilding have been far from smooth. The dimension of exile is providing unprecedented space for long-standing grievances and divisions to take centre stage. Simply put, the lack of a coherent message or strategy immediately following the coup allowed for struggles over legitimacy and leadership – and between members' agency and the organisation's hierarchical structures – to emerge, leading to the Brotherhood's fragmentation along ideological and organisational lines. This internal chaos is clearly reflected in the words of Ammar Fayed, former special secretary to Mohammed Morsi, who states 'Of course the organisation hasn't adapted to being in exile [...] in fact, we have failed to deploy effective opposition ever since the coup'.[29] The following chapters trace exactly what these divisions and patterns of disengagement look like, but for now it is necessary to acknowledge that a major source of this fragmentation lies in the fact that the unprecedented repression led to fundamental differences emerging within the Brotherhood on how to effectively respond to repression. In particular, during my fieldwork it became evident that there is a deep divergence between the 'classic' organisation – in this instance represented by the Historical Leadership and those faithful to them – and its members' responses to repression. These can be initially identified as tensions between stagnation and adaptation strategies, but they also tell a more compelling story: that the structures and mechanisms of control which kept the Brotherhood united for decades are being contested and, in the process, bear the potential for significant internal change and reformation.

The diasporic experience partially explains the quick disintegration of established chains of command in exile, as well as the emergence of questions regarding identity and belonging amongst Brotherhood members. Those who have been forcibly displaced from Egypt are brought together by shared traumas and experiences, in addition to the collective identity that binds them to the Brotherhood. While the shared experience of repression can indeed be a unifying one, diasporas can also be sites of contestation and offer individuals the opportunity to rethink their belonging to certain communities.[30] This is certainly the case for several of my interlocutors, who point to the experience of forced exile as the defining force that led them to rethink the terms of their membership with the Brotherhood and to question the movement's overarching control. This 'breakthrough' was described to me by Osama, a current member who thinks of himself as a dissenter:

> After the coup, when we came here [Istanbul], I realised that I had time to think [...] how did I get here? Why am I in this? Why am I a member of this organisation? Why should I keep listening to them [the Brotherhood's leaders] if I do not agree with what they are saying?[31]

Once a hardliner, when we first met Osama spoke harshly of those criticising the Brotherhood's leadership. As the years passed, each conversation showcased a more critical side of him and he now speaks openly of the often-painful process of having to rebuild his worldview. His testimony shows the extent to which some members have begun to question the hierarchical organisational structures and strict dogmas they have been socialised into for decades, rediscovering their individual voices and challenging the collective identity the Brotherhood historically relies on.[32]

This is not the case for everyone, as many seek comfort in the replication of the socialisation patterns and assigned roles that the Brotherhood relied on in Egypt. These go from the organisation of weekly *usra* meetings and regular social activities to the replication of the Brotherhood's social networks abroad, offering economic support and legal and bureaucratic advice to those who need it. These can be a lifeline for some members, while others complain that this 'copy and paste' process is making it harder for them to integrate into their new societies. This is the case of Abdullah, a primary school teacher from Alexandria, who initially found solace in finding the Brotherhood community abroad but soon started feeling constrained by it.

> So many people came here and the Ikhwan immediately found them a place to stay, and gave them a job [e.g. in the organisation's media channels], but they

never learnt Turkish, they never speak to anyone else [...] they have been here [in Istanbul] for five years, and if they leave the organisation they are lost.[33]

Abdullah is not alone in this, as there are growing numbers of current and former members who experience a sense of deep alienation. Yet, a significant novelty of the post-2013 context is that, while some give up their membership, others choose to stay and dedicate themselves to reforming the Brotherhood from the inside. Hussein, a Brotherhood member in his early thirties, is deeply frustrated by the lack of internal space for independent initiatives but refuses to leave the movement, as he believes it still represents his religious and political beliefs. Our conversations through the years tell a story of his personal battle for belonging, between not wanting to renounce his membership and his frustration at not being listened to. He admits to being close to leaving the Brotherhood behind in 2015, when leadership contests at the higher level became evident together with the lack of a clear strategy against repression. Yet, he chose to stay as he realised that 'There is not just one way to be a Brother (Ikhwani) anymore. I can do what I believe is right, for myself and for the organisation, and there are a lot of us who feel this way.'[34]

These patterns of fragmentation and dissent also show that, once again, to understand what is at the core of the movement's trajectories after 2013 it is necessary to differentiate between collective and individual responses. One therefore needs to focus the analysis on the level of the individual members, rather than on that of the organisation as a monolithic unit, in order to account for how emotions, personal experiences and grievances are shaping responses to repression in the aftermath of the coup. Doing so also draws attention to another pressing issue that underlines the research at the core of this book –the need to acknowledge that, just as the Brotherhood's unfamiliar circumstances require the group to significantly rethink its strategies and behaviours, it is our duty as scholars of the organisation to do the same. It is striking that, eight years after the coup, a rigorous analysis of how the Brotherhood's perceived political failure and the repression that followed is affecting the movement's own identity, structure and attempts at restructuring is only just emerging.[35] Similarly, there is an abundance of works examining the organisation's political behaviour while in power,[36] but only a limited number of scholars have begun to engage with the repercussions that repression is having on the relationship between the movement and its members.[37] This is probably due, in part, to the fact that the Brotherhood's trajectories in the aftermath of 2013 depart significantly from several analytical and theoretical approaches that are classically used to study the movement, therefore highlighting the need to adopt a new lens.

Immediately after the coup many predicted that the Brotherhood could only go one of two ways. Either the organisation was going to seek reconciliation with the regime, or several of its factions were going to radicalise and face the regime through the use of violence.[38] Yet, while there is evidence suggesting that both of these scenarios were at least partially pursued, neither of them has so far consistently materialised. Others have gone back to dominant debates within Social Movement Theory on the link between regime repression and opposition movements' responses to try and chart the Brotherhood's development after 2013.[39] However, while approaches such as the inclusion-moderation thesis and the repression-dissent nexus remain a popular lens through which to study how Islamists respond to conditions of exclusion, they largely fail to capture all of the different dynamics that are currently at play within the movement. Similarly, the Brotherhood's recent trajectories also notably depart from the argument that, while under repression, social movements tend to prioritise their survival and therefore are compelled to make organisational changes to adapt to repression.[40] In fact a large source of discontent within the movement is the exact opposite phenomenon, as a large portion of the membership claims that while they are asking for such transformations to take place, the Brotherhood is only implementing superficial changes that leave the organisation's hierarchical structures untouched.

Overall, while these approaches do provide some original insights, they mostly focus on the Brotherhood as a collective and therefore do not account fully for the role of individual initiatives in bringing about internal change. I argue that it is necessary to move away from the analysis of the movement's responses to repression from an organisational perspective and, instead, pay more attention to what the changing relationship between the movement and its members can tell us, as well as placing value on the role of individual emotions and initiatives. This is an emerging theoretical approach to the study of the Brotherhood that, as the work of Mustafa Menshawy, Erika Biagini, Khalil al-Anani and Carrie Rosefsky Wickham also show, allows for the study of how individual responses, and the fragmentation along strategic and ideological lines, are influencing the Brotherhood's metamorphosis in the aftermath of 2013.

Emerging debates and internal fragmentation

A closer look at the relationship between the movement and its members reveals that, even before the coup, the Brotherhood was deeply divided and struggling to maintain unity and obedience. Its partial politicisation during the last two decades of Mubarak's rule created deep rifts between those members who were more politically inclined and the leadership's reluctance to implement any changes or actually commit to a clear political manifesto, leading to patterns of disengagement along ideological, organisational and even personal lines. While these long-standing grievances were routinely suppressed before the 2011 uprisings, the disintegration of the Brotherhood's organisational structures of control in the aftermath of the coup brought them back to centre stage.

Immediately after the coup it became evident that the Brotherhood's celebrated ability to adapt to change and to alter its strategy to cope with new environments and struggles did not apply to such unfamiliar circumstances. The erosion of the very structures at the core of the *tanzim* and the lack of a cohesive and unified response to toppling and repression initiated the Brotherhood's gradual fragmentation along ideological, territorial and organisational lines. These unprecedented levels of internal chaos, further aggravated by the leadership's lack of control and decreasing legitimacy, allowed for two points of contention to clearly emerge, which would then go on to shape further internal schisms down the line. These are: the interpretation of the circumstances that led to the fall of the Morsi government, and the lessons that should be learnt from that experience; the need to stipulate a coherent narrative and strategy for the Brotherhood to move forward and re-group. Different individual positions vis-à-vis these points of contention are what broadly divides the Brotherhood between stagnation and adaptation strategies, but it is worth nothing from the beginning that these are not fixed or binary categories. Rather, what makes the post-2013 context so unique in the history of the organisation is the fluidity and changeability of its members' alliances, loyalties and personal positions. Overall, the aftermath of the coup has led many to embark on long processes of self-reflection that are still ongoing, leading to shifting perspectives, personal revelations and deep identity crises.

The movement's decreased control over its members is not only symptomatic of its internal chaos and lack of direction following 2013, but also reveals that its core principles and values are at stake. The questioning of values such as blind obedience, which for decades kept the Brotherhood united in the face of repression, is a clear indicator that the organisation needs to undergo some deep structural changes if it wants to avoid further defections. Members' grievances centred around the movement's ideological stagnation, and lack of pluralism and space for debate have old roots that long precede the events of 2011, but were undeniably catalysed by the Brotherhood's quick politicisation in the aftermath of Mubarak's removal. Mustafa Menshawy shows that different processes of disengagement from the organisation had already began in the early 2000s, but were often dismissed as individual occurrences rather than as a wider phenomenon.[41] Nevertheless, internal disagreements over the creation, running and political behaviour of the FJP, among other factors, greatly increased the number of defections, which have continued to grow. Tracing the core grievances behind these processes of disengagement and dissent, through a focus on the individual level, allows us to also begin outlining the main internal challenges that the Brotherhood faces in the aftermath of 2013. These are issues that the movement categorically needs to tackle if it wants to regain internal unity and develop a cohesive strategy against repression, yet, over seven years on, most of these remain largely unaddressed.

Old grievances, new challenges

A major source of defections and dissent both before and after the 2011 uprisings was the lack of a coherent position towards the Brotherhood's engagement in politics from its leaders, which was characteristic of much of the movement's behaviour throughout the last two decades of Mubarak's rule. More politically inclined members openly complain about their initiatives to develop a coherent political manifesto being shut down by their superiors. This was Mahmoud's experience, who in the mid-2000s was a Brotherhood supervisor in his medical school's Political and Media Committee:

> Actually, we were just a media committee [laughs], but I pushed for the political aspect to come through. I asked to also have a political committee and started to supervise some political training activities, but the problem was that I was not myself politically trained! I was just a medical school graduate who liked to read books about politics and social activities. [...] we needed real political training, I mean basic knowledge and skills starting from dialogue, negotiations, doing campaigns, guidance on how as a political activist you should develop your skills in this field. Of course the problem was that the programme was never implemented completely. I myself was not trained in political issues, so I asked the MB to provide me with someone from the MB political committee. So when I asked them, I went to the head of the political committee in Eastern Cairo and I showed him the programme that I had prepared, and said that please I needed support with that. He said he was impressed by it and that he was going to support us, but that support never came.[42]

Others look back at the Brotherhood's official political engagement prior to 2011 and retrospectively accuse the leadership of never fully committing to parliamentary politics, referring to how the movement never tried to match or even surpass the limit of representatives imposed on them by the Mubarak regime, even when its popularity was high and the parliamentary process clearly rigged. Such discontent only grew exponentially in the wake of the 2011 popular uprisings, as the Brotherhood refrained from taking sides or endorsing the protests until Mubarak's faith became clear. There is a consensus among former and current members that at this time the Brotherhood missed an excellent opportunity to take the lead in the uprisings and gain support as a revolutionary force, and a sense that the movement was simply 'not revolutionary enough', or even counter-revolutionary at times. Amr Darrag, who served as the FJP's Minister of Planning and International Cooperation, openly criticises the Brotherhood's ideological and intellectual stagnation towards the possibility of structural political change prior to 2011:

> The Ikhwan was not ready for the revolution, it did not plan for it, it did not even consider it as a possible scenario they should plan for. [...] The Ikhwan had a big responsibly being the largest and oldest opposition actor at that time. So this is the main thing, what I really mean when I said that we as the Ikhwan failed because we were not revolutionary enough. We had to continue on that path [the revolutionary, more proactive one] while the transitional period was allowing us to set the structures in place to eventually lead to major change. We had a lot of knowledgeable and expert people in the Ikhwan who participated in political life throughout Mubarak's time, but we lacked an overall strategy and agenda when it came to core questions like 'what do we need to do in terms of legislation, of dealing with the state, how do we handle the civilian-military relationship, how do we handle transitional justice?' We were simply not ready, and that cost us everything.[43]

This unpreparedness did not stop the Brotherhood's leadership from wanting to gain power once Mubarak was removed, which inevitably resulted in an incoherent and contradictory political discourse. This also explains why it was the Brotherhood's deep dive into national politics that further triggered the disengagement of many within its ranks. Controversies over the creation of the FJP, the Brotherhood's lack of transparency over the extent to which they wanted to participate in the transitional process, and the production of a contradictory and ambiguous political discourse further alienated a considerable part of the membership. This dimension remained central after the 2013 coup, especially given the perceived failure of the Brotherhood's political project.

Another related grievance is rooted in the Brotherhood's refusal to accommodate or even hear the pleas of its members both before and after the transitional period, which eventually hit the movement where it hurt the most. Indeed, it contributed to the slow erosion of the collective identity that for decades kept the organisation together. The suppression of independent thought and opinions that do not align with the Brotherhood's discourse is a core component of the movement's 'listen and obey' principle, which is also clearly embodied in its historical isolationist stance. Nevertheless, many Brotherhood members began engaging with secular and revolutionary groups during both the lead up to and the aftermath of the 2011 uprisings, seeking an avenue where their individual initiatives and political visions could be heard. In the process they became directly involved in Egypt's social and political transitions, and were exposed to discourses and narratives that had long been dismissed or forbidden by their leaders. This new dimension fed directly into ongoing or emerging processes of disengagement, and was instrumental in gaining autonomy from the movement as well as the courage to stand up against it. As Menshawy puts it 'members of the Brotherhood found themselves newly identifying as part of a collective identity that had long been rivalled by the Islamist one: a national identity'.[44] Anyone familiar with the Brotherhood's strict organisational structures and mechanisms of control will see that this is an unprecedented development, which directly hinders one of the main forces that kept the organisation united for decades. In Chapter 4 it will become clear that this partial refusal of an Islamist collective identity in favour of a national one was just the beginning of a much longer and more complicated process. There are many who in the aftermath of the coup began to engage in what are effectively processes of self-reflection, which are leading to the emergence of members' subjectivity vis-à-vis the Brotherhood's collective identity, posing a direct threat to its unity moving forward.

These processes of self-reflection and disengagement from the Brotherhood have taken centre stage in the years following 2013, but they also heavily disrupted the organisation's internal dynamics both during the lead up to and the immediate aftermath of the coup. The Brotherhood's political trajectory in the two years following Mubarak's removal exposed long-standing structural biases, such as the appointment of political or senior positions on a loyalty rather than expertise basis, or the fact that the movement was clearly led by an exclusive group of individuals gathered around Khairat al-Shater. These issues further catalysed members' discontent around the leaders' lack of accountability and ability to lead the movement, feeding into the erosion of their legitimacy and influence. Feeling betrayed by the leaders, individual members began to act on the personal requests and initiatives that had been shut down for years by those in the higher ranks of the organisation. For example, many refused to join the FJP despite being instructed to do so and openly challenged its heads over the incoherent political choices made by the party, while countless others left in order to create and join other political parties such as the Egyptian Current Party.[45] These behaviours clearly signal the pursuit of an unprecedented amount of individual agency, which goes hand in hand with the leadership's lack of control over the membership. The disruption of fixed hierarchies and the consequent increase of member-based initiatives has reached its peak in the post-2013 context, and is one of the main forces driving internal change and transformation.

Conclusion

It is clear that the 2013 coup and the unprecedented brutality of the wave of repression that followed dealt a heavy blow to the Brotherhood's unity and coherence. The movement was already deeply divided at the time, but the emergence of competing strategies to deal with the crackdown further fragmented the organisation. The Raba'a massacre, combined with the mass arrest of senior leaders and the scattering of members abroad enhanced these schisms. The aftermath of the coup also marked the first time the Brotherhood's General Guide and several members of the Shura Council and Guidance Bureau had been arrested since 1981.[46] Coupled with the leadership's already decreasing legitimacy and control over its members, as well as the movement's perceived failure to maintain power, this created an unprecedented wave of internal criticism and outrage. Therefore, rather than facing regime repression as a united front, the Brotherhood found itself in forced exile while also having to deal with unprecedented levels of internal chaos and discontent. I would argue that, in the aftermath of 2013, the most pressing challenges the Brotherhood faces are those coming from within the movement, rather than those linked to the dimension of forced exile and regime repression. The long-standing grievances just outlined were not only brought back to the fore by the events following the 2011 uprisings, but have since evolved into the main forces that are currently driving internal calls for reformation and change.

Another factor that highlights the Brotherhood's lack of a cohesive narrative is the fact that there is still a lack of internal consensus on what went wrong in 2013, or on whether or not the Brotherhood's erratic political behaviour is partially to blame for bringing about the coup. From this, there are new sources of discontent that emerged after the coup. First of all, members are still complaining about the lack of a coherent discourse and strategy to face repression, as well as the Brotherhood's unclear position on whether or not the organisation considers itself as a political actor in the aftermath of 2013. This directly feeds into increasing challenges to a top-down Islamist collective identity mostly centred around notions of victimhood and personal sacrifices, as many had already begun to disengage from it even before the events of 2011. In addition, as many feel increasingly betrayed and abandoned by the Historical Leadership, this discontent is directly eroding one of the Brotherhood's core principles, the 'listen and obey' commandment. What all of these internal grievances point to is the gradual – but apparently unstoppable – invalidation of the movement's historical mechanisms of control over their members. This development is a clear indication that the hierarchical structures and internal dynamics that for decades have kept the Brotherhood united in the face of repression are largely inapplicable to the post-2013 context. Despite the movement's attempt to replicate the structure of the *tanzim* abroad – a process that dissenters in Istanbul refer to as 'copy and paste' – the increased agency of individual members and their open disregard for the Historical Leadership's directives reveal that something has begun to change at the basic structural level of the organisation.

It follows that there is an overt call for the replacement of the old values at the core of the Brotherhood, such as blind obedience, in favor of new ones that emphasise pluralism, transparency and openness. Sources of individual legitimacy are also being transformed, slowly shifting from lengthy prison sentences to instead being linked to professional and intellectual skills. Nevertheless, this is not a smooth process nor a trend that is characteristic of the organisation as a whole. It is undeniable that both individual members and different factions have been consistently pushing from internal change and transformation since 2013, but have also been facing a fierce resistance from those representing the 'classic' organisation, as will become clear in Chapter 3. Yet, the increasing reclamation of individual agency after the coup helps to clearly identify what internal challenges lay ahead for the organisation as a whole. Perhaps unsurprisingly, the Brotherhood's overall trajectory since 2013 has lacked both a mission and a coherent strategy, leaving room for individuals to pursue competing approaches to exit repression. Indeed, the movement faces the daunting task of introducing the transformations necessary to better address popular demands for an inclusive, pluralist and egalitarian political space.[47] Even then, if the Brotherhood manages to somehow come out relatively intact, its ability to maintain unity of purpose and control over its ranks in the long term is growing weaker.

Notes

1 Author Interview with an FJP's Minister. London, 2016.
2 Author Interview with secular activist. London, 2016.
3 Muqtedar Khan, 'Islam, democracy and Islamism after the counterrevolution in Egypt', *Middle East Policy*, 21:1 (2014), 75–86, 83.
4 These are two of the most common criticisms against the Brotherhood at the time, by both the Egyptian population and its own members. They still drive a lot of the rank-and-file members' grievances against the movement today, and feature prominently in interviews and conversations with both current and former members.
5 This is something that several members who were in a position of power within both the Brotherhood and the FJP have come to admit.
6 Author Interview. London, 2016.

7 Lucia Ardovini, Simon Mabon, 'Egypt's unbreakable curse: tracing the state of exception from Mubarak to Al Sisi', *Mediterranean Politics*, 25:4 (2020), 456–475.
8 Julia Elyachar, 'History and anthropology upending infrastructure: Tamarod, resistance, and agency after the January 25th revolution in Egypt', *History and Anthropology*, 25:4 (2014), 452–471.
9 David Kirkpatrick, Kareem Fahim, 'Morsi faces ultimatum as allies speak of military coup', *The New York Times* (1 July 2013) www.nytimes.com/2013/07/02/world/middleeast/egypt-protests.html (accessed 14 June 2020).
10 'Rabaa: the massacre that ended the Arab Spring'.
11 Pargeter, *Return to the Shadows*, 14.
12 Al-Anani, 'Upended path: the rise and fall of Egypt's Muslim Brotherhood', 540.
13 See for example: Menshawy, *Leaving the Muslim Brotherhood*; Michel, *Political Parties*; McAdam, McCarthy and Zald (eds.) *Comparative Perspectives on Social Movements*, 12.
14 Zollner, 'Surviving repression'.
15 Al-Anani, *Inside the Muslim Brotherhood*.
16 Kandil, *Inside the Brotherhood*; Menshawy, *Leaving the Muslim Brotherhood*.
17 Ardovini, Biagini (eds.) 'Assessing the Egyptian Muslim Brotherhood after the 2013 *coup*'.
18 Vannetzel, 'The party, the Gama'a and the Tanzim', 211–226.
19 Nathan, Dunne, 'Unprecedented pressures, uncharted course for Egypt's Muslim Brotherhood' (accessed 3 March 2020).
20 Menshawy, *Leaving the Muslim Brotherhood*, chapter 4.
21 Amr Darrag, Steven Brooke, 'Politics or piety? Why the Muslim Brotherhood engages in social services provision: a conversation', *Brookings* (6 May 2016), www.brookings.edu/research/politics-or-piety-why-the-muslim-brotherhood-engages-in-social-service-provision-a-conversation/ (accessed 14 June 2020).
22 Brooke, 'Egypt', in Hamid, McCants, *Rethinking Political Islam*.
23 Lucia Ardovini, 'The Muslim Brotherhood in Turkey after the 2013 coup d'état: organizational renewal in the diaspora', in Dalia Abdelhady, Ramy Ali (eds.) *The Routledge Handbook of Middle East Diasporas* (Abingdon: Routledge, 2021) *forthcoming*.
24 Abdelrahman Ayyash, 'The Turkish future of Egypt's Muslim Brotherhood', *The Century Foundation* (17 August 2020) https://tcf.org/content/report/turkish-future-egypts-muslim-brotherhood/?agreed=1 (accessed 2 September 2020).
25 Shaima Magued, 'The Egyptian Muslim Brotherhood's transnational advocacy in Turkey: a new means of political participation', *British Journal of Middle Eastern Studies*, 45:3 (2018), 480–497.
26 Bilge, Kotan, 'An overview of Turkish-Egyptian relations since the Arab Uprising', *TRT World* (27 November 2017), www.trtworld.com/mea/an-overview-of-turkish-egyptian-relations-since-the-arab-uprising-12658 (accessed 14 June 2020).
27 Roel Meijer, Edwin Bakker, *The Muslim Brotherhood in Europe* (London: Hurst, 2012).

28 Ardovini, 'The Muslim Brotherhood in Turkey after the 2013 coup d'état'.
29 'Why the Egyptian Muslim Brotherhood needs to transform in order to survive', *World Politics Review* (20 February 2018), www.worldpoliticsreview.com/articles/24221/why-egypt-s-muslim-brotherhood-needs-to-transform-to-survive (accessed 14 June 2020).
30 Anthony Gorman, Sossie Kasbarian (eds.) *Diasporas of the Modern Middle East: Contextualising Community* (Edinburgh: Edinburgh University Press, 2015).
31 Author Interview. Istanbul 2017.
32 Ardovini, 'The Muslim Brotherhood in Turkey after the 2013 coup d'état'.
33 Author Interview. Istanbul 2019.
34 Author Interview. Istanbul 2017.
35 Ardovini, Biagini, 'Assessing the Egyptian Muslim Brotherhood after the 2013 coup'.
36 See for example: al-Anani, 'Upended path: the rise and fall of Egypt's Muslim Brotherhood'; El-Sherif, 'The Egyptian Muslim Brotherhood failures'; Kandil, *Inside the Brotherhood*.
37 See for example: Menshawy, *Leaving the Muslim Brotherhood*; Erika Biagini, 'The Egyptian Muslim Sisterhood between violence, activism and leadership', *Mediterranean Politics*, 22:1 (2017), 35–53; Jannis Grimm and Cilja Harders, 'Unpacking the effects of repression: the evolution of Islamists repertoires of contention in Egypt after the fall of President Morsi', *Social Movement Studies*, 17:1 (2018), 1–18; Samir, 'The Muslim Brotherhood's generational gap'.
38 Mohammed Ayoob, 'Muslim Brotherhood ripe for re-radicalization', *ISPU* (15 August 2013) www.ispu.org/muslim-brotherhood-ripe-for-re-radicalization-by-mohammed-ayoob/ (accessed 14 June 2020).
39 Al-Anani, 'Rethinking the repression-dissent nexus'.
40 Ibid., 1331.
41 Menshawy, *Leaving the Muslim Brotherhood*.
42 Author Interview. Istanbul, 2019.
43 Author Interview with Amr Darrag. Istanbul, August 2018.
44 Menshawy, *Leaving the Muslim Brotherhood*, 129.
45 Vannetzel, 'The party, the Gama'a and the Tanzim', 224.
46 Al-Anani, 'Rethinking the repression-dissent nexus', 1333.
47 Ashraf El-Sherif, 'The Muslim Brotherhood and the future of political Islam in Egypt', *Carnegie Endowment for International Piece* (21 October 2014), 1–44, 3.

3

The *tanzim*, shattered

The forceful removal of Mohammed Morsi and the ensuing scattering abroad of Brotherhood leaders and members alike represent a breaking point in the history of the organisation – most importantly, associated with deep trauma and loss of direction. The dimension of exile and the process of resettling abroad are significant challenges, which delivered an unprecedented shock to the movement, meaning that in the aftermath of 2013, Brotherhood members are facing ideological and identity crises. On the surface the movement has been relatively successful in rebuilding abroad, mostly relying on the replication of the *tanzim*'s (organisation) structure and on the creation of Guidance Offices outside of Egypt, meaning that the Brotherhood is now mostly being coordinated from Istanbul and London.[1] The Historical Leadership still officially rule over the movement as they control the Brotherhood's finances, negotiate alliances with other groups, and remain the international 'face' of the organisation. Nevertheless, the shock of exile means that something crucial has shifted in the way the movement historically resisted and even thrived under repression: rather than acting as a source of unity, the current crackdown is bringing back deep-seated internal issues and driving the organisation's fragmentation along ideological, strategic and structural lines.

A clear indication of the fact that the movement's classic tools of resistance do not apply to this new context is that fact that *mihna* (ordeal, tribulation) is now seen as a source of division rather than unity, significantly weakening one of the strongest markers of collective identity that kept the Brotherhood united for decades. This is a small but significant indication of a much broader problem that becomes apparent throughout most of my conversations with former and current Brotherhood members alike: removed from the Egyptian context, who actually are the organisation and its members? On top of obvious strategic and ideological issues, the organisation's unity is being fractured by deep questions about individual and collective identities that, apart from isolated episodes, have long been suppressed by its leadership throughout its history. Having been re-ignited by the controversies and discontent surrounding the Brotherhood's political path during and after the 2011 uprisings, identity questions took centre stage following the coup, and are not only driving fragmentation and divisions, but also the emergence of competing strategies and narrative against repression. Overall, their development has been made possible by the slow erasure and disintegration of one of the Brotherhood's key assets: the *tanzim*, with its fixed and hierarchical organisational structures.

As such, the new hubs of the Brotherhood in exile, such as in Turkey and the UK, have become the stage for ongoing conflicts over leadership, ideology and competing responses to repression. Throughout my fieldwork, many refer to the experience of forced exile and to processes of diasporic formation as the first time they had the opportunity to disengage from the movement and re-evaluate the organisation's overarching control over daily activities, careers and individual thought processes.[2] Osama, a current member who thinks of himself as a dissenter, stated on several occasions that 'after the coup, when we came here [Istanbul], I realised that I had time to think [...] how did I get here? Why am I in this? Why am I a member of this organisation? Why should I keep listening to them [the Brotherhood's leaders] if I do not agree with what they are saying?'[3] These words speak volumes, indicating that the novelty of life in exile is leading many to question, and even disregard, the very principles over which the Brotherhood historically rests. Statements like 'the time of following blindly is no more'[4] are common among both current and former members, especially when they are asked about the movement's perceived lack of an active response to the crackdown against the Brotherhood perpetrated by the regime of Abdel Fattah el-Sisi.

This chapter traces the sources and development of these dynamics of dissent, focusing on the ongoing clash between agency and structure within the Brotherhood – understood as the emergence of members' own subjectivities and initiatives vis-à-vis the movement's organisational structures and collective identity. These tensions are at the core of the organisation's fragmentation in the aftermath of the 2013 coup and pre-date the new dimension of exile, as they are embedded in the very principles over which the Brotherhood historically rests. As such, they are not a new phenomenon, but rather resemble previous significant splits within the movement such as the Wasat Party initiative in 1996.[5] Nevertheless, while these historical precedents have been thoroughly analysed, these dynamics have been left largely unexplored in the post-2013 context, the unfamiliarity of which is also leading to the departure from pre-existing categories and new fragmentation patterns. It is also worth noting that, while unpacking the sources and effects of internal divisions, literature on both the Brotherhood and Islamist movements more broadly focuses largely on its reactions to repression from an organisational perspective, therefore mostly understanding the movement as a monolithic unit. However, a focus on individual experiences and emotions is more suitable to capture the effects that repression is having on the Brotherhood as we knew it up until 2013.

Such an approach also allows us to look beyond the movement's overarching narrative and to identify two main points of contention dividing the Brotherhood in the aftermath of 2013: the interpretation of what went wrong during the FJP's experience in government and the lessons that should be learnt from it; and what strategy should be implemented to move past the current crisis. Those belonging to the more conservative fringes of the organisation mostly deny any responsibility or wrongdoing, largely blaming the coup on the military deep state and foreign conspiracies. This is the belief of Ahmed, a senior member in his late sixties who now lives in London with his family. He inspires authority and respect and has dedicated his entire life to the Brotherhood, serving several prison terms under Mubarak. He remains firm in his conviction that the FJP was doomed to fail because of an international conspiracy against it, regardless of how it acted when in power: 'From the first moment it was a conspiracy against political Islam. I believe the international community was not happy about the Ikhwan being in power, they feared a domino effect, they were scared we would export the revolution, which we never planned to do.'[6] Nevertheless, during our most recent encounter, he admitted that the Brotherhood should have been more responsive to warnings about popular discontent and the upcoming coup:

> It is a big lesson. For me what happened in 2011 is not a revolution, I am trying to convince people of it, we need to start from there. It was a conspiracy of the army to steal power from Mubarak, and we supported them, because we did not know. If the Ikhwan did not participate [in the uprisings] the army could not have stolen the power from Mubarak, but we did not realise at the time. The same happened in 1952, the military used us to take power from the king, and then they put us in jail. Then we should learn from this lesson! This is a very harsh lesson to learn. We lost thousands of people, we have 8,000 people behind bars, we have hundreds of people who had to leave their home, we have 18,0000 families who are suffering. It is a big lesson, which never happened before.[7]

This partial change of heart is indicative of a wider self-reflection trend, spurred by the events of 2013, pushing members to take stock of the circumstances leading to Morsi's removal. The result of this process is a rather insightful *mea culpa* that looks at the Brotherhood's own shortcomings as an accelerating factor for the failure of the FJP's government, also drawing on many of the internal critiques historically coming from the movement's own ranks. Chapter 1 identified four main reasons for the premature end of the Morsi government, these being the lack of a coherent vision for the Islamist project, the miscalculation of how much legitimacy the movement actually had, the appointment of political positions according to loyalty rather than expertise, and the failure to address the permanence of the deep state. In particular, the lack of professionalism as a leading cause of the Brotherhood's inability to successfully govern and reform internally is a key thread that runs through most of the fieldwork at the core of this book, and suggests that, while the Brotherhood undeniably had to rule in a deeply hostile political environment, its own political, ideological and organisational failure ultimately contributed to its downfall.

These kinds of internal critiques are not necessarily new, as there are several instances of discontent over the Brotherhood's overarching organisational structure leading to schisms and division, as embodied by the Wasat Party initiative.[8] Yet, the dimension of exile combined with the Historical Leadership's loss of legitimacy means that they are being articulated and discussed quite openly by members who still consider themselves part of the organisation, rather than just by outspoken dissenters or former Brothers. The pursuit of greater individual agency therefore also means that a growing number of members is reclaiming the space for debates within the organisation, creating avenues that had long been suppressed and that are, in turn, driving internal change. Indeed, some of the Brotherhood's own shortcomings that are more prominent within these discussions are the gap between ideology and practice made evident by the FJP's rule, as well as the inadequacy of the movement's fixed organisation structures and its unwillingness to reform to adapt to changing circumstances.

Therefore, the Brotherhood's rigid, hierarchical structure was a major factor in its downfall. The strict hierarchy that holds the *tanzim* together meant that the movement was incapable of adapting to its new circumstances and favoured ideological lethargy and internal rigidity over the dynamism and reforms needed to successfully overcome Mubarak's legacy and pursue the goals of the revolution. This is not a new phenomenon; however, prior to the FJP's rule, the Brotherhood's inflexibility had only directly affected its members. Under Morsi's presidency, the movement's isolationism, distrust towards grassroots initiatives and favouring of loyalty over expertise considerably contributed to furthering the popular discontent that powered the counterrevolution. In essence, the movement's refusal to reform its structures while in power worsened internal discontent over the lack of transparency and representation, while also irreparably alienating the people who voted them into power.

The rise of the second rank and the disintegration of the Guidance Office

An immediate consequence of the Raba'a massacre and of the indiscriminate arrests that followed the coup was the imprisonment of the majority of those sitting in the Guidance Office, which severely weakened the Brotherhood's established chain of command. Those who escaped persecution were either displaced or went into hiding, essentially leaving the movement without a clear leadership when it needed it the most. In such a fragile context, it was not long before competing leadership factions started to emerge, drawing from old grievances within the movement and dividing its ranks even further. This is where tracing a complete picture of the various leadership schisms dividing the Brotherhood after 2013 becomes complicated, given the high number of committees that were created and then dismantled, competing Guidance Offices catering to different audiences, and the quick rise and fall of leadership figures. Victor Willi does this remarkably well in his book, *The Fourth Ordeal*, and I build on the picture of internal divisions that he presents. What I want to convey is that, rather than uniting in the face of oppression after the coup, the Brotherhood grew more divided than ever and remains so today. The leadership struggles between three main entities – the Historical Leadership leading the International Organisation, the High Administrative Committee in Egypt, and the Crisis Management Committee in Istanbul – took the Brotherhood's fragmentation to the extreme, with open rifts further accelerating the disintegration of the *tanzim*, as outlined below.

After Raba'a and with most of the Guidance Office gone, the task of leading the Brotherhood fell upon the so called 'second rank', a group of individuals born in the mid-to-late 1950s who up until 2013 held secondary leadership positions within the movement. Almost overnight they were tasked with the highest decision-making powers, becoming responsible for guiding the Brotherhood through the greatest crisis it had ever faced. While taking on this daunting task the second-rank leaders were almost immediately accused of lacking strategic vision, a critique by members who would soon move to create the High Administrative Committee, or what is now known as the 'New MB'. This meant that, soon after Raba'a, the Brotherhood was already descending into leadership struggles over who was most fit to guide the organisation in Egypt.

The core of this 'revolutionary' leadership came together after the coup, uniting members committed to reorganising the Brotherhood's priorities and aims. Some of these leaders already sat in the Guidance Office, such as Mohammed Taha Wahdan, a medical doctor in his fifties who also headed the Section for Upbringing. Wahdan had a strong following among the rank and file and was rumoured to be one of the candidates to become the next General Guide.[9] The second was Mohammed Sa'd Aliwa, in his late forties at the time, who had served as head of the youth section and had sat in the Guidance Office since January 2013.[10] Once the security situation stabilised in early 2014, formal reorganisations activities began, and a committee was created to guide the Brotherhood through the crisis. Together with Wahdan and Aliwa this included other Guidance Office members such as: Mohammed Kamal, an agriculturalist in is late fifties; Abd al-'Azim al-Sharqawi, a close confidant of al-Shater; Abd al-Rahman al-Barr, head of the Da'wa Section; and Mohammed Abd al-Rahman al-Morsi, member of the Guidance Office since 2008.[11] They were joined by three more Brothers with no precedent leadership experience, but who were selected to the executive body thanks to their political activities and skills. These were: Ali Batikh, head of the Administrative Office in Giza; Hussein Ibrahim, former Secretary General of the FJP; and Abd al-Fattah al-Sisi, a member of the Section for Upbringing.[12] One of their first moves was to create the High Administrative Committee, headed by Kamal, which became the Brotherhood's official body in Egypt.[13] Kamal soon started arguing that the Brotherhood needed an entirely new leadership, given the fact that General Guide Mohamed Badie was in jail along with his deputies, and he quickly assumed control of the movement's activities in Egypt. Because of the Brotherhood's precarious circumstances this all happened at enhanced speed, but several of my interlocutors recall that while Kamal was not well-known, his charisma and enthusiasm soon gained him a considerable following. This was also thanks to the widespread impression that he would reshape the movement in significant ways, dismantling hierarchies and bringing forward a clear strategy against repression. Most of all, what attracted many to his side was not necessarily his revolutionary approach towards the regime, but rather his intentions to democratise the Brotherhood internal elections and structures, turning its top-down nature into a more inclusive organisation.

However, despite the popularity of the High Administrative Committee, the Brotherhood was becoming increasingly divided. The fact that its members had not been formally elected considerably undermined their legitimacy, and they also faced growing hostilities from Brotherhood leaders in exile. A point of major concern was Kamal's revolutionary ideas and calls for an open confrontation with the regime, which worried senior leaders in exile such as Secretary General Mahmoud Hussein, acting General Guide Mahmoud Ezzat and Secretary General of the International Organisation Ibrahim Mounir. As core representatives of the Historical Leadership, Hussein, Ezzat and Mounir administer the Brotherhood finances as well as heading its international relations, effectively remaining in control of the organisation as a whole. In an attempt to appease the growing tensions between the International Organisation and the High Administrative Committee, the 'Crisis Management Committee' was created in Istanbul in January 2015, bringing together revolutionary second-rank leaders loyal to Kamal and those aligning with Hussein in Istanbul, Munir in London and Ezzat in Cairo.[14] The committee included elected members based in Istanbul, namely Hussein al-Qazzaz, Gamal Heshmat and Yehia Hamid; Ayman Abd al-Ghany,

Taher Abd al-Mohsin and Mohammed al-Beshlawy, based in Qatar; and Hafiz al-Sawi in Malaysia and Osama Sulayman in Sudan. Three more members were appointed by the High Administrative Committee: Amr Darrag, Minister of Planning and International Cooperation under the FJP, who took charge of political activities; Ahmed al Watidy, responsible for the committee's coordination with the International Organisation in London and Adb al-Rahman, appointed as the formal head of the Crisis Management Committee.[15]

Yet, international discord between the Historical Leadership and second-rank leaders continued to develop. A major point of contention was the fact that, while emerging leaders wanted to see the Crisis Management Committee take on more responsibilities, the Historical Leadership had no intention of relinquishing their administrative powers. Most of all, Secretary General Hussein's refusal made it clear that the Historical Leadership lacked a vision for how the Brotherhood should adapt itself to its new circumstances both in Egypt and abroad; nor did it have a clear strategy to face repression or the regime. Following a trend that I identify as 'stagnation', the Historical Leadership hence refuses to implement internal reforms and wishes to maintain the Brotherhood as it is, focusing efforts on strengthening members' moral and spiritual foundation. This is also evident through my numerous conversations with Mohamed Soudan who, during our last meeting in London in 2018 said:

> These people [those in the High Administrative Committee and in the Crisis Management Committee] do not have enough experts who give them guidance on how to do this. They do not have any experience and they make a lot of mistakes. So the senior leaders heard about this [the call for internal reforms and for open confrontation with the regime] and they said that this is not our strategy. Because our strategy is to be peaceful, struggle is our way, even after what happened to some of our sisters, of our women, we need to be patient and we need to solve our problems with wisdom. Because Sisi and all his companions are just waiting for the Ikhwan to turn to violence, for us to argue with each other. They are trying to push us in this direction, so that they have another excuse to kill even more of us.[16]

Yet, as this statement suggests, this strategy openly clashes with that of those loyal to Kamal, who believe that significant organisational changes are needed at all levels. Moreover, this is not an opinion that only second-rank leaders hold, but is also widespread across a growing portion of the membership who, now in exile, feel constrained by the inactivity of the Historical Leadership.

This struggle over legitimacy and leadership reached its peak in 2015, when the High Administrative Committee conducted unsanctioned elections in Egypt and announced that that the Brotherhood had abandoned its commitment to peaceful means, thus initiating 'open confrontation' with the regime.[17] This was perceived as an act of treason by the Historical Leadership, who immediately denounced such actions and reiterated the subordination of the committee to the Guidance Office. They quickly moved to freeze the membership of leaders and rank-and-file members faithful to Kamal, in an attempt to communicate that they remained in charge of the International Organisation. Nevertheless, the fact that these schisms were openly taking place represented a public relations disaster for the Brotherhood, whose leaders on both sides were quickly losing legitimacy in the eyes of both its members and international supporters. Several attempts to reach a compromise and avoid further defamation were made throughout 2015, with little success. Rather, the clashes went public and the struggle between these two factions started to involve the rank-and-file members, who up until then had been largely unaware of the debates dividing the leadership. As accusations spread through social media, members started to pledge allegiance to different sides, dividing the movement even further along both vertical and horizontal lines.[18]

Reconciliation talks took place in Doha in March 2016, where the Crisis Management Committee was represented by Darrag, Batikh and al-Rahman, while Munir and Hussein spoke for the Historical Leadership. Perhaps unsurprisingly the talks failed, allegedly because of the Historical Leadership's refusal to compromise, prompting a new cycle of public accusations and insubordinations from the High Administrative Committee in Egypt. Tensions between the two factions were briefly dampened by Kamal's assassination in 2017, but eventually culminated into what Willi identifies as the 'Third Founding'. In an attempt to establish a new organisational hierarchy abroad, second-rank leaders announced the formation of the 'Founding Body of the Muslim Brotherhood Abroad' in September 2017, with Ali Batikh as its chairman. He claimed its foundation meant that 'the Brotherhood society has come back to its order' and that the conflict over leadership which erupted in 2015 had been contained and resolved at the top level. He continued to say that the only unresolved issue remaining was that, while some still favoured revolutionary means, others wanted to go back to peaceful political opposition, but reiterated that there was no disagreement over the fact that the Brotherhood was 'a complete and comprehensive social movement whose members were united by one idea and whose mutual relationships were marked only by love, respect, *da'wa* and the *tanzim*'.[19] Yet, such a statement fails to mask the fact that the Brotherhood remains in deep disarray, with each faction still attempting to delegitimise the other. This has a direct impact on members, who are subordinated to different chains of command or instead remain fragmented and alienated. More importantly, this state of deep internal divisions was aided by the Brotherhood's organisational structures and by its strict, pyramid-shaped *tanzim*. The ongoing fragmentation therefore not only has negative implications for the unity of members in Egypt, but also heavily weakened the integrity of its ranks in exile. At present, while it is hard to quantify, interviews point to almost half of those living in exile remaining faithful to the Historical Leadership, one third favouring more revolutionary approaches, and the remaining members being suspended in a state of alienation and confusion.

Cultivating the Brother, building the *tanzim*

The fragmentation and competition for leadership at the highest ranks of the organisation reveal the existence of deep schisms preceding 2013, which were accelerated by the internal chaos following the coup. Those representing the Historical Leadership are also facing significant challenges coming from the movement's lower ranks. Indeed, one of the major takeaways from the movement's time in government is that, organisationally, the Brotherhood was incapable of adaptation when it was most needed. This is a critique that members have been making of the leadership for decades, but has historically been side-lined for the sake of dealing with more urgent needs, namely surviving routine crackdowns and ongoing repression. Nevertheless, the two most significant forces that are driving the Brotherhood's internal restructuring in the aftermath of 2013 are indeed the call for adaptation to the movement's new circumstances and the individual pursuit of greater agency vis-à-vis the hierarchical structures that kept them bound for decades. Therefore, in order to fully grasp just how significant the revival of these trends is, it is necessary to take a step back and look at the recruitment, cultivation and mobilisation processes that are at the core of the *tanzim* and that, today more than ever, are being disputed and dismantled by its members.

The Brotherhood's organisational structure is, in the words of Nathan Brown, 'the most notable feature of the Muslim Brotherhood model'.[20] Its high levels of sophistication distinguish the Brotherhood from other Islamist and secular social movements, and historically allowed it to endure regime repression while expanding its activism and social networks at the same time. Indeed, the repressive environment under which the Brotherhood developed and politicised partially explains the strictness of its internal structures – built to maximise survival – but nevertheless led to criticism for being too totalitarian and severally lacking internal democracy and representation. In this sense, the potency of the Brotherhood's organisational structure is a double-edged sword: while it undoubtedly allowed the movement to endure decades of crackdowns, it became so central to the Brotherhood's own organisational identity that the preservation of the *tanzim* has long become one of the main objectives in itself. It is also quite telling that al Banna established the Brotherhood's structure before he developed its ideology and that, to this day, the organisation's hierarchy remains much clearer and more prescriptive than the ideology itself.

Again, the fact that the Brotherhood existed under illegality for most of its history explains, in part, the strictness of these hierarchical structures, as well as the lengthy process that is required to achieve full membership. The movement's recruitment machine is arguably unrivalled, but at the same time great care is taken when selecting potential members in order to avoid infiltration from the regime. Membership in the Brotherhood is therefore highly selective and dependent upon years of cultivation and scrutiny (*tarbiyya*), leading many to assert that 'the movement selects its sons' rather than the other way around.[21] Those who make it through the years that it takes to become a fully-fledged Brother emerge from this cultivation process entirely socialised into a strictly defined collective identity that is at the very core of the Brotherhood's functioning and survival. As a social movement, and especially as one that operates under strict repression, the Brotherhood requires its members to internalise its ideology, norms and values as a fundamental step to creating a sense of belonging and commitment (*iltizam*), which leads individuals to willingly sacrifice their time, effort, money and even lives to achieve the group's objectives.[22]

The literature on social movements tells us a great deal about the fundamental role that the construction of a collective identity plays in keeping a movement like the Brotherhood together and running despite decades of repression. In particular, the scholarship of collective identity and collective action highlights the mutual relationship between these two forces: movements rely on activism to construct their identity and, in turn, collective action allows them to sustain their identity and cultivate a sense of belonging among their members.[23] Alberto Melucci highlights three more key functions of collective identity for a social movement, as its successful construction allows it to 1) regulate membership; 2) set the criteria for joining the movement; 3) draw on the criteria members use to recognise themselves and to be, in turn, recognised by others.[24] Therefore, one can see that for an Islamist movement like the Brotherhood producing a strong and clearly defined Islamic identity is key to recruiting new members, expanding their constituency and sustaining their activism. This constructed identity brings together different forces that, in turn, forge members' worldview, behaviours and attitudes, such as a codes of value, norms, rituals and emotions.[25] Furthermore, this Islamic identity also provides a frame of reference that goes beyond recruitment and activism but is also instrumental to preserving a movement's own existence, as it leads individuals to identify themselves as part of a robust and meaningful entity and gives them a sense of differentiation and recognition from the rest of society.

Indeed, one of the movement's key features has been its ability to capitalise on its status as an illegal organisation by turning repression into a marker of its identity. As Zollner correctly stated, repression (*mihna* – ordeal) became 'the glue' that bound all Brotherhood members together, providing a shared experience that boosted their resolve against authoritarianism and reinforced the movement's status as a legitimate opposition actor.[26] This shared ordeal further contributed to the creation of a strong collective identity that, along with a strict organisational structure, allows the movement to project a cohesive message while also promoting unity and coordinating its membership. Other aspects that encourages loyalty and obedience to the Brotherhood and its political mission are the intertwining of members' ideological indoctrination to their advancement in the organisation's hierarchical system,[27] and the tying together of members in Brotherhood-only emotional, material and biological networks.[28] Members marry within the organisation and the ideological pressure of unity is grounded in personal and emotional networks, such as marriage and kinship ties that result in the full immersion into a parallel society. It is also common to hear members even describe how they built their homes to reflect their belonging to the organisation, taking care to make sure that they had rooms devoted to group prayers and to the hosting of weekly *usra* meetings. Indeed, a former member who willingly left the movement in 2012 complained that his house was a constant, painful reminder of the social connections he lost once he decided to renounce his membership.[29] Hence, all these elements combined are at the core of the strong collective identity that allowed the Brotherhood to present a united front despite recurrent waves of state-led crackdowns and long-standing internal debates, up to the reshuffling of the status quo brought about by the 2011 uprisings.

With this in mind, it is easy to recognise these patterns of behaviour throughout the foundation, development and running of the Brotherhood's organisational structures, which also allows us to unpack what makes the *tanzim* one of the movement's most valuable assets – and indeed one than needs to be protected at all costs in the eyes of many. Ashraf El-Sherif refers to the Brotherhood's organisation as a 'parallel state', built to survive its decades in opposition and therefore resting on ideological adherence to Islamist principles, an inflexible structure and led by leaders intolerant of differences and dismissive of criticism.[30] Two of the core principles binding members to the organisation are 'listen and obey' and 'blind obedience' towards the leadership, both necessary elements not only to create an all-encompassing collective identity, but specifically one strong enough to survive and thrive under decades of harsh repression.[31] From this, the starting point to understand the ongoing struggle between the Brotherhood and its members since 2013 is that, as Hazem Kandil points out, 'one cannot choose to join the Brotherhood; one has to be chosen'.[32] In fact, when asking members how long they have been a part of the movement it is common for them to be unable to pinpoint an exact moment in which they made the active choice of joining, as many are either born into Brotherhood families or selected for the process of socialisation and cultivation from a very young age. This explains numerous statements such as 'My father was a member and also my two uncles [...] So this is my family, I was a child in this environment, it was something normal for me to be an *Ikhwani* child'.[33] Similarly, a now former member, recalls:

> I joined the Ikhwan apparently [laughs] in the early 1990s. I was a polite boy who just wanted to pray regularly, and there was a small mosque beside our home, which was different. They had a lot of activities [...] and the ones organising them were very capable, very charismatic. [...] Until 1996 we just did some activities in this mosque or with our friends in other mosques in the same district. So at the time I thought [this was based] just on personal relations, the person responsible just had relations with the other so they organised activities, it was not a hierarchy, it was actually personal relations and things happened like that. At the time it was very informal, and we went through the process of socialisation softly, without even mentioning the Ikhwan, we just focused on religious teachings, the Quran, and a lot of activities and morality.[34]

Moreover, as I mentioned previously, even for those who make an active choice of embracing the movement this is hardly a rapid process. Rather, they have to first go through a lengthy process of intense socialisation that Al-Anani refers to as the 'incubation model', which aims at transforming an individual's views to make them conform to the Brotherhood's ideology, norms and objectives.[35] Before granting individuals full membership the Brotherhood trains and vets candidates for a period of three years, during which they progress through a multi-tiered membership system designed to test and maximise their loyalty and commitment.

This model allows the movement to effectively achieve four key objectives: 1) it familiarises new members with the Brotherhood's rules and regulations; 2) it creates cohesiveness and unity between old and new members; 3) it allows the movement to maintain control over its ranks and files; 4) it allows the movement to continue its activities despite regime repression. As they progress through the vetting period candidates are eventually assigned to collective activities, apprentice groups and study units aimed at further familiarising them with the Brotherhood and its principles, as well as creating a sense of comradery and emotional bonds with their fellows. If they are successful, prospective members are then asked to swear an oath of allegiance (*bai'a*) to the General Guide (*al-murshid al'am*), during a ritual that marks their transformation from a devotee into a Brother.[36] Building on al Banna's idea of comprehensiveness as a core value of Islam itself, the oath of allegiance contains ten pillars that form the value-system informing the Brotherhood's thinking and worldview. These are, in order: understanding, sincerity, action, effort, sacrifice, obedience, perseverance, resoluteness, brotherhood and trust.[37] Therefore, by the time someone is deemed pious enough to officially become a member, the movement has already deeply socialised them into its daily activities, hierarchical structures, and values, cultivating the collective identity and subscription to internal roles and dynamics that are key to the Brotherhood's survival.

Yet, the gradual process of socialisation (*tarbiyya*, shaping an individual's identity through practice) is so central to the Brotherhood's ideology and structure that it does not stop once one becomes a member, but continues for as long as one is affiliated with the movement. Al Banna viewed *tarbiyya* as a 'rope that binds brothers together'[38] and it is indeed through this continuous cultivation process that the Brotherhood can further strengthen its members' new identity and ensure their loyalty and commitment. *Tarbiyya* also defines a certain set of values that members need to subscribe to and integrate into their daily lives, such as obedience, confidence in leadership, loyalty, sincerity, sacrifice and commitment.[39] Therefore, the socialisation and cultivation processes are fundamental to tie together identity and values for the ranks and files. Together with the Brotherhood's religious ideology, which directly shapes its norms, regulations and values, the movement's leaders rely on *tarbiyya* to consolidate their position and maintain control over the membership. Nevertheless, the Brotherhood's decades under repression have led to the organisation remaining highly aware of possible infiltrations and of the need for its members to completely subscribe to the movement's aims and objectives, which means that internal scrutiny and top-down directives do not stop once one becomes a member. Rather, the hierarchical structure designed by al Banna is built to continuously scrutinise members' commitment and personal development. Because of this, several former members refer to the Brotherhood as an 'army', citing a 'quasi-military' educational system propagating 'loyalty, obedience, organisational discipline, secrecy'.[40]

The *tanzim* relies on a pyramid structure based on five different membership tiers, with the promotion from one to another being dependent on a complicated set of monitoring mechanisms. While these evolved through the years, the five levels in the current membership system are *muhib* (sympathiser), *mu'ayyid* (supporter), *muntasib* (associate), *muntazim* (regular or registered), and *'amil* (active or operating member).[41] In addition to different membership tiers, the Brotherhood is also divided into seven administrative levels: *usra* (family or cell), *shu'ba* (division or branch), *mantiqa* (district), *maktab idari* (administrative office), *Majlis al-shura* (the Shura Council), *Maktab Al-Irshad* (the Guidance Bureau), and *al-murshid al-'am* (the General Guide).[42] Both Willi and Al-Anani offer a complete and detailed breakdown of the role and duties of each of these levels – which will not be unpacked here – but for now it is sufficient to say that this extremely hierarchical and strict structure is governed by bylaws determining the responsibility and power of each organisational level, and aiming to enable the Guidance Bureau and Shura Council to best achieve the Brotherhood's goals.

While the Brotherhood's fixed membership system and hierarchical structures allowed it to survive and even thrive under repression, it also means that the movement's decision-making process is highly centralised and completely dominated by senior members and the leadership. Decisions are made by the small and exclusive circle of leaders who sit in the Guidance Bureau – who I mostly refer to as the 'Historical Leadership' – who then task lower- and middle-ranking members with implementing such decisions. While a system of checks and balances and internal elections to the Brotherhood's governing bodies is in place, the high levels of repression that the movement faced under Mubarak meant that the Shura Council was often unable to meet regularly, essentially devolving most of the decision-making power to the Guidance Bureau. This imbalance of power further widened the gap between those at the top of the organisation and its members, feeding into already existing power struggles and creating discontent over the lack of internal representation and space for different voices to be heard. These are some of the key complaints advanced by those who want to reform the Brotherhood's structure in the aftermath of the coup, as I have been told many times. When asking a former member what he thought about the internal elections that do take place, he rolled his eyes and just said 'all these elections, they are just like decorations. They pretend they do elections but in reality there are no elections, it is all about connections and about networking. *Khalas.*'[43] As demonstrated later in the chapter, these tensions have much older roots and stem directly from the strictness of these organisational structures and the historical unwillingness to alter the nature of the *tanzim*.

Another result of these strict pyramidal structures is the stagnation and inertia of the Brotherhood. The historical attention paid to ensure unity and integration over allowing some space for debates and individual agency came at the cost of internal vibrancy, meaning that the Brotherhood had long ago lost its chances to create a healthy organisational environment. Rather, the culture that Brothers are socialised into has created a submissive and subservient membership, who are largely unwilling to challenge the leadership at the cost of potentially being marginalised, demoted or expelled. The combination of the intense socialisation process, as well as the hierarchical structures at the core of the *tanzim*, means that Brotherhood members become embedded into ideological, emotional and biological bonds, which further reinforce their strict collective identity and put them under constant surveillance, making both critiquing or leaving the movement a very difficult task. Indeed, over the decades the Brotherhood's leadership has gone to great efforts to minimise independent thinking and activities that might go against the movement's overarching ideology and aims. Yet, they never quite managed to fully eradicate the forces that are now back at the centre of the organisational debates in the aftermath of the coup.

Anti-intellectualism and the silencing of individual voices

The strict hierarchy at the core of the Brotherhood organisation and the unwillingness to reform the *tanzim*'s structures to adapt to changed circumstances played a major role in the 2013 downfall. It meant that the movement's leaders kept on prioritising loyalty over expertise, and apparent unity over diversity of ideas, at a time when what the Brotherhood needed most was the implementation of creative, flexible and smart policies to fully eradicate Mubarak's legacy. The Brotherhood reacted to its newly found political power by sticking to what they knew rather than diversifying, which translated into ideological lethargy and organisational rigidity.[44] Overall, its unwillingness to reform internally and to tackle long-standing frustrations over the lack of internal democracy and transparency further exacerbated the challenges that the movement was already facing from the outside.

Old habits are hard to break, and for decades the Brotherhood relied on a unifying set of rules, ideological tenets and values in order to present a united front against continuous regime crackdowns. This meant that there was very little space to allow for internal debates and for competing views to emerge, as that would have considerably weakened the unquestioned authority of its leaders as well as the collective identity on which the movement relied for unity. Indeed, the unwillingness to allow space for individual thought or agency is built into the very organisational structures outlined above, starting with the recruitment and cultivation process of prospective members. Throughout the decades the Brotherhood has been rather successful in curbing internal discontent – with the exception of significant incidents such as the Wasat Party split in 1996 – by what Kandil refers to as 'anti-intellectualism'. This approach is deeply ingrained into the cultivation process and puts value on privileging sentiments and practices over ideology, the methodical censuring of arguments and the overt avoidance of those with a background in the social sciences.[45] In particular, there are three main ways in which the Brotherhood is designed to patrol and control the thoughts of its members: the recruitment process, its cultivation curriculum, and the lack of clear ideological precepts. I will return to this last aspect in the next chapter, as ideological hollowness is directly linked to recurring grievances relating to the lack of professionalism and accountability.

As discussed above, the process of becoming a Brother takes years and those selected are usually born into Brotherhood families or recruited from a very young age. This means that they are either already socialised into the movement's structures and values or that their personal and intellectual development follows *tarbiyya* and the cultivation curriculum, which is key to making members from different backgrounds subscribe to the same ideological message. Older candidates are usually selected based on their religious fervour rather than competences, with a marked preference for those with a modest knowledge of history, politics and religion. The organisation therefore looks for individuals who are passionate and active believers without being too inclined to independent learning, as it is understood that the individual pursuit of knowledge invites arguments, which would then, in turn, create internal debates and rifts. In his analysis of disengagement patterns from the Brotherhood, Menshawy reports that the culture created by anti-intellectualism is a key factor in driving more intellectually engaged members away, with many saying that 'the Brotherhood has no mind', that orders are passively accepted without being questioned and that members are 'without mind and always share a herd mentality'.[46] Such internal dynamics create an environment in which members' frustrations with the movement are perceived as their own spiritual shortcoming, and any attempt at expending the Brotherhood's curriculum to address the lack of particular skills or knowledge is understood as an attack against the movement's integrity and that of its leaders. A former member who, in the early 2000s, acted as a supervisor for Cairo University's Brotherhood Political and Media Committee recalls that he approached his superiors with a detailed plan on how to improve the political knowledge and training of its fellow members. Perhaps unsurprisingly, 'of course the programme was never implemented. I asked for guidance from the Brotherhood political committee in Cairo and I was just told that they would look into it, and that I should just focus on my studies'.[47]

It therefore becomes clear that the individual pursuit of anything that falls outside of the official cultivation curriculum is actively discouraged and portrayed as unnecessary, with particularly proactive Brothers being reprimanded, reminded of their oath of compliance, and then overloaded with other duties. When these measures are not enough, recruits can have their probation period expanded while full members can face disciplinary measures such as having to answer to investigation committees with the power of suspending or expelling them.[48] Hence, both organisational structures and the threat of marginalisation are employed to patrol and censor instances of independent thought.

Of course, these measures can only work if the right members are recruited in the first place. This is why there is a predilection for those with either low levels of education or members who specialise in scientific disciplines such as natural sciences, engineering or medicine over those with a background in politics, sociology or philosophy. While the side-lining of social scientists is intended to circumvent dissent, over time this has become a significant problem for the Brotherhood when it comes to issues of professionalism.[49] Not only does the movement lack prominent public intellectuals – which is a growing criticism and source of splits in the aftermath of 2013 – but the professional composition of the membership means that the organisation as a whole lacks the necessary knowledge and skills required to fully engage in the political process. Following Mubarak's removal and the founding of the FJP, the Brotherhood's political programme was widely criticised for being an assortment of incoherent policy proposals underpinned by religious fervour. This was evident during the rule of the FJP and in the fact that Morsi himself was an engineer, and part of the reason why now, after the coup, there is a considerable proportion of the membership who are enrolling back at university to provide what they perceive as a knowledge gap that partially drove their removal in 2013. I will explore this in more details in the next chapter when I will also trace the Brotherhood's post-coup fragmentation into two broad camps, stagnation versus adaptation, but for now it is important to point out that this is an issue with much older roots than the current circumstances.

Another tool of control that the Brotherhood's leaders historically rely on to curb the emergence of dissenting voices and control the agency of its members is the movement's ideology and values. Despite being one of the Islamist organisations par excellence the Brotherhood is, in fact, ideologically weak and has often been criticised for lacking a clear ideological vision, precepts and ideologues. Indeed, there are many who, in the fragmentation following the 2013 coup are calling for the complete rewriting of the movement's cultivation curriculum and for a return to al Banna's original teachings, which they argue have been misinterpreted to make the Islamist ideology he theorised fit with the organisation's erratic behaviour, as shown in Chapter 5. Al Banna repeatedly claimed that the movement's ideology 'liberates the mind' and 'respects different views', and the first pillar of the oath of allegiance required to become a member is 'understanding'.[50] Nevertheless, the rules and principles at the core of the movement's structures go directly against these claims, calling for the opposite: *al-sam' wal t'a*, hearing and blind obedience to unquestioned orders, which is the sixth pillar of the oath.[51]

The Brotherhood's lack of a clear ideology historically favoured its leaders, as it allowed them to adapt the movement's values to the particular circumstances to which they needed to quickly react. The lack of a clearly articulated ideology also made it possible for the Brotherhood to mobilise and include wide segments of the population and Muslims from different backgrounds without threatening its unity. Therefore, despite being a doctrine-based movement, the organisation's apparatus has historically been more crucial for its success and survival than its ideology, and its preservation has hence always been prioritised.[52] Indeed, having a concrete ideological programme would deprive the movement of one of its greatest assets: flexibility. Intellectual depth is hence sacrificed in favour of organisational strength, which meant that discouraging independent thinking and suppressing new ideas become crucial to maintaining internal unity. However, this 'intellectual bankruptcy' and ideological hollowness come with a high price, as the movement did not survive the challenges posed by policy-making.[53] It was easy for the Brotherhood, while in opposition, to disseminate general principles that could garner public support on religious and cultural bases. But it was far more difficult for the group's leaders to express specific viewpoints on divisive policy issues, including the economy and social welfare.[54] Most notably, this is yet another factor behind the leaders' control over individual thinking, as they fear their ideological hollowness being displayed.

Breaking away from the *tanzim*

When considering the strictness of the Brotherhood's organisational structure and the emotional, biological and intellectual constraints it imposes on its members, one of the most significant shifts that characterises the movement's transformation in the aftermath of 2013 is the belief that an individual member has the agency and the power to change the organisation from within. In the past, the movement's strict socialisation and control mechanisms meant that dissenting voices were either repressed or expelled. However, the fading legitimacy of the Historical Leadership that followed the coup means that they are now prominent within the movement. The novelty of forced exile and the shock that it delivered to both the movement as a whole and to individual members is leading many to question, and even disregard, the very principles on which the Brotherhood historically rests. As mentioned, in my ongoing conversations with both current and former members statements such as 'the time to follow blindly is no more' are becoming increasingly common, signalling that the dimension of exile marks the first time in which individuals have the opportunity to disengage from and re-evaluate the Brotherhood's control over daily activities, careers and individual thought.

Simply put, the diasporic experience is offering members an unprecedented space to reclaim their agency against the Brotherhood's strict hierarchical structures, leading in some cases to their disengagement from the movement and the emergence of individual identities and subjectivity.

Questioning the very structures in which an individual is socialised throughout their life, as well as the values and ideology associated with them, is not an easy or quick process. It is also not uniform, as individuals who already held grudges against the Brotherhood prior to 2013 might react differently to the novelty and opportunities offered by forced exile than those who did not. There is not a clear pattern to these different dynamics of disengagement and dissent; however, what I noticed through almost seven years of ethnographic fieldwork was the gradual emergence of deep, fundamental questions about identity, belonging and ideology. Many are hesitant to express these at first, both to me as an outsider as well as to their peers, as the questioning of the Brotherhood's core values can lead to the severing of social, biological and emotional ties. This is particularly challenging when living under forced exile, as expulsion from the movement also means the cutting off of the elaborate support system that the Brotherhood provides its members with, ranging from economic and bureaucratic to emotional guidance. As well as these external constraints the questioning of such an encompassing collective identity also comes with an intricate process of self-reflection and soul-searching, which requires such extensive emotional work that it might seem unattainable when coupled with the reality of having to resettle abroad after being forced to leave Egypt. Nevertheless, the unprecedented space for individual thought that comes with the diasporic experience and the inevitable mixing with different realities, ideologies and values cannot be ignored in the long run.

As I have argued elsewhere,[55] the Brotherhood's experience in exile departs from the classic understanding of what constitutes a diaspora as the main element bringing its members together is not only a shared homeland, but also the belonging to an ideological group. This means that the processes of identity-formation and value-change that are usually associated with the diasporic experience are grounded, in the case of the Brotherhood, in the cultural, ritual and spatial markers that come with the connections and community that its membership entails. Nevertheless, conceptualising members' experience of exile within the diaspora framework further facilitates the understanding of the movement as a heterogeneous rather than unitary entity. Rogers Brubaker claims that the diaspora experience is marked by a conception of identity characterised by hybridity rather than unity and stillness, therefore seeing diaspora communities as heterogeneous entities bringing together groups with different needs, experiences and agendas, which consequently have competing internal voices and trends.[56] This does not mean that such communities are necessarily emancipatory projects: as such, in the case of the Brotherhood, many still depend on their elite leadership to shape and represent their interests in the host states. Nevertheless, living in a diaspora can indeed be a liberating experience and this is particularly true of communities where religion and the diaspora dimension are tightly intertwined, but nevertheless see the emergence of subjectivity vis-à-vis top-down collective identities.[57]

There is a growing body of literature that deals with the issues surrounding the shifting and formation of identities within a diasporic context, highlighting their hybrid and ever-changing nature. As Stuart Hall states, 'diaspora identities are constantly producing and reproducing themselves anew, through transformations and difference',[58] meaning that some, while being part of a diaspora, find it hard to reconcile their original beliefs and values with the new context they find themselves in. This, in turn, can lead to the emergence of diasporic subjectivity, which describes the process through which the dislocation from one specific national context and the (forced) relocation to another results in changes in identity construction and sense of belonging. The ensuing state of unfixed identity can therefore result into the challenging of fixed notions of origin and collective identity, leading to processes of disengagement from the 'original' community just like in the case of individual members within the Brotherhood. A key thread underpinning most of my conversations with current and former members is what Bauman refers to as a 'war of liberation', understanding the emergence of subjectivity as a perpetual state of unfixed identity and a pursuit of freedom.[59] Menshawy similarly writes of several Brotherhood members who left the organisation and its tight-knit community after experiencing Istanbul's social freedoms, which is a widespread phenomenon I also came across during my own fieldwork. Additionally, I have met several others who, while remaining affiliated to the Brotherhood, have begun to pursue greater individual agency and have become openly critical of its hierarchical structure and the levels of social and ideological control the movement seeks to impose on its members. While these processes are still in flux, they have already started to reshape the values at the core of the movement and have initiated deep internal change.

Agency and individualism

These patterns of dissent and disengagement are still limited to a proportion of the Brotherhood's membership, but their impact on the movement as a whole is already becoming visible and will have significant long-term consequences on its message and ideology. The reclamation of agency – understood as the emergence of members' own subjectivities and initiatives vis-à-vis the movement's organisational structures and collective identity – as well as the belief that an individual member has the power to challenge the very structures they are socialised into are directly linked to the diasporic experience and to the opportunities posed by this new reality. The struggle between members' agency and desires and the movement's hierarchical structure has taken centre stage under forced exile, and centres around points of contention such as what lessons need to be learnt from the premature end of the political experience and what changes need to be implemented to move past the current crisis. Yet, these tensions build on historical objections internal to the Brotherhood that were re-ignited by the rapid rise and fall of the movement in the aftermath of 2011, and have now found an avenue thanks to the eroding legitimacy of the Historical Leadership and to the consequent weakening of the *tanzim* in communities abroad.

The Brotherhood's narrow and controlled intellectual environment, which has historically been key to maintaining unity in the face of repression, has also long deprived members of their agency and is a source of deep-rooted discontent. This had already become apparent in the past and especially after the Brotherhood's foray into electoral politics in the 1980s, which exacerbated tensions between those who resisted innovation and change and those who were unwilling to 'listen and obey'. The 1996 Wasat Party Split was a clear manifestation of these tensions, seeing a considerable number of Brotherhood members leaving the movement to create their own political party over claims of 'feeling muzzled' by the *tanzim*'s top-down structure.[60] Since then, political engagement has become a channel through which members could express frustration towards their lack of individual freedoms and an avenue in which they had the possibility to challenge the Brotherhood's restrictive structures. It also showcased the movement's overarching control over its members, as any activity to raise the profile of the organisation and the competences of its members to enhance its political ambitions was quickly shut down, adding to the already growing internal frustration. As I have shown elsewhere,[61] in the decade preceding the 2011 uprisings more and more members began to pursue individual projects disregarding the leadership's orders and started to pursue alliances with secular groups, as well as enrolling in university courses to study political sciences and fill the professionality gap that they had identified.

This is evident in the words of Abdullah, a Cairo-based Youth leader before the 2011 uprisings, who recalled how his discontent towards 'the organisational issues, the strategy, openness, transparency from within the organisation, the quality of the leaders, all of this stuff' made him began to question his loyalty to the movement as far back as 2003. Perhaps naively, he still believed that the Brotherhood would eventually listen to its members and therefore set out to acquire the skills that he thought the organisation lacked: 'I started studying political science [in secret] in 2009, because I told myself "you can't just blame them [the political committee] for not being professional and you are like them, you are just reading books". So I started studying political sciences and for a diploma in civil society, so I said "let's take the initiative, I will start to be professional!"'[62] His hopes for internal renewal never quite materialised and Abdullah eventually left the movement after relocating to Istanbul in 2014. However, there are many others who, having started to pursue individual initiatives prior to the uprisings, remain a part of the Brotherhood and are pushing to implement change from the inside.

These accounts are particularly common amongst politically active Brothers, who report being routinely shut down by those in higher positions when asking to pursue political activities and education outside of those prescribed by the Brotherhood's curricula. Mohammed, who prior to 2011 was part of the movement's political committee at Cairo University, is a medical doctor by training and recalls repeatedly asking his superior permission to enrol back at university to pursue a course in political sciences, without success. When his requests continued to be denied, he eventually went directly against the wishes of the movement:

> And by the way, the interesting thing is that I went to Cairo University in the School of Economics to apply for this postgraduate diploma. I went with one of my friends, but then I discovered another three Ikhwan's members who came to apply to the same course and for the same reasons! We were five in this diploma, and we were driven by this idea: that we needed to be professional in politics.[63]

Just like Mohammed, others confirm that instances of individual agency had started developing before the outbreak of the 2011 revolution, and therefore found an avenue in the opening of the political space that followed Mubarak's removal. This shows that the tensions dividing the Brotherhood today are not necessarily a new phenomenon, but rather embody the evolution of long-standing, cross-generational grievances between the rank-and-file members and the Historical Leadership. The events of 2011 acted as a spark for members' pursuit of individual freedom, building on internal tensions that had long been brewing beneath the movement's surface. One of the founders of the Egyptian Current Party (*Ḥizb al-Tayyār al-Maṣrī*), who left the Brotherhood after the foundation of the FJP, described the feeling of excitement that he felt after Mubarak's removal as he saw the new path ahead as a chance to reform the movement:

> The revolution actually was a time in which there is no excuse for procrastination: if you want to change the organisation, this is the time! I remember my conversation with Dr Morsi at this time, after the revolution, I told him in a meeting frankly that there is no excuse now. Now we need to really change

within the organisation, I know that it is a huge organisation and that change can take time, but let's start from this point and let's agree on the direction of change! So during this meeting I told him two things: either we need to start now rebranding the Ikhwan within society and restructuring the Ikhwan as an organisation, or leave people to take their own initiatives under the Ikhwan umbrella! We can't keep the organisation to itself and even forbid members to take their own initiatives, this is too autocratic, something too rigid.

However, their dreams were short-lived. The controversial foundation of the FJP, as well as its political trajectory and the exclusion of Youth and activist members from its activities, soon revealed that the Brotherhood was not ready to reform itself.[64] The consistent purging of members who tried to influence the political choices of the FJP and called for a more cautious and well-thought out approach to the transitional period also sent a clear message: the leadership would not tolerate independent thinking or insubordination.[65] Nevertheless, it was too late to back down. As would become increasingly clear in the years following the 2013 coup, a growing number of members are now unwilling to relinquish the increased freedom that they experienced and refuse to unquestionably follow the leadership's orders.

Therefore, while the Brotherhood's violent removal and persecution, and the novelty of forced exile, are a significant source of trauma for many of its members, in the aftermath of 2013 the organisation is witnessing the unconstrained emergence of individual agency. The tensions outlined above are but one manifestation of this phenomenon, as members from across the organisational spectrum report that 'we think that this pyramid structure is not effective. Something has to change' and that 'the time of following blindly is no more'.[66] And things are changing indeed. As the Historical Leadership fails to put forward a cohesive strategy to move past the current crisis, the Brotherhood is growing increasingly fragmented. These internal divisions go beyond the formation of alternative Guidance Offices – which is still deeply significant – but are also manifesting in the formation of cross-ideological and cross-generational alliances within the organisation's membership, which will be explored in the next chapter.

Conclusion

These dynamics show that the Brotherhood entered the biggest crisis of its history after the 2013 coup. The significant challenges that it faces come not only from the relatively new dimension of forced exile – the most significant ones are embodied by the calls to renegotiate the relationship between the movement and its members. The partial disintegration of its established chains of command means that the Brotherhood is experiencing fragmentation and divisions at all levels. In such a context, while old grievances come back to the fore, a significant finding is that dissenting members now operate from within the organisation, vocally asking for structural changes and for more representation and transparency.

Even more importantly, as members reportedly have acquired the opportunity to pursue individual initiatives for the first time and are now openly disregarding the leadership's orders, they have also begun to challenge the collective identity that they have been socialised into. This process is infinitely more complex than enrolling back at university or building alliances with secular actors, and challenges the very sense of self of many of these members. It is traumatic too – as the search for their own individual identities and individualism often comes at the cost of personal and emotional bonds – but this phenomenon is already underway and does not only apply to those who have left the organisation, but also to the many who remain members but have started to question their loyalty to the Brotherhood's structure. Mohammad, a young journalist residing in Istanbul, described to me the deep identity struggle that he is facing as he tries to unlearn and break free from the constraints that he was socialised into:

> So this was my turning point [the 2011 revolution]. I can say that I have a lot of problematic questions with the Ikhwan since 2011, after the revolution. And it is getting bigger day by day, year by year [...] if you are in such an organisation since you were a child, you don't know anything about the other worlds, about the outside. It is problematic for us. When you see these worlds face to face you will consider yourself as a fool. [sighs] Yes, I have overcome all of this. Now I am free actually, I feel it.[67]

These trends reveal the extent to which the Brotherhood's core principles are being contested by its own members, adding to the significant challenges posed by the task of reuniting while in exile. As these grow more prominent within the organisation, it increasingly looks like structural changes need to be implemented to avoid further mutiny and fragmentation. Yet, it might be too late to go back to the movement as we knew it, and throughout my fieldwork I got a sense that this option might now be entirely off the table. The deeps cracks that are emerging within the movement along strategical and ideological lines might be fixed, but the seed of change and independent thinking that has now been planted might be just too hard to uproot.

Notes

1 Victor Willi, 'The Egyptian Muslim Brotherhood in 2016: scenarios and recommendations', *German Council on Foreign Relations* (15 March 2016) https://

dgap.org/en/think-tank/publications/dgapanalyse-compact/egyptian-muslim-brotherhood-2016 (accessed 19 July 2020).
2 Ardovini, 'The Muslim Brotherhood in Turkey after the 2013 coup d'état'.
3 Author Interview. Istanbul, 2017.
4 Author Interview. Istanbul, 2018.
5 See for example: Carrie Rosefsky Wickham, 'The path to moderation: strategy and learning in the formation of Egypt's Wasat Party', *Comparative Politics*, 36:2 (January 2004), 205–228; Wickham, *The Muslim Brotherhood*.
6 Author Interview. London, 2016.
7 Author Interview. London, 2018.
8 Wickham, 'The path to moderation'.
9 Willi, *The Fourth Ordeal*, 317.
10 Ibid.
11 Ibid., 318.
12 Ibid.
13 Yasser Fathy, 'From confrontation to division: the Muslim Brotherhood in Egypt from 2013–2016', *Al Sharq Research Papers: Political Islam Movements* (16 October 2019), 1–42, 31.
14 Tamer Badawi, Osama Al-Sayyad, 'Mismatched expectations: Iran and the Muslim Brotherhood After the Arab Uprisings', *Carnegie Middle East Center* (March 2019), 1–6, 5.
15 Willi, *The Fourth Ordeal*, 328.
16 Author Interview with Mohammed Sudan. London, 2018.
17 Tamer Badawi, Osama Al-Sayyad, 'Iran and the Egyptian Muslim Brotherhood: heading towards development or simply repair?' *Al Sharq Research Papers: Political Islam Movements* (September 2018), 1–62, 45–49.
18 Mokhtar Awad, Mostafa Hashem, 'Egypt's escalating Islamist insurgency', *Carnegie Middle East Center* (October 2015), 8–11.
19 Willi, *The Fourth Ordeal*, 369.
20 Al-Anani, *Inside the Muslim Brotherhood*, 103.
21 Ibid., 67.
22 Ibid., 68.
23 See for example: William A. Gamson, 'Commitment and agency in social movements', *Sociological Forum*, 6:1 (1991), 27–50; Sheldon Stryker, Timothy Joseph Owens and Robert W. White (eds.) *Self, Identity, and Social Movements* (Minneapolis: University of Minnesota Press, 2000); Francesca Polletta and James M. Jasper, 'Collective identity and social movements', *Annual Review of Sociology*, 27 (August 2001), 283–305, 285.
24 Alberto Melucci, *Challenging Codes: Collective Action in the Informative Age* (Cambridge: Cambridge University Press, 1996), 75.
25 Al-Anani, *Inside the Muslim Brotherhood*, 44.
26 Zollner, 'Surviving repression'.
27 Al-Anani, *Inside the Muslim Brotherhood*.
28 Kandil, *Inside the* Brotherhood; Menshawy, *Leaving the Muslim Brotherhood*.
29 Author Interview. Istanbul, 2018.

30 El-Sherif, 'The Egyptian Muslim Brotherhood's failures', 17.
31 Nora Medhat Abdelkader, 'Islamist parties and social movements: cases of Egypt and Tunisia', *Review of Economics and political Science*, 4:3 (July 2019), 224–241.
32 Kandil, *Inside the Brotherhood*, 5.
33 Author Interview. London, 2017.
34 Author Interview. Istanbul, March 2019.
35 Al-Anani, *Inside the Muslim* Brotherhood, 84.
36 Kandil, *Inside the Brotherhood*, 6.
37 Willi, *The Fourth Ordeal*, 24–26.
38 Hassan Al-Banna, *A Collection of Hasan Al-Banna Messages* (Cairo: Dar Al-Da'wa Publications, 2002), 44.
39 Al-Anani, *Inside the Muslim Brotherhood*, 85.
40 Menshawy, *Leaving the Brotherhood*, 88.
41 For a more detailed analysis of each membership tier see Al-Anani, *Inside the Muslim Brotherhood*, 94; Willi, *The Fourth Ordeal*, 33–49.
42 Al-Anani, *Inside the Muslim Brotherhood*, 103–106.
43 Author Interview. Istanbul, 2017.
44 El-Sherif, 'The Muslim Brotherhood failures', 17.
45 Kandil, *Inside the* Brotherhood, 10.
46 Menshawy, *Leaving the Brotherhood*, 82.
47 Author Interview. Istanbul, 2016.
48 Kandil, *Inside the Brotherhood*, 25.
49 Ibid., 34.
50 Willi, *The Fourth Ordeal*, 24–26.
51 Ibid.
52 Abdelrahman Ayyash, 'Strong organization, weak ideology: Muslim Brotherhood trajectories in Egyptian prisons since 2013', *The Arab Reform Initiative* (29 April 2019), 1–23, 4.
53 Kandil, *Inside the Brotherhood*, 42.
54 Ayyash, 'Strong organization, weak ideology', 15.
55 Ardovini, 'The Muslim Brotherhood in Turkey after the 2013 coup d'état'.
56 Rogers Brubaker, 'The "diaspora" diaspora', *Ethnic and Racial Studies*, 28:1 (2005), 1–19; Bahar Baser, Amira Halperin, 'Diasporas from the Middle East: displacement, transnational identities and homeland politics', *British Journal of Middle Eastern Studies*, 46:2 (2019), 215–221, 216.
57 Manuel Vasquez, 'Diasporas and religion', in Kim Knott, Sean McLoughlin (eds.) *Diasporas: Concepts, Intersections, Identities* (London: Zed Books Ltd, 2010), 128–134; Gorman, Kasbarian, *Diasporas of the Modern Middle East*, 9.
58 Stuart Hall, 'Cultural identity and diaspora', in Jonathan Rutherford (ed.) *Identity: Community, Culture, Difference* (London: Lawrence and Wishart Ltd, 1990), 244.
59 Zygmund Bauman, 'Identity for identity's sake is a bit dodgy', *Soundings: A Journal of Politics and Culture*, 29 (2005), 12–20.

60 El-Ghobashy, 'The metamorphosis of the Egyptian Muslim Brotherhood', 385–387.
61 Lucia Ardovini, 'Rethinking the *tanzim*: tensions between individual identities and organizational structures in the Muslim Brotherhood after 2013', *Middle East Law and Governance*, 13 (2021), 130–149.
62 Author Interview. Istanbul, 2018.
63 Author Interview. Istanbul, 2019.
64 Vannetzel, 'The party, the *Gama'a* and the *Tanzim*' 218.
65 Samir, 'The Muslim Brotherhood's generational gap', 43.
66 Author Interviews. Istanbul, 2018.
67 Author Interview. Istanbul, 2019.

4

Lessons learnt? Stagnation vs adaptation

The unprecedented nature of the repression that the Brotherhood faces in the aftermath of 2013, and specifically the shock that comes with the dimension of exile, is paving the way for internal fragmentation, power shifts and divisions along strategic and ideological lines. The internal dynamics that we see at play within the movement now – such as the emergence of members' agency vis-à-vis the Brotherhood's organisational structure – draw on pre-existent grievances that were catalysed and brought back to the fore by the events following the 2011 uprisings. Most importantly, forced exile and the uncertainty that comes with the diasporic experience are playing a fundamental role in shaping the movement's trajectories in the aftermath of 2013, especially when it comes to internal polarisation over different responses to repression and competing strategies on how to move forward.

There is a burgeoning literature on exile and its potential to effect social transformations, stemming from Edward Said's seminal work *Reflections on Exile*.[1] Much like in the case of diaspora, exile is better understood as a process rather than as a fixed entity and, as can be seen in the case of the Brotherhood, the experience that comes with it is not just painful but also creative.[2] Forcibly displaced from their homeland, some individuals see their new reality and the challenges that come with it as an opportunity to develop new values and identities and to question pre-held ones, engaging in a process of self-discovery that is as painful as it is revolutionary.[3] This is indeed the case for a portion of the Brotherhood membership, which sees members who resettled abroad beginning to air long-standing objections against the movement's strict structures and values, therefore reclaiming their own agency and subjectivity vis-à-vis the top-down collective identity they have been previously socialised into.

As pointed out earlier in the book, the real novelty in these dynamics is the fact that, while prior to 2013 dissenting members would be expelled or leave the organisation at their own will, in the aftermath of the coup we are seeing the emergence of the belief that a single, individual member has the capability and the right to influence changes within the Brotherhood.

Once again, while these trends and dynamics are not necessarily new in the long history of the Brotherhood, it is their scale and momentum that is potentially revolutionary. This is due to the unfamiliarity of the wave of repression the movement is currently facing that, combined with the unprecedented dimension of exile, is drastically altering the ways in which the Brotherhood historically responded to repression. Therefore, before I analyse the two broad responses that started developing in the aftermath of the coup, it is worth noting that the experiences of Brotherhood members with repression are also pointing to the need to rethink how we approach the study of repression and its effects on social movements.

There is a long, ongoing debate on the study of the effects of state repression on social movements and political participation, which is characterised by often conflicting findings and explanations. Some have argued that repression silences social movements,[4] others find that it enhances political participation and mobilisation,[5] while another trend focuses on the curvilinear effect of repression and claims that it can lead to alternative forms of expressing political discontent.[6] Yet, these studies do not usually account for the wide variation of responses to repression that emerge within the same movement or political community. There is a considerable gap in the research when it comes to the analysis of individual responses to repression or, as Ali Honari puts it:

> repression studies neglect the fact that individuals, even though embedded within similar networks and structural contexts, perceive and interpret repression differently: different options are available to each person, and thus each responds differently to repression. Equally importantly, individuals are strategic actors and have agency, so they can act independently of repression. Thus, the outcome of repression largely depends on how people respond to it.[7]

Overall, as individuals have the capability to act independently despite repression, agency should be taken into account when investigating the effects of repression on a particular social movement.

While there is an increasing emphasis on the necessity to acknowledge this, most of the existing debates still focus on reactions to repression from the perspective of movements and parties as a whole, therefore failing to account for how individuals respond to the same circumstances. As the case of the Brotherhood shows, in order to get a more objective picture of the various forces and dynamics at play after 2013 one needs to shift the analysis to the level of individual members, seen as actors with the agency to develop their own strategies in response to repression. Most importantly, one also needs to account for the role that emotions, individual experiences and trauma play in shaping these individual responses to repression. In line with the affective turn in social and political sciences this trend is gaining increasing traction and the study of the Brotherhood's current trajectories directly speak to this literature, drawing on insights about how individual perceptions of repression shape tactical changes and political activities.[8]

In turn, individual experiences of repression also have the potential to drastically alter an individual's social identity, leading to polarisation both within and between different social groups and movements. This is evident in the case of the Brotherhood, which sees a considerable number of members in the aftermath of 2013 contending with the collective identity the movement socialised them into – with competing results: some leave, others stay but with a refreshed perspective, and others effectively go 'dormant' and put their membership and activities on pause. The literature on social psychology, while still primarily focusing on groups as a main unit of analysis, offers a compelling analysis of how the effects of repression impact processes of group identification. It understands identity as being shaped by emotional attachments to a particular group rather than adherence to a specific ideology, which is a fairly constant factor.[9] From here, a focus on the individual level reveals that it is lived experiences that ultimately shape processes of identity formation, creating or updating beliefs that ultimately shape preferences and attitudes.[10] Once again, this supports the value of focusing on the individual level in order to begin to understand what forces are driving the Brotherhood's transformation in the aftermath of 2013.

The Brotherhood is far from being a monolithic movement, despite its rather successful attempts at portraying itself as such. The organisation's leadership and senior members are the ones who historically bore the price of repression, being routinely arrested and detained by the regime, from which they derived increased legitimacy and social clout. Many are unwilling to let go of the status quo that comes with those experiences, as it became clear during a particularly emotional conversation with a senior leader in the UK. When asked about dissenting members trying to reshape the movement from within, he sadly commented 'I have been imprisoned many, many times but I never hid. I always came back to the Ikhwan straight away. Who do you think is more committed to the Ikhwan, someone like me, or like them?'[11] Yet, the brutal repression that followed Morsi's removal affected leaders and rank-and-file members alike, fundamentally shifting the movement's internal hierarchies and balance of power. Members who had never experienced active repression before were imprisoned, forced to hide and to leave the country in order to escape al Sisi's crackdown. It is this unprecedented experience and the trauma that comes with it that is leading individual members to take charge of their own agency and of the vision that they have for the movement, therefore leading to the emergence of competing strategies against repression and to subsequent polarisation and internal fragmentation.

Exile and shifting balances of power

Immediately after removing Mohammed Morsi from power, the counter-revolutionary regime led by al Sisi set out to eradicate the Brotherhood once and for all. The regime's repression strategies were mostly based on their understanding of the movement as a heavy, top-down hierarchical organisation and on the belief that, if this pyramidal set-up was incapacitated, it would inevitably lead to the disintegration of the Brotherhood as a whole. Al Sisi therefore initiated an all-encompassing campaign aimed at destabilising the movement's main sources of power, proscribing it as a terrorist organisation and arresting those sitting in the Guidance Office and the Shura Council. This dealt a significant blow to the movement's historical chains of command, as only a few managed to escape into exile. Meanwhile, the rank-and-file members were also being targeted by an unprecedented wave of regime brutality, leading to thousands being arrested, while those who could also fled Egypt to escape persecution. Therefore, the severity of the post-2013 wave of repression, combined with the novelty of exile significantly destabilised the movement, as discussed. Yet, the biggest challenges to its established values and chains of command come from within the organisation itself.

Amid an aggravating security crackdown and a chain of arrests that upset the established balance of power within the Brotherhood, different factions and coalitions started to emerge causing internal fragmentation and organisational splits. As pointed out earlier in the book these internal schisms developed along two main points of contention, namely the interpretation of what went wrong during Morsi's tenure and the appropriate strategy to confront and exit repression. The significant disruption to the Brotherhood's chain of command and the arrest of most of those who sat in the Guidance Office, combined with the dimension of exile, provided an unprecedented opportunity for disgruntled middle-rank members to advance their positions, therefore generating an internal battle for power. This took place in two different geographical contexts, Egypt and abroad, which were thus driven by widely diverse dynamics and needs. In Egypt a group of mid-rank individuals led by Mohammed Kamal, an agriculturalist from Asyut, formed the High Administrative Committee in February 2014, bringing together seven Guidance Office members and three technocrats.[12] Most commonly known as the 'New MB', the High Administrative Committee capitalised on the frustration and desperation of rank-and-file members who remained in the country and is known for advocating revolutionary measures against the military regime.

This committee and its activities are vocally denounced by the so-called Historical Leadership, composed of figures associated with the Brotherhood's Historical Leadership who effectively remain in charge of the movement's activities and finances. These include Secretary General Mahmoud Hussein, former General Guide Mahmoud Ezzat, official spokesperson Mahmoud Ghozlan and London-based Ibrahim Mounir, who is generally recognised as the official face of the Brotherhood in the West having lived in exile since 1981.[13] Other high-ranking members in exile, such as Amr Darrag and Yahya Hamid, constituted the 'Crisis Management Committee', while the 'Founding Body of the Muslim Brotherhood Abroad' relocated the movement's centre of power abroad, mostly in Istanbul and London.[14] Nevertheless, even if al Sisi's repressive strategies seemed to be effective at first, in the aftermath of the coup the Brotherhood is definitely divided but far from being annihilated. What in 2015 looked like a generational clash between a revolutionary Youth wing and an orthodox Old Guard was really a clash between different approaches to repression, further exacerbated by the Historical Leadership's attempts to maintain power and legitimacy. From this, we see the emergence of cross-generational and cross-ideological alliances and factions that do not conform to the historical internal schisms which are well documented in the literature on the movement.

These debates are still ongoing and are arguably among the most significant forces shaping the Brotherhood's trajectories and internal renewal in the aftermath of the coup. On the surface, the Historical Leadership remains in control of the Brotherhood's administration and continues to represent the organisation abroad, yet, the movement's vertical command structure is slowly being replaced by non-hierarchical factions and networks of communication.[15] This has created the space for relatively younger or previously silenced members to start reclaiming space within the movement, with these individuals now playing a crucial role for the Brotherhood's renewal and survival. The Brotherhood has therefore proven to be highly resilient, despite the disintegration of its internal lines of command. These significant changes to its circumstances and to the ways in which the Brotherhood survived in the Egyptian context makes it rather complicated to trace its trajectories and strategies in the aftermath of the coup. Mostly, this is due to the fact that for a long time after the coup the movement was so worried about surviving that there simply was no time to formulate a clear message on how to move forward. Yet, as various factions of the Brotherhood started to resettle abroad this confusion over future directions continued. In particular, the combination of the shock of exile and of the disintegration of vertical chains of command severely threaten the unity of the movement.

While the movement's Historical Leadership strongly denies internal fragmentation, throughout several rounds of fieldwork I began to observe the ways in which competing strategies against repression began to create a rift within the organisation. Much like I have highlighted above, it became increasingly clear that a growing number of members were going through the process of exile alone, as single individuals rather than as part of a collective, meaning that their personal trauma, emotions and perspectives directly shape their view on how the movement should react to its current circumstances. In turn, this results in a detectable gap between collective and individual responses to repression. Overall, what I have found is that the organisation as a whole has been implementing changes and strategies to accommodate repression while avoiding sweeping changes to its structure and hierarchies, and individual members are taking advantage of their newfound space to put forward independent thinking and initiatives. Therefore, one can say that while members are adapting to their new circumstances, the Brotherhood as an encompassing, unitary movement remains largely immobile.

Scholars like Al-Anani have argued that since 2013 the movement as a collective unit has been making organisational and strategic changes to adapt to its new circumstances, while members' individual tactics mostly range from political apathy to confrontation with the regime. While this might appear to be the case at a quick glance, a deeper analysis of the internal dynamics of the Brotherhood reveals a very different scenario. Competing approaches to the two points of contention that I have previously identified – these being the interpretation of the circumstances that led to the fall of the Morsi government and the need to stipulate a coherent narrative and strategy for the Brotherhood to move forward – are driving the Brotherhood's fragmentation into two overarching factions, dictated by the preferred strategies against repression. I named these the 'adaptation' and 'stagnation' camps, for reasons that I am about to unpack. Before I do so, however, a disclaimer is in order. These divisions over strategies are ongoing and arguably represent one of the most significant challenges to the Brotherhood's unity and message in the aftermath of 2013. Because of this, I understand these as broad 'trends' encompassing different strategies driven by similar perspectives, rather than attempting to offer an alternative categorisation of internal divisions currently dividing the movement. These competing trends are a useful way to look at what the main debates are currently, but they do not necessarily reflect the proliferation of ideological and cross-generational alliances that emerged within the movement after the coup. Rather, they reflect the dynamism that has come to characterise alliances and loyalties, now more than ever. As such, they are a useful tool to identify and begin to outline the main internal challenges and debates that are shaping the Brotherhood's responses to repression. Lastly, I employ this terminology as these are the most common terms with which my interviewees themselves refer to the competing approaches under examination. For the purpose of clarity, while 'stagnation' can be seen as having an inherently negative connotation, in this context it can also be thought of as 'endurance' or 'steadfastness'. Similarly, 'adaptation' refers to the pursuit and emergence of change in the movement's strategies, tactics and structures.

Stagnation

The stagnation camp encompasses strategies and approaches against repression that are in line with the Brotherhood's historical tools of resistance, and is headed by the Historical Leadership and those who remain faithful to them. Championing the 'classic' Brotherhood's approach the actions – or lack of thereof – that fall under this trend heavily draw from the movement's historical experiences and particularly from those of its leaders, who endured repression and repeated arrests throughout the regimes of Nasser, Sadat and Mubarak. Pre-2011, time spent in prison was a key factor that contributed to the legitimisation of leadership and reinforced hierarchical lines within the movement, also further strengthening the unifying narrative of endurance against repression that is at the base of the Brotherhood's collective identity. Nevertheless, when talking about historical tools of resistance it is necessary to note that the Brotherhood's notable survival skills and strategies against repression have not always been fixed, but have indeed evolved overtime to adapt to the socio-political circumstances in which the movement had to operate. These strategies have not always been unanimous and, similarly to the dynamics that we see playing out within the movement after 2013, there are old internal disagreements over which path to pursue to survive repeated crackdowns and illegality. These historically manifested into two competing currents, a confrontational one epitomised by Sayyd Qutb and a more accommodative one articulated by former General Guide Hassan al-Hudaiby.[16] Today, the struggle between the 'New MB' hands-on approach against the regime and the Historical Leadership's call for patience can be seen as an echo of these old tensions. However, the multi-layered dynamics that are at play within the movement after the coup – and their scale and impact on the organisation as a whole – mark a clear element of novelty when compared to the Brotherhood's past experiences.

The movement has historically resisted repression by employing a set of well-defined strategies, which is what I refer to when I talk about tools of resistance. First of all, the Brotherhood's pyramidal structure and its reliance on principles such as 'listen and obey' made for a strong collective identity, in which continued repression acted as a source of unity and endurance. Cut off from officially participating in political life, the movement built its assets and popular base through the provision of social services, as well as charitable and preaching activities, by gaining a strong following within universities and syndicates, and by establishing a strong public presence through various media channels and outlets. These tools were key to the Brotherhood's growth into one of Egypt's most powerful civil society actors and to its subsequent embedment into social and political life. However, while previous waves of repression allowed for these activities to take place to varying degrees, the brutality of the crackdown enforced by al Sisi's regime after the coup has all but annihilated them. Some of the counter-revolutionary regime's first moves after toppling Morsi were the seizure of the Brotherhood's social associations, education and medical centres, the freezing of its financial and economic assets, and the indiscriminate arrest of its leaders, rank-and-file members and supporters.[17] The designation of the movement as a terrorist organisation for the first time in its history in December 2013, coupled with the mass killing of thousands of its followers during the Rabaa' and Nahda' massacres clearly marked the end of an era for the Brotherhood, throwing the organisation into a drastically changed political, social and even geographical context.

The fleeing of thousands of Brotherhood members and leaders is yet another novel element for the movement, as the dimension of forced exile had historically only included its leaders. The unfamiliarity of the events that followed the coup, together with the unprecedented challenge of having to reform while abroad, therefore largely invalidated the efficacy of the tools of repression that the movement had relied on up to 2013. This is particularly significant when looking at the narrative surrounding *mihna*, which historically acted as a source of unity against repression. I keep coming back to *mihna* because it is a fundamental component of the Brotherhood's existence under repression that needs not to be overlooked, as it is key to the movement's historical ability to capitalise on illegality and even thrive because of it. By this I am referring to the Brotherhood's turning of repression into a binding tool and as something to be used for its own benefit, ranging from generating internal solidarity and public support, to strengthening organisational coherence and even marginalising Reformist voices.[18] The reference to *mihna* as a call for patience, persistence and fortitude still plays a central role in the narratives of the Historical Leadership after 2013, reaffirming the need for internal unity and tenacity against authoritarianism. It is therefore not surprising that the current crisis is perceived as just another period of hardship, which the organisation will eventually survive if they wait it out for long enough. In the words of Mohammed Sudan, former Foreign Affairs Secretary of the FJP:

> I believe that 2013 is the biggest crisis we have ever had facing the Ikhwan. [The strategy] is resistance. This is just a stage of life. If you study the history of the Ikhwan, you will see that they thought we were done in 1954, and then 1965, they thought that we were finished. And then we woke up again in 1971, and then we became very strong, we spread from Egypt to all the Arab

countries. If you think that we are done, that is not true. Because we are just a thought. [The Brotherhood] is a thought from generation to generation, we know to keep going with this. [...] All of us, we are coming back to the mother organisation. So this is a time for re-gathering, for re-grouping.[19]

This emphasis on unity against adversity is a clear attempt to draw a parallel to the past, but today is wielding largely different results and generating frustration towards the perceived inactivity of the leadership.

Therefore, those belonging to the stagnation camp are characterised by the refusal to acknowledge the novelty of the post-2013 context and the subsequent need for new ways to face the current wave of repression. During my conversations with those subscribing to this approach, ranging from leaders to rank-and-file members, when I asked about the movement's strategy to move past the current crisis I was almost unanimously met with affirmations like 'This is just another period of hardship, we need to be patient. We survived before and we will survive again'.[20] Such an approach means that, overall, the higher ranks of the organisation are not calling for any specific strategies to respond to repression but rather require members to be patient and wait for things to evolve. In essence, the leadership seems to believe that the regime cannot further target the Brotherhood as long as they remain inactive. This has been described to me as a 'wait and see' strategy by frustrated members who call for a more proactive response moving forward, also suggesting that the inaction of the Historical Leadership is further contributing to their quickly decreasing legitimacy. Discontented members also recognise the historical continuity of this stagnation, as explained to me by Hussein, a young Brother who since coming to Istanbul in 2015 has been actively advocating for internal reforms. Having been a prominent member of the Youth division prior to the coup, Hussein has dealt with the pushback from the Brotherhood's higher ranks before. When recalling the years immediately following 2013, he said:

> the decision-makers within the Ikhwan took the decision not to activate [...] not because they are afraid, but because this is their mentality. [...] I think this has been the main strategy of the Ikhwan since the 1950s [laughs]. I have internal peace that there is no hope in the Leadership. When I came to Istanbul 4 years ago I was very proactive and tried to start and get involved in a lot of initiatives, but the Leadership is not going to change. So it is up to us to make it happen.[21]

Nevertheless, a stark difference from previous times of repression is the extent to which individual members are reacting with their own initiatives against the immobility and orders of the movement's top ranks.

It is worth pointing out here that the Brotherhood as a whole is not completely immobile, and that the stagnation I identify here is mostly ideological – meaning a refusal to acknowledge that changed circumstances require new strategies, even if at the cost of making significant changes to organisational structures and hierarchies. This is the case as the adoption of a 'wait and see' strategy largely benefits those in the higher ranks of the movement, allowing them to maintain power and to replicate the Brotherhood's internal structures abroad, while also aligning with their shared personal experiences of imprisonment and repression.[22] This is not new for the Brotherhood, as ideological stagnation and anti-intellectualism have old roots in the movement and are directly linked to the need to preserve chains of command through the refusal to adapt values, narrative and practices.[23] If anything, its renewed suppressed status has pushed the Brotherhood to fall back even more on its doctrinal core, relying on the reproduction of its ideological and religious character against this new existential threat.[24] This means that, while organisational changes have been made, over seven years after the coup the movement still lags behind when it comes to the urgent need to formulate doctrinal and intellectual revisions. This is not necessarily surprising, as there is a vast body of literature documenting that during repression waves, opposition movements tend to focus on their survival as the key objective, prioritising it over political activism or other activities, so the Brotherhood is no exception.[25] In order to do this, movements are usually required to implement some degree of organisational change to adapt to their new environment which, in the case of the Brotherhood, means that this time around the source of this changes is renewed repression rather than inclusion in formal politics.

From this, it is undeniable that some changes have taken place at the organisational level since 2013, even though they are too limited in scope to be included in the 'adaptation' camp. What I mean by this is that there are detectable adjustments to the Brotherhood's new circumstances that have been implemented by the Historical Leadership, but in a way that leaves the movement's structures, ideology and core message fundamentally unchanged despite the dimension of forced exile. The most significant of these is undeniably the fact that the movement has been forced to decentralise and to relocate administrative activities abroad, especially with Turkey, London and Qatar being centres where the exiled leadership is out of the reach of the Egyptian regime. The Brotherhood's most significant Guidance Office is now the External Egyptian Brotherhood Office, located in Istanbul, from which decisions are made and then communicated to members regardless of their location. The geographical shift goes hand in hand with a breakdown of hierarchical lines within the movement, especially after the arrest of high-level leaders and members of the Guidance Bureau. Both in Egypt and abroad, this gave increased leverage to lower tiers of membership and allowed a more fluid progression through the movement's ranks.[26] As I will show later, this process goes hand in hand with the resurfacing of old grievances between the movement and its members and is allowing for the slow dismantling of established hierarchies and pyramidal structures.

The dimension of exile has also forced the movement to at least partially rethink its means of political mobilisation, highlighting the need to establish some form of transnational activism. This is happening along two main lines, which are largely dependent on the geographical contexts in which members have settled since the coup. Looking at the UK context, it appears that members who belong to senior ranks and generally reside in London are now acting as the Brotherhood's official 'face', representing the movement in their engagement with international bodies and governmental institutions.[27] Because of this, they are usually referred to as the Brotherhood 'PR office' (in a mocking manner) by those residing in Turkey. A mid-rank Brotherhood member in Istanbul explained this by saying 'These "leaders" [air quotes], they think they speak for the Ikhwan, that they represent us, but no one asked them to. They appointed themselves, they are just doing publicity', echoing a sentiment that many others also expressed.[28] Nevertheless, they do act as the public face of the movement and take part in international efforts to de-stigmatise the Brotherhood in Western contexts, as evidenced in the 'Muslim Brotherhood Review' commissioned by the UK government in 2015.[29]

On the other hand, Turkey and its government's continuous support for the movement also allows for activism and mobilisation to take place across different media channels, which is in line with the historical tools of resistance successfully employed by the Brotherhood in the past. Beyond Facebook and online portals such as Ikhwanweb, pro-Brotherhood satellite television stations such as Rabea TV, Mekammelyn, Al Sharq, Misr al'n and al-Watan are crucial outlets through which to transmit ideas, keep lines of communication open and connect the leadership with grassroots members.[30] More importantly, they are allowing the exiled Brotherhood to perform political opposition from abroad by deploying a narrative that is Islamic, anti-regime and based on self-victimisation.[31] These outlets also broadcast to different publics, allowing the movement to virtually reach out to different segments of society, therefore replicating *da'wa* strategies and techniques in the media realm. For example, in her in-depth study of the Brotherhood's 'media empire' Noha Mellor identifies that al-Watan targets hard-core members, while Mekammelyn is aimed at young Egyptian revolutionaries who supported the 2011 uprisings.[32] Another channel named al-Hiwar TV provides a platform for leaders in the UK – such as Ibrahim Mounir – to discuss the future of the movement and has been instrumental in sustaining the Brotherhood's discourse after the coup.[33] Yet, while allowing the Brotherhood a platform from which to initiate transnational activism and project an anti-regime rhetoric, these media channels have a rigid top-down hierarchy which is dominated by the old guard and fails to showcase the diversity of membership and views within the movement, causing yet more discontent among the younger presenters chosen specifically to portray a 'revamped' version of the movement. Hence, despite the variety of outlets, there does not seem to be a unified communicative strategy among the Brotherhood, which is once again a reflection of the lack of a coherent and cohesive strategy against repression. This immobility, combined with the decreased legitimacy of the Historical Leadership and the growing emergence of agency, is leading many within the Brotherhood to disregard the official narrative, and to set in motion more proactive strategies of adaptation.

Adaptation

Despite the overarching ideological immobility of the stagnation camp – and the refusal of the Brotherhood as a whole to renovate its values and practices to fit the new circumstances it finds itself in – the movement undeniably demonstrated resilience against the regime's brutal crackdown. Opposition and political mobilisation continued after 2013 through the use of satellite television and new media outlets, as well as the relocation of administrative activities and communication lines abroad. Yet, the leadership seem to remain anchored in the understanding of history as a repetitive series of events and invokes *mihna* waiting for the current crisis to subside, alienating many within the movement in the process. Therefore, while this strategy undeniably kept the Brotherhood united in the face of adversity in the past, it is failing to do so in the post-2013 context. As I have said before, the events of 2011 and 2013 accelerated internal discontent and grievances that had long existed within the movement, especially in relation to the dismantling of established hierarchies, the lack of space for debate and the demands for more transparency and accountability. Moreover, the fact that the current phase of repression and forced exile come after the Brotherhood's failed experience in government is yet another element that makes the contemporary crisis different from those in the past. In fact, the sudden and premature removal of the FJP has led many to question the viability of the Islamic project, along with the suitability of the Brotherhood's ideology to formal politics.

Altogether, after the shock of exile, these different forces made it possible for established lines of command to be challenged and for individual members to start voicing their own thoughts and opinions, capitalising on the partial disintegration of the Historical Leadership's legitimacy. The post-2013 context therefore saw the development of a variety of viewpoints among Brotherhood activists in exile in Turkey, the UK, Qatar and elsewhere in Europe and the

Middle East, which are often openly opposed to the narrative of the 'classic' Brotherhood. It is worth noting here that the lines between these worldviews are blurred and people easily shift from one side to the other, considerably complicating the effort to identify established categories and groups. Indeed, this is not what I aim to do here, but rather to highlight the outstanding levels of dynamism and intellectual exchanges that characterise certain factions of the Brotherhood after the coup. This caveat is important as the adaptation camp encompasses a range of approaches against repression that are even conflicting at times, ranging from more revolutionary tactics to quietist ones, but they all depart from the same point: the unwillingness to blindly follow the order of the Historical Leadership and the belief that, in order to overcome the current crisis, a more proactive approach is needed.

While these dynamics tap into old tensions within the Brotherhood, they have been made possible to this extent by the disruption of established organisational structures that came with the reality of forced exile. In the years immediately following the coup it appeared as if the Brotherhood had become split between two, easily identifiable lines: those who remained in Egypt and those in exile. Scholarship on the movement quickly identified two opposing camps, constituted of a confrontational subgroup in Egypt – generally referred to as the 'New MB' – arguing for a hostile approach against the regime, and by a second faction made up by leaders in exile who quickly condemned more radical approaches and focused on survival instead.[34] Even though the revolutionary momentum in Egypt was short lived, this was the first instance of a broader fragmentation within the Brotherhood organisation and a clear manifestation of deep fissures in a system that historically relies on obedience and controlled decision-making. Looking back, these initial tensions were just a prelude of the further fragmentation along strategic, organisational and ideological lines that was to come, and an early instance of deep internal inconsistencies that, to this day, jeopardise the process of a smooth, unified comeback.

This revisionism is symptomatic of ongoing processes of self-reflection that are only detectable if we focus the analysis at the individual level. The temporary suspension after the coup of the Brotherhood collective identity that members had been deeply socialised into meant that many went through repression alone, rather than as followers of a unified social and ideological body. The response to repression of individual members is therefore shaped by their emotions, trauma, personal experiences and grievances. Such levels of individualism had been kept restrained in the pre-coup era, as they were seen as a threat to the unity of the movement, but speaking to members in exile it becomes clear that the traumatic process of having to resettle abroad gave many the opportunity to stop and think clearly for the first time since they joined the movement. This process was also facilitated by the suspension of the Brotherhood's daily activities and tasks, which have since resumed, but in the years immediately following the coup it gave members unprecedented time to reflect upon their experiences vis-à-vis the movement. In the words of Mohamed, a member who now resides in Istanbul:

> Particularly after the coup, people who left Egypt realised that there is a lot of time to think because you can do very little. So the result was that the people became more vocal, they were expressing themselves about these issues [referring to strategies to rebuild, reunify and exit the crisis that still favoured established lines of command]. Myself, I realised that there is not just one way to be an Ikhwani anymore. I can do what I believe is right, for myself and for the organisation, and there are a lot of us who feel this way.[35]

Therefore, without going into generalisations, there are processes of self-reflection that have started to take place among some factions of the Brotherhood, along with a willingness to acknowledge past mistakes in order to learn from them, at least at the individual level. Together, these are a clear marker of strategies and approaches that belong to the adaptation camp.

The reference that many members make to finally having time to think independently is a direct challenge to the Brotherhood established anti-intellectualism, which is also one of the organisation's historical strategies to preserve unity and repression. Particularly when it comes to the ideological stagnation that I have outlined above, this taps into long-standing issues regarding freedom of thought, expression and debates within the movement. There are many who make direct reference to this unprecedented space to engage in individual thought, describing the process with very powerful statements. Abdullah, a member now residing in Istanbul, always leaned towards more reformist and proactive approaches to politics, but never personally advocated for them as he feared his membership would be frozen or terminated. Reflecting on what has changed, he said to me: 'Up until the revolution there was no space outside the Ikhwan, so we had no choice but to operate within it [...] you were like trapped. But after the revolution there was space, so we said that this is the time to renegotiate what it means to be an Ikhwan'.[36] What is really striking here is the common referral to a deeply traumatic event – forced exile – as an avenue that provided unprecedented space for members to breathe and question their belonging to the movement. The opportunity to 'stop and think' is identified by many as an empowering moment that allowed them to disengage from the overarching, top-down narrative of the Brotherhood and consider the options ahead of them. From this, these processes of self-reflection are leading to widely different results, ranging from some members completely disengaging from the movement to others choosing to retain their membership and work towards implementing internal change. On this, the work of Mustafa Menshawy offers a fascinating insight into dynamics of disengagement and ex-hood, highlighting how many refer back to the decision of leaving the movement as the moment in which they regained 'independence of mind', pointing to the Brotherhood's anti-intellectualism as one of the core elements at the base of their disillusionment.[37]

Nevertheless, what is uniquely new about the post-2013 context is that these same thought processes are also common among members who, despite their disillusionment, decide to stay in the movement and to use their dissent to bring about internal change. The scale of this phenomenon is quite simply unprecedented, as historically members who expressed dissent or showcased too high a level of individualism were either reprimanded, demoted, expelled or willingly left the organisation to join other projects that were more compatible with their worldview. Therefore, one of the most significant shifts that happened after the coup is the belief that a single member has the ability and indeed the right to change the movement from within, imbuing the Brotherhood with the values, strategies and structures that they most see fit.

Different tactics of adaptation stem from this belief and, despite their difference, are driven by processes of self-reflection, the interrogation of what went wrong in 2013 and by the questioning of what needs to be done for the movement to exit the current crisis and move forward.[38] As described to me by Amr Darrag, former Minister of Planning and International Cooperation with the FJP:

> After the coup there were internal discussions about what went wrong and why did this happen. [...] The leaders are getting very old, they are not allowing young people to be part of the decision-making process, a lot of young people are very active, but they are excluded from the strategic planning. [...] The general feeling is that there should be more freedom to take an active part in the decisional process, and maybe this hierarchical structure does not work anymore. This are some very radical questions, and this is why they are causing all these differences. That is why some people left, others are very unhappy. Others, including myself, started pushing to have these kinds of changes taking place within the organisation, we have this kind of resources, structures, history, influence in many countries [...] this should not be wasted! We should learn from our mistakes and implement changes.[39]

Darrag's position is shared by many and reflects a portion of the membership that is growing increasingly proactive and pragmatic, showing willingness to take matters into their own hands regardless of the Historical Leadership's lack of approval. From this, there are some key areas that have been identified by those belonging to the adaptation camp as issues that need resolving for the Brotherhood to move forward, even though the strategies to tackle them widely vary. These are: the examination of what went wrong in 2011–2013 and the lessons that should be learnt from it; the issue of professionalism; the need for ideological renewal; the push for the radical transformation of the structures underpinning the *tanzim* to promote transparency and inclusivity; and the call for more liberal values. Altogether, these issues are signalling the need for a drastic transformation of the Brotherhood's core values, structures and activities.

To begin with, the interpretation of what mistakes were made during the FJP's rule and the lessons that should be taken from it moving forward is one of the main points of contention dividing the Brotherhood in the aftermath of the coup, and a clear marker of the strategies that belong to the adaptation camp. Generally speaking, those who subscribe to the movement's official narrative see the events of 2013 as the culmination of a 'long coup' that started with 2011 and mostly refuse to take responsibility for what happened. This is evident in statements such as 'For me what happened in 2011 is not a revolution, I am trying to convince people of it, we need to start from there. It was a conspiracy of the army to steal power from Mubarak, and we supported them, because we did not know.'[40] While many still hold this view, I started noticing a significant shift in attitudes towards this topic around 2018, when I resumed conversations with current and former members who I had been in contact with previously. Up until then, when talking about the factors that might have led to the 2013 coup the most common reaction I encountered was the almost immediate rejection of the assumption that the FJP could have done anything wrong. Instead, many went to great lengths to point me towards international conspiracy theories, foreign involvement and lack of opportunities as the real reasons behind Morsi's removal. Then, when I started fieldwork again in 2018 I noticed that almost all interviews contained some degree of self-reflection and awareness of agency. Participants started outlining a series of mistakes committed by not only the Brotherhood as a whole, but also by themselves as members, that they believe played a considerable part in the failure of the movement's political project. Some of the most common issues that they identify are the lack of political proficiency and professionalism and the appointment of political positions on the bases of loyalty over expertise, which made for a cabinet formed by hardcore Brotherhood loyalists with little political experience. In the words of Mohammad, a member who now lives in the UK and has enrolled at university to study political sciences, 'the Ikhwan was not ready to govern Egypt because they didn't have enough skills, leaders, statesmen who can really run the country, they didn't even have enough vision to do that.'[41] From this, according to most interviewees the issue of professionalism is one that needs urgent addressing.

The lack of professionalism and of a diverse skillset are not new to the Brotherhood, and are attributable to its historical commitment to anti-intellectualism and the regard of those coming from the social sciences as potential dissenters and revisionists. Its membership body is therefore mostly composed of engineers, lawyers and medical doctors and the organisation historically pushed back on individual initiatives to widen its political curriculum, as evidenced by various members' experiences that I outlined in the previous chapter. These dynamics have begun to change in the post-2013 context, as members have started investing in self-development activities and are enrolling back at universities, establishing research centres and undertaking professional courses in order to gain the skills they perceive as lacking. Some concrete examples of this are the Egyptian Institute for Studies based in Istanbul, along with other institutions based in Turkey, such as the Egyptian Revolutionary Council, which focuses on political activism and international advocacy.

Members' pursuit of self-development and individual initiatives despite the lack of endorsement of the Historical Leadership goes hand in hand with their decreasing legitimacy, which is directly linked to the perceived lack of professionalism. Indeed, the Leadership's failure to appoint political positions on expertise bases and to react to the changing political tides in Egypt led members to question their once undisputable abilities and political cleverness.[42] Once again, issues of accountability are not necessarily new but what differs in the post-2013 context is the extent to which they are being openly and vocally addressed. Several members speak of the early 2000s as the moment in which they realised that maybe the movement's leaders were not as untouchable and omniscient as they thought, saying that 'we started looking more closely at the leaders and at their behaviours, and we started criticising them ... it was impossible not to! We realised that the leaders are very average people. There was obedience [to the ideology of the Brotherhood] but not performance'.[43] Building on this, others refer to the FJP's performance in government as the moment that 'put them [the Leadership] on the stage and turned on the lights', revealing the lack of a concrete plan to bring about the Islamic project and the lack of the leadership's governing skills and political insight. Indeed, this reckoning dealt a heavy blow to the Brotherhood's fixed hierarchies and prompted many to begin challenging the structures of the *tanzim* more forcefully.

In such a context, the lack of political skills is being remedied by those who have actively enrolled back into education, established research centres and are engaging in dialogue with secular opposition groups. Yet, another issue that is considerably harder to tackle is that of ideological hollowness and of the perceived gap between ideology and practice. The fact that the Brotherhood's ideology is purposely broad and unspecific is not new, and indeed historically allowed the leadership to adapt the movement's religious message to their decisions and to maintain control over the membership.

However, after 2013, this is a position that is being vehemently criticised by many who take issue with the lack of a clear, focused vision and message. One self-identified hardliner member, whose loyalty to the Brotherhood is determined by its religious rather than political activities, complained that 'there are even leaders who do not know the ideas of Hassan al Banna, even though they claim to be fighting for them [...]. This also explains why we have all of these problems with the current leadership, because most of these leaders have not read the literature of the Ikhwan, are not familiar with it.' Shaking his head, he half-muttered, half-joked: 'the only difference between Al Sisi and our current leaders is that they have beards, and Sisi does not'.[44]

Denouncing the fact that the Brotherhood has not had any new thinkers in decades, many members now also point to the need for ideological renewal. This concept means different things depending on who you speak to, with some calling for a return to al Banna's original writing and message while others argue that 'We need to sit down and re-visit our ideology in light of the current crisis. This is not defection, this is necessary for our survival'.[45] This lack of agreement even within the adaptation camp is leading to varied outcomes, with some taking upon themselves the task of rewriting the Brotherhood's curriculum to be more representative of al Banna's original message, and others revisiting the old debate between politics and *da'wa*. I will return to this in more details in the next chapter, but for now it is worth noting that this second faction in particular sees the failure of the FJP's experience in government as the proof that the Brotherhood cannot be both a religious and a political movement, and argues for these activities and messages to be kept clearly separated. Statements like 'Yes, Islam is a comprehensive religion, but this does not mean that the *Ikhwan* should be a comprehensive organisation. In order to work in politics there are specialised institutions for that: political parties'[46] are becoming more common and raise fundamental questions about the nature of the movement going forward. I will further unpack the struggle between politics and *da'wa* and its significance for the movement's future trajectories below, but for now, one can see how the lack of agreement on such a fundamental issues further hinders the chances of a unified narrative coming out of the Brotherhood.

Conclusion

Analysing responses to repression by looking at individual experiences and strategies reveals that, in the aftermath of the coup, the Brotherhood is growing increasingly fragmented along ideological, strategical and organisational lines. While internal divisions and disagreements are not new, the movement is now mostly split between stagnation and adaptation strategies.

The Historical Leadership's refusal to implement significant changes to adapt to the Brotherhood's new circumstances has brought old grievances back to the fore, causing it to clash with a variety of proactive approaches calling for new strategies to be implemented. Overall, the main issue is that, eight years after the coup, the Brotherhood still lacks a unified, coherent message and plan of action bringing its members together. Even more importantly, another finding is that the very values and core principles that have been at the centre of the Brotherhood for decades are now being challenged. This is incredibly significant as, even though the adaptation camp encompasses a wide range of different strategies, they overarchingly share a call for the need of drastic, internal reforms and for greater pluralism, transparency and participation within the movement. Indeed, these processes have already begun to take place and the Brotherhood is in a unique position to undergo internal change and ideological renewal, as it faces its mistakes and attempts to learn from past experiences. A main challenge confronting the Brotherhood members is therefore that of advancing the intellectual reforms the movement has long refrained from. Going forward, the movement's position towards democratic principles and ideological renewal is fundamental to address, but so are its political project and manifesto.

Notes

1. Edward Said, *Reflections on Exile and Other Essays* (Cambridge, MA: Harvard University Press, 2001).
2. Ibid., p. xiv; Amy Kaminsky, *After Exile: Writing the Latin American Diaspora* (Minneapolis: University of Minnesota Press, 1999), xviii.
3. Paul Allatson, Jo McCormack, 'Introduction: exile and social transformation', *Portal Journal of International Studies*, 2:1 (2005), 1–18.
4. Wood, 'The emotional benefits of insurgency in El Salvador', 267–281; Boykoff, *The Suppression of Dissent*; Brockett, 'A protest-cycle resolution of the repression/popular-protest paradox'.
5. Almeida, 'Multi-sectoral coalitions and popular movement participation', 65–99; McAdam, *Freedom Summer*.
6. Francisco, 'The dictator's dilemma', 58–81; Lichbach, 'Deterrence or escalation?' 266–297; Moore, 'Repression and dissent', 851–873; Kevin O'Brien, Yanhua Deng, 'Repression backfires'.
7. Honari, 'From "the effect of repression" toward the "response to repression"', 950–972.
8. George, 'Emotions in Politics'; Goodwin, Jasper and Polletta. 'The return of the repressed'; Jasper, 'Emotions and social movements'.
9. Christopher Achen, Larry Bartels, *Democracy for Realists: Why Elections Do Not Produce Responsive Government* (Princeton, N.J.: Princeton University Press, 2017), 228; Janine Clark, 'The conditions of Islamist moderation: unpacking

cross-ideological cooperation in Jordan', *International Journal of Middle East Studies*, 38:4 (2006), 539–560; Wickham, 'The Path to Moderation: Strategy and Learning in the Formation of Egypt's Wasat Party'.
10 Elizabeth Nugent, 'The Psychology of Repression and Polarization', *World Politics*, 72:2 (April 2020), 1–44.
11 Author Interview. London, 2017.
12 Willi, Ayyash, 'The Egyptian Muslim Brotherhood in 2016: Scenarios and Recommendations'.
13 Ibid.
14 'Egypt's Muslim Brotherhood announce new board for members abroad', *Middle East Eye* (20 April 2015) www.middleeasteye.net/news/egypts-muslim-brotherhood-announce-new-board-members-abroad (accessed 12 September 2020).
15 Zollner, 'Surviving Repression'.
16 Ibid.
17 Brooke, 'Egypt'.
18 Al-Anani, 'Rethinking the repression-dissent nexus', 4.
19 Author Interview with Mohammed Sudan. London, 2017.
20 Author Interview. Istanbul, 2019.
21 Author Interview. Istanbul, 2018.
22 Ardovini, 'Stagnation vs adaptation', 14.
23 For a further breakdown of anti-intellectualism see: Kandil, *Inside the Brotherhood*; Menshawy, *Leaving the Brotherhood*.
24 El-Sherif, 'The Muslim Brotherhood and the future of political Islam in Egypt', 8.
25 See for example: Clark, 'The conditions of Islamist moderation'; Dana Moss, 'Repression, response, and contained escalation under "liberalized" authoritarianism in Jordan', *Mobilization*, 19:3 (2014), 261–286; Sumita Pahwa, 'Pathways of Islamist adaptation: the Egyptian Muslim Brothers' lessons for inclusion moderation theory', *Democratization*, 24:6 (2017), 1066–1084.
26 El-Sherif, 'The Muslim Brotherhood and the future of political Islam in Egypt', 6.
27 See for example: House of Commons Foreign Affairs Committee, '"Political Islam", and the Muslim Brotherhood Review. Sixth Report of Session 2016–17' (1 November 2016), https://publications.parliament.uk/pa/cm201617/cmselect/cmfaff/118/118.pdf (accessed 30 December 2020).
28 Author Interview. Istanbul, January 2017.
29 House of Commons Foreign Affairs Committee, 'Muslim Brotherhood Review: Main Findings' (17 December 2016), https://assets.publishing.service.gov.uk/government/uploads/system/uploads/attachment_data/file/486948/53163_Muslim_Brotherhood_Review_-_PRINT.pdf (accessed 30 December 2020).
30 For a further analysis of the Brotherhood's usage of media, see Magued, 'The Egyptian Muslim Brotherhood's transnational advocacy in Turkey'; Mellor, *Voice of the Muslim Brotherhood*.
31 Magued, 'The Egyptian Muslim Brotherhood's transnational advocacy in Turkey', 489–492.

32 Mellor, *Voice of the Muslim Brotherhood*; Yotam Feldner, 'Turkey-based Muslim Brotherhood TV channels – an emerging hotbed of extremism, Jihadi ideology, and antisemitism', *MEMRI Inquiry & Analysis Series*, 1431 (8 January 2019), https://bit.ly/2mju4fm (accessed 12 September 2020).
33 Feldner, 'Turkey-based Muslim Brotherhood TV channels'.
34 Georges Fhamy, 'Resilience against violent radicalization: why haven't more Islamists taken up arms in Egypt since 2013?' *EUI Working Papers* (March 2020), 1–27; Georges Fhamy, 'How can religiously inspired ideas explain violent extremism in Egypt?' *Open Democracy* (November 2020) www.opendemocracy.net/en/global-extremes/how-can-religiously-inspired-ideas-explain-violent-extremism-egypt/ (accessed 30 December 2020).
35 Author Interview. Istanbul, 2018.
36 Author Interview. Istanbul, 2018.
37 Menshawy, *Leaving the Brotherhood*, 83.
38 Ardovini, 'Stagnation vs adaptation', 14.
39 Author Interview with Amr Darrag. Istanbul, August 2018.
40 Author Interview. London, 2016.
41 Author Interview. London, 2018.
42 El-Sherif, 'The Muslim Brotherhood and the future of political Islam in Egypt', 25.
43 Author Interview. Istanbul, September 2018.
44 Author Interview. Istanbul, June 2018.
45 Author Inteview. London, 2019.
46 Author Interview. London, 2018.

5

Divided, together

> A group that does not renew itself through thinking, it does not have a future.[1]

Eight years after the 2013 coup and the harsh repression that followed, the Brotherhood has proven to be highly resilient despite the numerous declarations that it was at its end. As Zollner argues, the Brotherhood's ability to survive through long periods of persecutions lies in the specifics of its organisational structure that, while under threat, is still allowing for lines of communication to remain intact.[2] This is the case despite ongoing confrontation between competing leadership factions, as both second-rank and historical leaders remain committed to the preservation of the movement. The transfer of central's decision-making and crisis-management to trusted members in exile contributed to the partial survival of the *tanzim*'s pyramidal structure. This means that the Office of the Supreme Guide and the Guidance Office remain the movement's symbolic centres of power, reinforced by members' devotion to its message and ideals. While in exile, the loyalist members who make up the Brotherhood's main body work alongside those who, despite their frustration at the organisation's official narrative, maintain their affiliation while pushing for internal change. This is the case because, as I have shown, commitment and loyalty can look radically different in the post-coup reality. Die-hard, hardline members who piously follow the curriculum now sit on committees and *usra* meetings with dissenters who would have been expelled prior to 2013, but are now kept together by the same objective: ensuring the Brotherhood's survival. The strategies to reach this end goal undoubtedly look different, as the partial disintegration of the Brotherhood's vertical structure has created the space for rank-and-file members to play a decisive role in the movement's survival. Indeed, it has become clear that in order to exit repression the movement needs to adapt to its changed circumstances and, in turn, transform itself despite the reticence to do so. After all, these members who openly express dissent and push for internal renewal might be the Brotherhood's main asset going forward.

Repression of social movements, even of those as ideologically driven and internally structured as the Brotherhood, can lead to contradictory strategies to exit a situation of crisis. Collective responses are indeed important to analyse, but this focus often overlooks the significance of contradictory strategies, discourses and tactics. The case of the Brotherhood shows that, for some movements, the potential for real change and survival lies in the responses that get dismissed or suppressed as they do not align with the official ones. Furthermore, these reveal another dissonance between collective and individual strategies. While the Historical Leadership and those who remain faithful to them are focused mostly on survival, members belonging to the adaptation camp have a more long-term vision and, crucially, they ask what kind of organisation the Brotherhood wants to be as it moves forward. This is what I mean when I say that the Brotherhood's biggest challenge comes from within its own ranks. Those who remain loyal to the movement's historical structures and hierarchies have undoubtedly been key to its survival so far, but the individuals who push for internal reforms, new values and internal dialogue are instrumental for the Brotherhood doing more than just surviving in the future, and instead start rebuilding the prestige and popular base it once had. This is not an easy process and resistance to this sort of change is high, but looking at individual experiences, emotions and activities reveals that some processes of internal transformation are already underway. Overall, the divergence between stagnation and adaptation strategies shows that, in order to go beyond survival, the Brotherhood needs to rethink what its purpose and message are. This is a need that is expressed by loyal and dissenting members alike, as the failure of the political project has brought these questions back to the fore.

Therefore, to deal with its current crisis, the movement needs to overcome renewed internal debates over ideology and practice, as well as settling the ensuing schisms. The Brotherhood has arguably never been so divided, and the decreasing trust in the competing leadership factions, combined with the dimension of exile, has created the conditions for members to bring forward independent initiatives, many of which go against the core principles and structures on which the movement historically rested. At present, different sub-groups of members, all claiming their affiliation to the Brotherhood but often pursuing different strategies against repression, are engaged in the process of rebuilding a fragmented organisation. Yet, there is no consensus on what kind of organisation the Brotherhood should be in the future. What is apparent, however, is that there is a significant process of value-change which many within the movement are experiencing in the context of forced exile. While this phenomenon is not necessarily new in itself, I would argue that its scale, along with the internal changes that have started to happen, marks the novelty of the post-2013 context.

Yet, this process goes against one of the Brotherhood's main assets, that is, its comprehensive nature and ideological message. In the past, this allowed the movement to recruit members across different societal, political and economic backgrounds and also contributed to the flexibility and adaptability of its narrative. Nevertheless, in the light of the internal fragmentation that followed the coup, the lack of a specific and cohesive voice is costing the movement the internal unity that previously kept it afloat in the face of repression. This is the case as members' different motivations for joining the Brotherhood result in competing opinions on what should be done to face the regime and on what sort of activities the movement should focus on in order to rebuild. Hence, while the comprehensiveness of the Brotherhood's message is indeed one of its key resources, the wide difference in the reasons why members join the movement represents a clear obstacle when it comes to developing survival strategies in the post-2013 context. This was eloquently explained to me by Essam who, now in his forties, joined the organisation while he was a university student at al Azhar. His personal motivations for becoming a Brother were, and remain, anchored in his faith and in his belief that the Brotherhood's ideology is in line with his worldviews and outlook on life. Nevertheless, since fleeing to Istanbul in 2015 he has grown increasingly concerned by the lack of an encompassing message and strategy to exit the current crisis.

> A question that should be asked in the light of the events of 2013 is actually who entered the Ikhwan for the ideology, and who for other reasons? The Ikhwan is very comprehensive in its scope, so many people enter because of different reasons –spirituality, politics, social solidarity, activism, revolution and change, family ties – these reasons very often have nothing to do with ideology itself.[3]

Essam is concerned that the Brotherhood is losing its ways because of the current immobility, and fears that those who argue for active engagement with secular opposition actors will end up compromising the organisation's original message. His concerns are mirrored by members on the other side of the spectrum, who instead worry that the Brotherhood's ideological immobility will cost the organisation its legitimacy going forward. This is clear across my recurring conversations with Tamer, who I first met in London in 2014. He joined the movement while studying for his engineering degree in the years leading up to the 2011 uprisings, attracted by the high levels of organisation of the Brotherhood committee at his university. Coming from an activist background even before getting involved in Brotherhood activities, Tamer believes that the only way forward is to renounce isolationism and establish cooperation with other opposition actors in exile. Explaining to me why he believes that the movement needs to urgently open up in order to survive, he said 'Theoretically the Ikhwan is a human community, and there is no human community that is going to continue forever. There might be someone who comes along and renews it, there is a chance that it might just die'.[4] The poignant silence that followed reinforced his statement even more.

Yet, internal reconciliation over these debates does not seem to be on the cards and, for now, the Brotherhood and its members remain divided, but together. Nevertheless, despite the reluctance of its leaders, the movement has already undergone significant internal transformations since it was ousted in 2013. While the growing space for individual voices, dissent and agency are yet to reform the Brotherhood's message, these dynamics have already begun to reshape the relationship between members and the movement. While it is too early to speculate as to what the end result might be, it is possible and indeed important to trace the debates over values and ideology that now characterise the movement, to start mapping the currents that are beginning to take shape within the movement and the future directions that they delineate.

The search for a new direction

Political engagement and value-change within highly hierarchical organisations are discussed at length in the literature on social movements, even though they are usually applied to the analysis of secular rather than religious groups. Scholars such as Nancy Bermeo, Jeffrey Checkel and Nathan Brown observe that new forms of political engagement and new political experiences can indeed produce shifts in the commitment of political actors, as a result of new experiences and/or exposure to new information and ideas.[5] These dynamics can trigger a process of soul searching as well as a critical re-examination of rigid ideological certainties that are central to a certain movement, also generating internal debates over their ultimate goals and purposes. Carrie Wickham notes that such a process is also present within Islamist groups, where leaders and rank-and-file members alike can criticise the 'culture of obedience', lack of internal dialogue, transparency and isolationism that are characteristic of an organisation such as the Brotherhood.[6] Just as in the case of the Brotherhood, this process of value-change occurs first and foremost at the level of individual actors and can lead to the questioning of not just the means, but also the ends of ideologically oriented movements.

Reforming the Brotherhood also means reforming its ideology. Indeed, I have been told on several occasions how the lack of ideological renewal has long stopped benefitting the movement, but, rather, contributes to members feeling alienated, disengaged and lacking an overarching sense of purpose. This point of view is of course not shared unanimously across the movement, but it has been fascinating to hear it being voiced by members who belong to opposite sides of its ranks. While members see this need playing out in different ways and for different purposes, any sort of renewal of the Brotherhood's ideology would have repercussion across the entire movement and its activities. This is the case as ideology is central to the functioning of many social movements and opposition groups. A strong ideological commitment serves different functions, which include explaining, repressing, integrating, motivating and legitimating.[7] Explaining and motivating primarily targets the broadest support base for the group by attempting to shape their worldviews. Integrating is more specifically aimed at official group members – though group members are targeted by the explaining and motivating functions as well. Finally, repressing and legitimating are primarily aimed at supporting the tenure of group leaders and other connected elites. Therefore, as Francisco Sanin and Elizabeth Wood explain, ideology is fundamental for the internal life of social movements, which spend significant time and resources producing, transmitting and discussing ideas.[8] Yet, while leaders are therefore reticent to implement any change, ideologies are not fixed and indeed transform in response to changed political contexts, constituencies and needs.[9] This is a costly process but, as in the case of the Brotherhood after 2013, often necessary for a group's survival.

Ideological change: da'wa vs politics

When looking at the strategies and demands that fall under the adaptation camp in Chapter 4, I began to outline a key question in ongoing debates about the Brotherhood's ideology and message, concerning the balance between political and religious activities. Calls for separating religion and politics within the Brotherhood are not new, and neither are internal schisms caused by this very issue. These competing visions are indeed at the root of significant divisions such as the Wasat Party schism in 1996, which saw middle-generation leaders who were frustrated with the Historical Leadership's ideological rigidity leaving the movement to form a separate political party, while openly arguing that 'The Brotherhood's activities should be limited to *da'wa*.'[10] These are existential debates and, as such, they have been brought back to the fore by the experiences of 2011 and 2013.

The notion that the Brotherhood is a religious movement with political aims is rooted in the idea of *shumuliyyat al-islam* (comprehensiveness of Islam), which is embedded in the Brotherhood's ideology and constitutes an integral part of its collective identity. However, it is also at the source of the cognitive dissonance – or 'founding defect' – ingrained in the movement's very nature and message.[11] According to al Banna, any attempt at separating Islam from politics should not be tolerated, and a key driver behind the Brotherhood's creation was indeed that of implementing both societal and political changes.[12] Therefore, as a religious movement, the Brotherhood calls for an understanding of Islam as a comprehensive system that governs both public and private spheres and does not draw a line between political and religious activities. Its purpose was never limited to *da'wa* – from the very beginning it incorporated calls for political reforms with a religious character and advocated the view of Islam as *deen wa dawla* (a religion and a state).[13] From this, the Brotherhood historically trains its members to be not only preachers, but also social activists and politicians. Yet, despite basing its mission on *da'wa* as a way of implementing *shari'a*, the Brotherhood never quite succeeded in developing a clear manifesto outlining how this could be practically implemented in the political sphere, as became evident during the FJP's rule.

Another aspect that further complicates this ongoing debate is the fact that political engagement also constitutes a key element of the Brotherhood's collective identity. As such, it is at the basis of its appeal to Muslims from different backgrounds, who seek to join the movement not just because of its religious character but also because of its social, political and educational activities. As Al-Anani puts is, 'politics is a key component of the Brotherhood's DNA, impossible to remove without changing the nature of the movement'.[14] This politicised identity, along with values that transcend religion, are also one of the key pillars of the Brotherhood's indoctrination (*tarbiyya*) and socialisation programmes. Therefore, any attempt to genuinely separate religion and politics would have drastic implications for the movement's organisation and message, as religious ideology shapes its internal values, rules and code of conduct. This has led to Shaykh Abdul Khaliq Al-Sherif, head of the Brotherhood's Da'wa Division, to state on numerous occasions that 'The Brotherhood has been created for nothing but *da'wa*',[15] which, in turn, also becomes a religious duty that every member has to fulfil. For these reasons, the Historical Leadership is obviously reluctant to consider any reshuffling of these key components. When asked if *da'wa* and politics should be kept separated in order to allow for internal renewal and maximise the movement chances of survival, a senior member got visibly agitated and stated

> No. That [the jointness of the religious and political project] started in 1928, this is our ideology. There are some who think we should just stay in the mosque and teach people the Quran, but this is not the ideology of the Ikhwan. It is to work in every field, in every field. We will never give up in this, we will never change our ideology.[16]

Nevertheless, questions on how to best achieve the balance between preaching and political activities have always existed within the movement, leading to divisions and schisms, meaning that their resurfacing has deep implications for both its organisational structures and overarching collective identity.

As I said above, while the comprehensiveness of the Brotherhood's message is indeed one of its key resources, the wide difference in the reasons why members join the movement also represents an obstacle when it comes to settling the debate between *da'wa* and politics. During another conversation with Essam on this very topic, he expressed his discontent towards the Brotherhood leaders' instrumental use of ideology that, in his opinion, departs significantly from al Banna's message:

> the Ikhwan has a very broad vision, and that, in turn, means that within the membership many do not care about or are not educated in the ideology. There are even leaders who do not know the ideas of Hassan al Banna, even though they claim to be fighting for them! These factors make the ideological aspect almost disappear. This also explains why we do not trust the current leadership: they have not really read the literature of the Ikhwan, they do not know it, yet they claim to be fighting for it!¹⁷

Essam is part of a group of members who believe that politics should be removed from the Brotherhood's activities and that, in order to rebuild, the movement needs to go back to al Banna's original words and purpose – focusing on the individual first rather than on society as a whole. This would also require a rewriting of the Brotherhood's curricula to be more faithful to its original message, as well as the stripping of any amendments made throughout the decades to fit with the Historical Leadership's choices and narrative.

These members think that the Brotherhood's official ideology has become hollow over the decades, a phenomenon that they attribute to the lack of thinkers and ideologues. As explained above, ideological vagueness is a key tool that allows the leadership to maintain control over the movement, but the voices asking for a re-writing of the Brotherhood's religious curricula are also advocating for more space to be created for new thinkers to come forward. This was explained to me by Mohammad, a member in his fifties who had held several senior positions within the movement and that, prior to 2013, aligned himself with the Historical Leadership and the conservative wing headed by Khairat al-Shater. After the coup he fled to Qatar and Malaysia before eventually resettling in Turkey, an experience that forced him to reconsider the fixed beliefs he had held for most of his life. Meeting and observing other Islamist movements during his travels shaped his belief that ideological renewal is fundamental to the Brotherhood not only surviving, but also thriving despite the current circumstances:

This is very crucial. Of course we have a lot of people who can think and can produce a lot of good thoughts, but because of the way in which the organisation is designed, these people are not given the space they need. They either have to leave the group, or they have to be quiet. If you look at the main thinkers without the Islamist space and domain, over the past 30 years, none of them belonged to the Ikhwan. Many of them used to be leftists and then turned Islamists, because they were free to think and flourish. If they were bound by the rules of the organisation, they would have never done that. This is why we don't see new ideas and new ideologues within the Ikhwan. If anyone starts developing new ideas, they are looked at very suspiciously, and they are isolated and their membership is frozen and so on. But this cannot go on. A group that does not renew itself through thinking, it does not have a future.[18]

Such an approach would require radical changes for the movement, with consequences impacting its hierarchy, indoctrination and mobilisation strategies. Moreover, calls for intellectual renewal are not just limited to ideology. There are others who, while still addressing the issue of the balance between *da'wa* and politics, put the focus more on civil society and activism. This position appears to be popular among members who, following from the FJP's removal, recognise that the Brotherhood lacks the basic skills to engage in formal politics. Rather than abandoning the political project altogether, however, the goal is to start rebuilding from the basics and focus on the grassroots level. This was explained to me by Hussein, an active member of the Brotherhood Youth who played a role in coordinating with secular activists before and during the 2011 uprisings. Despite his frustrations with how the political experience was handled – from the formation of the FJP to the exclusion of younger and more Reformist members – once he had fled to Istanbul he kept his membership and believes in the possibility of reforming the Brotherhood from within. While he does not think that the political project is within reach, he said to me that 'the goal now is to turn back towards society, regardless of the discourse about whether we should go back to power or not', therefore rebuilding the movement's popular base both in Egypt and abroad.[19] Hussein also recognises the lack of professionalism as one of the factors that accelerated the FJP's fall, and argues that focusing on civil society would give willing members the time to acquire the skills they need to successfully return to politics if the chance ever arises. He is himself studying for a degree in Political Sciences, and believes that:

The goal is not only to return to the grassroots, but after the 2013 experience we should get back into society with different tools. In the past the Ikhwan mostly focused on charity as a means to get involved in civil society, but now having a functional and effective media outlet is also very important. [...] The Ikhwan discovered that they are lacking, especially among the cadets, people that are qualified in the social sciences, in politics, philosophy, media, it is now important to recruit and educate cadets to be statesmen, to build expertise. We need people who are educated and trained in these fields.[20]

There are many among the Brotherhood members in exile who have gone back into education, or are retraining in different ways. Some, like Hussein, therefore believe that while the political project is not yet achievable it is their duty and right as members to undertake individual development to prepare for it, should another occasion arise.

These are significant developments and, while they are indeed beginning to trace potential future directions for the Brotherhood, it should be noted that these trends to not represent fixed categories or groups. On the contrary, the processes of self-reflection these members are engaging in mean that their positioning often changes over time, creating great dynamism and cross-contamination between these different currents. During the most recent round of fieldwork, I sat through several conversations indicating that there are growing conversations around a more formal separation of religious and political activities. Osama, a dissenting youth member who considered renouncing his membership at a time when younger and more Reformist members were excluded from the FJP, has since been vocally arguing for the formation of a more inclusive political wing:

> The Ikhwan should differentiate between the preaching part and the political one, even at the intellectual level, they don't mix well with each other. [...] This is a very popular opinion within the organisation now. Even the leadership might adopt this opinion, but it is not appropriate to declare the separation of the two activities now, they are reluctant to do so. It is about the idea of division itself, unfortunately this is not the time to divide the Ikhwan, but I don't agree.[21]

This is another current that is gaining more prominence within the debate around value-change. It showcases the extent to which individuals within the Brotherhood are engaging in a critical re-examination of rigid ideological certainties that are central to the movement, therefore also questioning its ultimate goals and purposes. This is represented by those who claim that the Brotherhood is indeed not a political movement, but rather is a reformist social group wishing to implement gradual changes at the social, political and religious levels. It follows that, while the idea of *shumuliyyat al-islam* (comprehensiveness of Islam) is not up for debate, the religious and political missions should be kept clearly separated. This is not an opinion held just by young, frustrated members, but is also shared by some who, like Mahmoud, had a senior position within the Brotherhood for a number of years. He was directly involved in the foundation and running of the FJP, and now believes that the party's dependency on the movement was one of its key weaknesses, leading him to state that:

> For example, one of the main ideas that the Ikhwan is proposing, which of course in our view is correct, is that Islam is a complete religion, it covers all aspects of life and it should rule the life of a good Muslim, whether it is economy, politics, and so on. The Ikhwan interprets this by understanding that as an organisation we should be working on all these issues all together, and it should all be governed and controlled by the same leadership. And this in my opinion is really wrong. Yes, Islam is a comprehensive religion, but this does not mean that the Ikhwan should be a comprehensive organisation.[22]

These views are rooted in the belief that the lack of professionalism played a big part in the FJP's poor political performance, as well as in the acknowledgement that the Brotherhood's membership is notably lacking in those trained in social and political sciences.

> In order to work in politics there are specialised institutions for that: political parties. The person who is fit to work in a NGOs is not necessarily fit to be a politician. This is why in many situations you find people who are good and have expertise, are charismatic, but they are being pushed to be in politics, to be in parliament and so on, so they failed because they are not qualified. On the other hand, somebody who is qualified to be a politician does not perform as well in a mosque, in a poor area and so on. [...] So the whole structure does not need to be comprehensive. It is more appropriate at this time to have separate organisations.[23]

While these voices do not reject the political mission at the core of the Brotherhood, they argue that the movement is simply not ready to take part in competitive politics. Instead, it should support political parties that are aligned with its values and maintain the religious and political mission clearly separated in order to exit the current crisis.

> In my opinion it does not make sense for the Ikhwan as a movement to establish political parties in the way in which it was done. So I am of the opinion that the Ikhwan should not get involved into partisan competitive politics. We can of course be involved in politics by lobbying, applying pressure, and demanding things and so on [...]. The Ikhwan should not establish a political party, and should not prohibit its members from joining other political parties, as long as they are compatible with its message.[24]

While the popularity of such debates is hard to measure, a dissenting member who I met several times in Istanbul also said:

> That the movement and an eventual party should be kept clearly separated is a very popular opinion among those who are calling for changes. The other side [the Historical Leadership] looks at this separation as yet another way to lose control over the group – if you allow somebody else to control the politics, your public agenda, then you will be less powerful. These are all major differences! Because of these schisms over core issues, I am not sure that right

now it is possible for the Ikhwan to undertake reforms, or whether this will result in the formation of different groups, I don't know. But definitely, the group is in a very different place now than where it was before the revolution.[25]

Overall, it is too early to assess whether or not the renewed struggle between *da'wa* and politics will lead to a tangible transformation of the Brotherhood's message and goals. Yet, the simple fact that these opinions are openly being voiced speaks volume and reveals the extent to which processes of value-change are ongoing within the movement. Of all the debates currently dividing the movement, the one regarding the fragile equilibrium between religious and political activities is one to watch, as separating religion and politics would require a complete transformation of the Brotherhood's ideology, strategy and organisational structure. In turn, doing so runs the risk of alienating a considerable part of its membership and of even shattering the movement going forward.

Old grievances, new context

In parallel with the ongoing debate over ideology and practice, analysing individual responses to repression vis-à-vis collective ones reveals the multiplicity of approaches that fall within the adaptation trend. Members' individual experiences of repression and exile are shaping a variety of strategies to react to the current crisis, some of which are informed by old grievances while others point to the emergence of new issues in the relationship between the movement and its members. Altogether, they are driven by the growing tensions between members' desire for change and the Historical Leadership's commitment to immobility and restraint. The proliferation of competing strategies to move forward and the growing agency of individual members go hand in hand and also reveal that, while the *tanzim* partly survives, the decreasing legitimacy of competing leadership factions is causing members to grow disillusioned and prompting them to take matters into their own hands. Despite efforts to limit the struggle to the top ranks, since 2015 members have grown increasingly aware of just how divided the Brotherhood is. Combined with the increased freedom and disruption of hierarchies in exile, this realisation has enhanced the space for members to bring forward independent initiatives, many of which go against the core principles and structures on which the movement historically rested. At present, various sub-groups of members, all committed to the Brotherhood's survival, are implementing different initiatives in an attempt to rebuild a fragmented organisation. Those who have been traditionally marginal actors within the Brotherhood, such as women, the Youth and Reformist members, are taking advantage of the lack of coherent narratives and hierarchical structures to advance their position and put forward their own strategies and desires.[26] In the process, these members are creating cross-generational factions and imbuing the organisation with new values, which largely draw on more democratic and pluralistic ideals.

These initiatives are driven by the two main points of contention that characterise the Brotherhood after 2013, these being the lessons that should be learnt from the FJP's experience and what strategies should be implemented to move forward. Currently, the ongoing fragmentation and competition for leadership mean that there is a notable lack of a common vision regarding what kind of organisation the Brotherhood should strive to be in order to survive its current crisis. Nevertheless, looking at the old and new grievances that are shaping members' strategies to move forward, it is possible to identify the main internal issues that are informing internal debates over the reformation of the Brotherhood's structures. Perhaps unsurprisingly, these are mostly centred around loyalty and the way in which the movement is administered and run.

One of the main issues that emerged after 2013, and that is driving members' grievances, is the disillusionment caused by the trickling down of the leadership contest to the lower sections of the movement in 2015. This prompted fundamental questions about loyalty, specifically to what and to whom, which, in turn, further drives internal splintering. Loyalty to the Historical Leadership, to the New MB, to the Crisis Management Committee or to the principles of the movement as outlined by al Banna all lead to different directions and visions for the future. Once again, while members and leaders alike are committed to the Brotherhood's survival, they are envisioning competing scenarios of what such a thing would look like. Coupled with ongoing processes of self-reflection, this is causing members to grow confused and frustrated, with many beginning to wonder what their purpose is and whether or not their membership is still valid. This is the case for Osama, a member is his thirties who lost a brother in Raba'a and who, since relocating to Istanbul, is questioning his belonging to the Brotherhood.

> After 2015, they [the Historical Leadership] froze the membership of everyone who disagreed with them. What does this mean for us? Who is a Brother and who is not? I want to see the Ikhwan come out of this victorious, but if I want more freedom, does this mean that I am not a part of it anymore?[27]

Osama is referring to the Historical Leadership's attempts to maintain power after the leadership crisis became evident in 2015, prompting the Guidance Bureau to freeze or suspend the membership of those who aligned with the High Administrative Committee in Egypt and their supporters abroad.[28] While prior to 2013 individual members would have been formally notified of this, the scale of insubordination in 2015 forced the Historical Leadership to condemn this phenomenon as a whole, leaving many to wonder whether or not this applied to them. During one of my conversations with Mohammed Sudan, I asked him whether or not he thought that such a move was counterintuitive, as it raised more questions about who, or which factions, represented the 'real' Brotherhood in the eyes of members, dividing unity even further. He took a long time to reply, and seemed saddened by my question, eventually saying:

> We are the Guidance Bureau, and this is the legal leadership. Whatever they say, that's fine. The majority of the Ikhwan in the world, they are under the umbrella of the Guidance Bureau, this is the real organisation. In Turkey there are people whose membership has been frozen. If they change their mind and they regret these thoughts, the door is open, we need them to come back.[29]

The uncertainty surrounding questions of loyalty and belonging are directly linked to the other overarching issue driving grievances and competing strategies to move forward in the aftermath of the coup – that is, the way in which the Brotherhood is administered and run. The testimonies collected in this book, especially those belonging to individuals undergoing processes of self-reflection, point to the growing belief that in order to survive, the movement needs to reform its internal structure and hierarchies. As discussed, members' desires for more space and freedom within the movement have roots in the pre-revolutionary period, but they have been accelerated by the failure of the political experience and by the increased space for individual agency in exile. Calls for internal reforms are central to the movement's internal debates and they need to be urgently addressed. This is especially the case as, in the aftermath of the coup, values and structures that previously kept the movement together, such as blind obedience and its pyramidal structure, are having the opposite effect. As members grow more disillusioned and alienated by the Brotherhood's strict hierarchies, they are asking for internal monitoring, consultation, accountability and fairer elections. This is a fundamental point of contention between the Brotherhood and its members and puts its leaders in an impasse, as the accommodation of such demands implies the reformation of the *tanzim*, while their dismissal would lead to more members disengaging from or leaving the movement.

This conundrum partially explains the reasons why the Historical Leadership appears to be more open to dialogue in the post-2013 context, allowing dissenting members to remain active within the movement and not condemning individual activities as would have been the case in the past. Yet, rather than a capitulation, these circumstances are dictated by the need to avoid further defections and by the limited capacity to dictate members' activities in exile. This opening therefore seems to be driven by the movement's historical pragmatism rather than a commitment to accommodate demands for internal reforms. Senior leaders are aware of the need to maintain numbers and at least apparent unity – thus explaining their tendency to allow members' pursuit of independent activities as long as they do not directly threaten organisational cohesion. Sudan's statement about the Leadership being open to welcoming back those members whose membership has been frozen further highlights their efforts to attract those who have already left, and to retain those who are considering disengagement. Pragmatism is also behind the increased freedom that individual members have to gain professional and educational skills, despite the Historical Leadership's refusal to openly acknowledge that the lack of professionalism was one leading factor in the failure of the political experiment. Nevertheless, this is leading to the accommodation of members' desires for individual development after 2013, as it is likely to benefit the movement going forward. The growing inclusion of Youth members and women in the Brotherhood's official media also reflects further attempts to contain internal discontent, but is far from representing a shift in the movement's internal hierarchies.[30] Overall, the Brotherhood has always relied on pragmatism in the face of hardship and the post-coup situation is no different. While tolerance for independent initiatives is growing, this does not necessarily signal a direct change in the movement's structures and ideology. Yet, as toleration for these activities grows and they become more embedded into the Brotherhood's daily life, the chances of going back to the pre-2013 hierarchy significantly decreases. In a way, this is a manifestation of internal change beginning to take place within the movement, initiating a transformation process that will be almost impossible to reverse. When I asked Osama if he would ever go back to the way in which the organisation was run in Egypt he immediately laughed. Then, he became serious and slammed his hand on the table while saying 'There is no way. I am not going back to being a sheep.'[31]

Ongoing fragmentation and future directions

Grievances around loyalty and the *tanzim*'s administration, along with intensifying debates over *da'wa* and politics, confirm the existence of deep cracks within the organisation. The contest for leadership that became evident after 2015 further weakened the movement and, on its ninetieth anniversary in 2018, the Brotherhood was more divided than ever. Those who remain faithful to the Historical Leadership continue to deny the extent of these divisions, which is a recurring point during our conversations. In 2018, a senior leader who I met several times in London became visibly agitated when discussing my recent round of fieldwork in Turkey. Senior members tend to display a keen interest in what I observe in my role as a researcher, and I was explaining to him how intrigued I was at all the competing points of view and strategies that I had recently encountered during that trip. When I asked him what he thought about these developing internal divisions he abruptly interrupted me, saying:

> No, no! We cannot say that the organisation is divided. [hesitates] We can say that there are groups in Istanbul, and in Sudan, and in Egypt, who are against the big organisation, but when we talk about hundreds against millions, it is nothing. That's nothing. Don't listen to them.[32]

While this is not necessarily surprising considering the stance of the Historical Leadership, this statement suggest that the top ranks of the movement are indeed worried about the ongoing fragmentation, regardless of whether or not they are willing to openly acknowledge it. One senior member who, after holding a conservative view all his life, has gradually embraced more reformist views since fleeing Egypt, suggested that the Historical Leadership is so disconnected to what is happening within the ranks and files that they might not be aware of just how divided the movement is:

> You as a researcher, you are an outsider so you need to dig deeper to find out [what the factions are]. But even some people from the inside, from the leadership, are blind to just how many divisions there are. One of the old people in the leadership was shocked when I told him what I am about to tell you, even though he is supposedly very powerful.[33]

While it is hard to measure the extent to which this statement is true or not, he was not the first to identify a growing disconnect between the movement and its members. In addition, what comes out of years of fieldwork is the indication that ongoing debates centred around value-change and intellectual renewal are splitting the membership into a number of factions, whose loyalty to the Brotherhood does not necessarily equal loyalty to its leaders. Yet, the fact that the Brotherhood is internally divided, or that the ongoing fragmentation does not show any sign of slowing down, is not a new finding in itself. The movement has always been divided and this has been well documented in the literature on the organisation.[34] What is different about the current schisms is how they expand those identified prior to 2013, what they can tell us about the potential future directions of the Brotherhood, and how they identify the points of contention and key issues that might lead to significant internal transformations. Once again, I am not suggesting that these are fixed categories or even groups established well enough to be considered as such. Rather, they are fluid trends that members freely move in and out of, showcasing the high dynamism on the ongoing processes of self-reflection that many are engaged in. Indeed, these divisions are so fluid that there are many more than I can identify and present here, and maybe even too many for members themselves to keep track of. I once had lunch with two Brothers in a packed mall in Istanbul and, after asking them to identify the different factions for me, I had to sit back while they argued with each other over which ones there were, which were even worth mentioning, and which trends themselves and their friends identified the most with. Therefore, while I hereby present some subgroups that in my fieldwork appear as the most prominent, more work is definitely needed to analyse this ongoing phenomenon.

The different groups that have formed within the Brotherhood since 2013 are usually determined by three main criteria: the strategy that their members think should be pursued to challenge repression; what kind of organisation they want the movement to be moving forward; and how they position themselves vis-à-vis the Brotherhood as a whole. This is why their analysis can give us an insight into what the future directions of the movement might be, and into the key issues that are being discussed.

The first group, which for now remains the most popular one in terms of followers, is represented by those who remain faithful to the Historical Leadership and to the Brotherhood's core historical values. They mostly refuse to take responsibility for the mistakes made by the FJP and see Morsi's removal as the culmination of a long coup that began with the 2011 uprisings. They are committed to the replication of the Brotherhood's structures and hierarchies in exile – what dissenting members call a 'copy and paste' process – and embrace the historical concept of *mihna*, believing that the current crisis is another period of hardship that will eventually pass. Another senior leader who I often met in London and who served as a minister with the FJP firmly believes in this, having dedicated his entire life to the Brotherhood and having endured various prison sentences under Mubarak. Talking about whether or not the Brotherhood should adapt its historical tools of resistance to better fit the circumstances of forced exile, he slowly shook his head and took a deep sigh before saying:

> We are the Ikhwan, this is our way. This is just a stage of life. If you study the history of the Ikhwan, you'll see that they thought we were done in 1954, and then in 1965, they thought that we were finished. And then we woke up again in 1971, and then we became very strong, we spread from Egypt to all the Arab countries. If you think that we are done, that is not true [...] Because we are just a thought, from generation to generation, and we will keep going with this.[35]

Those belonging to this group therefore subscribe to the so-called 'wait and see' strategy, avoiding a proactive response to regime repression and focusing their activism and political mobilisation into the Brotherhood's media channels. Most of all, they challenge calls to reform the organisation and seek to maintain its pyramidal structure, principles and values, as these remain a fundamental marker of their collective identity and a critical tool for the leadership to maintain control over members.

The second, most prominent faction is composed of those who identify as dissenting members but choose to maintain their affiliation and seek to reform the movement from the inside. While this would not have been possible to this extent prior to 2013, their numbers are growing and bring together individuals of different backgrounds, ages and membership ranks. These members are usually those who, after 2013, saw forced exile as an opportunity to rethink their commitment to the Brotherhood and are engaged in various processes of self-reflection. They contest the Brotherhood top-down collective identity and actively seek more agency against its outdated hierarchical structures. While still respecting the leaders, they lost trust in their ability to guide the movement through the current crisis and are instead taking matters into their own hands, refuting principles such as blind obedience. Having identified the lack of professionalism and political competencies as one of the accelerating factors behind the coup, these members are engaged in various processes of individual development, such as further education, changes in career paths and so on. They are strongly critical of the first group's immobility and 'wait and see' strategy, arguing that the movement needs to re-invent itself to not only survive, but also to thrive despite the current wave of repression. Similarly, they also support a more clearly defined administrative separation between *da'wa* and political activities.

In doing so, they channel long-existing objections about the lack of space for dialogue and representation and call for a radical rethinking of the relationship between the movement and its members. They believe that internal reforms addressing principles of democracy, transparency and pluralism are needed and seek a greater, consultative role in the Brotherhood's decision-making processes. They long to establish an organisation that is transparent and open to its members. This group show great dynamism because of the self-reflection processes that they are engaged in, and their loyalties often change, meaning that they move from one group to another. This is the case of Mohammed, a member in his late fifties who, prior to the coup, played an active role in the FJP. He is a strong believer in taking a proactive approach to face repression and in keeping political and religious activities clearly separated to maximise the Brotherhood's chances at excelling in both. After 2013 he briefly aligned with Kamal's revolutionary High Administrative Committee, then rescinded his membership from the Brotherhood altogether, but since 2017 he has slowly began to re-engage with its activities in Istanbul. Speaking of what he believes are much needed internal reforms, he said:

> To me, to achieve freedom [within the movement] is the number one objective. In the light of freedom everything can be done. But if you start to overlook this, just to preserve the organisation, you lose the organisation and you lose your popular base. The Ikhwan is also by definition a very open society, it flourishes in the light, not in darkness. It is not an underground movement. This is what I always say: we should not be afraid of freedom, it will allow us and everybody else to express themselves. The leadership is scared of this, they say it is too big of a sacrifice. But they are always telling us to sacrifice ourselves! [for the good of the movement] So how is this any different?[36]

This shows that, while members who fall within this faction are strongly critical of the way in which the Brotherhood has always been run, they also recognise the value of its message and rather than leaving the movement altogether they seek to reform it internally to better suit the circumstances it is now forced to operate under.

Another faction that is gaining more traction is represented by those who, while maintaining their membership, have grown disillusioned with the Historical Leadership and believe that the organisation has long deviated from its purpose as articulated by al Banna. They see proof of this in the failure of the political project and, while they remain loyal to the movement, their priority is not the Brotherhood as an organisation in itself but rather its religious and ideological message. They therefore believe that the Brotherhood should abandon political aspirations and activities, at least for now, and focus back on ideology and on its Islamic mission. They are strongly critical of those who joined the movement to achieve personal or political aims and believe that the movement should be purified from members who do not prioritise Islam over politics. These members are most active within the grassroots ranks of the Brotherhood and do not necessarily endorse calls for internal reformation of the movement's principles and structures, which they believe are fundamental to its survival.

An ever-growing and multifaceted faction is that composed of ex-members, including those who left of their own volition and those who have been expelled following insubordination. Individuals who willingly leave the Brotherhood do so for a wide variety of reasons, ranging from intellectual, ideological and political disengagement, to long-standing objections, personal identity crises, and those who leave in order to create a separate but parallel organisation, such as the New MB. I have shown before that several members began to question their belonging to the movement after being forced into exile, leading many to leave the movement in order to gain greater freedom and experience independent thinking for the first time. Meshawy has also documented at length the ways in which disengagement processes tap into ideological and identity issues, leading to widely different results.[37] This is often a traumatic and painful process, as questioning a worldview that one has been socialised into for their entire lives comes at a great cost. In the case of the Brotherhood, this goes beyond the already troubling process of disengaging from a collective identity, and also implies the cutting off of emotional, biological, social and organisational ties. Every individual experience of disengagement is different and many struggle to come to terms with life outside of the movement. Mohammad, a doctor in his forties who spent half of his life dedicating himself to building the Brotherhood's political curricula and activities, willingly left the movement in 2012 following the disputed foundation of the FJP. At the time he openly denounced the party's lack of inclusivity and representation and was given a warning from his superiors. Eventually, he decided to leave of his own volition:

> It was hard, it still is. I had to re-invent myself and find a new sense of purpose. My wife stayed in the movement for a few more months after I left and that also made things very hard between us. [...] Of course I miss my friends, my Brothers. But I had to leave, I knew in my heart that this was not the movement I joined anymore, and I had to stay true to myself and to my beliefs.[38]

While all of those who willingly leave do so following specific grievances – often related to the lack of representation and inclusivity within the movement – there is another cohort of members who takes things a step further. This is the case of those who renounce their membership to create a parallel organisation, modelled on the Brotherhood's ideology and message but with a reformed and more democratic structure. The New MB that formed in Egypt after the 2013 coup is a prime example of this, with its leaders claiming to be the 'real' Ikhwan and therefore attracting a considerable number of discontented members. However, while the New MB and its revolutionary approach to repression enjoyed a surge of popularity in the couple of years immediately following the coup, its inability to achieve pre-set goals, coupled with heightened repression in Egypt, led to many leaving its ranks and either returning to the International Organisation or disengaging altogether.

This leads to the last faction, which is the hardest one to quantify but arguably one of the most significant for the future of the organisation. This is the growing group constituted of members who go dormant, meaning that they have disengaged from the movement's activities and ranks. They are not ex members as they have not formally renounced their membership, nor they have been expelled, but they have chosen to take a step back and put their affiliation on pause. There are several reasons behind the choice of going dormant, beginning with the traumatic experience of repression and exile or the high risk associated with belonging to such a persecuted organisation. Others have lost faith in the current leadership and choose to focus on themselves rather than on the movement as it is now, but would consider re-activating their membership if reforms are eventually implemented. There is also a more opportunistic cohort of dormant members who, no longer able to benefit from their affiliation to the Brotherhood, have disengaged from it completely. While, for obvious reasons, I never had the chance to meet a dormant member myself, their presence has been pointed out to me as a point of concern by members belonging to different factions. A cleric who has long acted as a confidante for those in the higher ranks of the Brotherhood, and who since 2013 has become one of their harshest critics, stated that many come to him for advice when considering whether or not to temporarily disengage from the movement. While it is hard to gain concrete numbers, he believes that dormant members might be close to representing almost half of the Brotherhood membership as a whole, an estimate also confirmed by others.[39] Therefore, while their number represents a threat to the movement's unity, this group of members is also a considerable resource. This is due to the belief that these members might consider re-joining the Brotherhood in the future if their grievances are addressed, be it in the form of a more favourable political environment, the formulation of a clearer direction and strategy or a reformation of its internal structures. If it is true, whichever faction manages to mobilise the dormant members might gain the loudest voice within the movement.

Conclusion

To conclude, addressing the processes of value-change and the ideological debates that have emerged within the Brotherhood since 2013 reveal that the movement is now more divided than ever. Repression does not always lead to cohesion, and, in the specific case of the movement, the post-coup disillusionment with the Historical Leadership has led to a disintegration of its collective identity and hierarchical structures. Overall, there is a shared sense that the Brotherhood needs to rethink its ideology and message, along with the ways in which the movement is run, in order to adapt to its changed circumstances and find a cohesive way to move forward.

The Brotherhood's fragmentation into different but unfixed factions gives us an idea of the core issues that will need to be addressed sooner or later. Demands for more internal representation and pluralism clash with the desire to return to the movement's original ideological message and with the leadership's unwillingness to acknowledge the need for internal reforms. Overall, this shows that while all members are committed to the Brotherhood's survival, there is a marked difference between those who just aspire to it and those who instead want to see the movement thrive despite the ongoing repression. The latter consequently argue for internal reforms and changes that would allow the Brotherhood to adapt to its current circumstances, and which are fundamental not only to allow its members greater freedom and autonomy but also to begin rebuilding a popular base and establish much needed cooperation with other opposition actors in exile.

Yet, despite ongoing divisions and schisms between competing Guidance Offices, the Historical Leadership ultimately remains in charge of the International Organisation. They control the Brotherhood's finances and represent the official face of the movement in the international arena. Even more importantly, despite the high levels of internal dissent, they still have the loyalty of the majority of the movement's followers. This is not necessarily because members both in Egypt and in exile believe that they are fit to guide the organisation through the current crisis – rather, it is quite the contrary – but because there is not a real alternative. According to Abdullah, a dissenting member in his late thirties who led the Youth faction's fight against the movement during the foundation of the FJP, this is the case because:

> Kamal, the New MB, they made promises that they could not keep such as 'we will have another revolution'. After some time people saw that they did not achieve anything and were also adopting an increasingly confrontational discourse against the state. The spokesman used strong words, he used to say that 'we will respond to the regime harshly' but he did not achieve anything, so the discourse did not match the reality and people's alliances shifted towards the old leadership again. People are turning back to the old leadership not because it is good, but because they do not want to leave the Ikhwan so they would rather stick with the devil they know. They don't admire the leadership, but they know what to expect from them.[40]

This is also confirmed by Shuruq, a well-known member of the Muslim Sisterhood, who for decades has been campaigning for more inclusion within the Brotherhood's ranks:

> I want to say that I am still with the Old Ministry, with the Old Leadership. Because there are no differences between them and the 'new' Bureau in Egypt that claimed they wanted to implement changes after the coup. So I stand with the Old Bureau, but I maintain good relationships with the 'new' one.[41]

Overall, it is hard to differentiate between those who remain active members because of opportunism or because they really believe in the movement's message. There is an inevitable component of self-interest in belonging to the Brotherhood, even under the current circumstances and particularly in exile, as it provides its members with social ties, emotional bonds and a solid support network that include bureaucratic and economic assistance. For others, it is often the case that the Brotherhood is the only reality they have ever known and therefore they remain faithful to the movement, but not necessarily to the leaders. Altogether, these factors lead to very different scenarios and desires regarding the type of movement that the Brotherhood should be moving forward. Because of this, it is too early to speculate on whether or not the process of internal renewal that has partially started will have tangible results. What is certain is that, for now, the Brotherhood remains consumed by its internal identity crisis.

Notes

1. Author Interview. Istanbul, 2018.
2. Zollner, 'Surviving repression'.
3. Author Interview. Istanbul, 2018.
4. Author Interview. London, 2018.
5. See for example: Nancy Bermeo, 'Democracy and the lessons of dictatorship', *Comparative Politics*, 29:3 (1992), 273–292; Nathan Brown, *When Victory is Not An Option: Islamist Movements in Arab Politics* (Ithaca, N.Y.: Cornell University Press, 2012); Jeffrey T. Checkel, 'Social construction and integration', *Journal of European Public Policy*, 6:4 (1999), 545–560.
6. Wickham, *The Muslim Brotherhood*, 12–15.
7. John Gerring, 'Ideology: a definitional analysis', *Political Research Quarterly*, 50:4 (1997), 971–972.
8. Francisco Gutierrez Sanin, Elisabeth Jean Wood, 'Ideology in civil war: instrumental adoption and beyond', *Journal of Peace Research*, Anniversary Special Issue, 51:2 (March 2014), 213–226.
9. Jillian Schwedler, 'Can Islamists become moderates? Rethinking the inclusion-moderation hypothesis', *World Politics*, 63:2 (2011), 347–376.
10. Wickham, *The Muslim Brotherhood*, 81–85.
11. Khalil Al-Anani, 'Egypt's Muslim Brotherhood faces a dilemma: religion or politics?' *The Washington Post* (20 June, 2016) www.washingtonpost.com/news/monkey-cage/wp/2016/06/20/egypts-muslim-brotherhood-faces-a-dilemma-religion-or-politics/ (accessed 23 January 2021).
12. Mellor, *Voice of the Muslim Brotherhood*, 15.
13. Ibid.
14. Al-Anani, 'Egypt's Muslim Brotherhood faces a dilemma'.
15. As quoted in Al-Anani, *Inside the Muslim Brotherhood*, 71.
16. Author Interview. London, 2019.
17. Author Interview. Istanbul, 2018.
18. Author Interview. Istanbul, 2018.
19. Author Interview. Istanbul, 2019.
20. Author Interview. Istanbul, 2017.
21. Author Interview. Istanbul, 2018.
22. Author Interview. London, 2018.
23. Author Interview. London, 2018.
24. Author Interview. London, 2018.

25 Author Interview. Istanbul, 2018.
26 Biagini, 'The Egyptian Muslim Sisterhood between violence, activism and leadership'.
27 Author Interview. Istanbul, 2018.
28 Willi, *The Fourth Ordeal*, 359.
29 Author Interview with Mohammed Sudan. London, 2018.
30 Mellor, *Voice of the Muslim Brotherhood*, 53.
31 Author Interview. Istanbul, 2018.
32 Author Interview. London, 2018.
33 Author Interview. Istanbul, 2017.
34 See for example: Wickham, *The Muslim Brotherhood*; Al-Anani, *Inside the Muslim Brotherhood*; Samir, 'The Muslim Brotherhood's generational gap'.
35 Author Interview. London, 2017.
36 Author Interview. Istanbul, 2017.
37 Menshawy, *Leaving the Brotherhood*.
38 Author Interview. Istanbul, 2019.
39 Author Interview. Istanbul, 2019.
40 Author Interview. Istanbul, 2019.
41 Author Interview. Istanbul, 2018.

Conclusion

On 30 June 2013, the one-year anniversary of Mohammed Morsi's inauguration as Egypt's first president without a military affiliation and the first to come from within the Brotherhood's ranks, millions of Egyptians took to the streets to demand that he step down. On 3 July 2013, he was removed by a coup d'état staged by the country's military forces, which brought a premature end to the Brotherhood's first experience in government. What followed was a wave or repression and persecution that indiscriminately targeted the movement's leaders, members and supporters, forcing those who escaped arrest and murder to forcibly flee the country and seek refuge abroad. The dimension of forced exile marked the beginning of a new era in the history of the Brotherhood, one characterised by the invalidation of its historical tools of resistance and by the partial breakdown of its established chains of command. Since 2013, as old grievances relating to the relationship between the movement and its members returned to the fore, the Brotherhood has grown increasingly divided between two main points of contention, which, in turn, are driving internal debates and further fragmentation. These are: what factors led to the fall of the Morsi government, and what lessons should be learnt from that experience; and what strategy should be implemented to face the current crisis and move forward. These fundamental questions, combined with the unprecedented brutality of repression, are creating deep schisms within the Brotherhood, as individual responses openly clash with the movement's official narrative, further widening the disconnect between those at the top of the organisation and the rank-and-file members. There are growing tensions between calls for the movement to adapt to its changed circumstances and the refusal to implement internal reforms, indicating that a key issue that needs to be renegotiated is the changing relationship between the Brotherhood and its members.

Despite its changed fortunes, the Brotherhood is famously resilient. Eight years after the coup, the movement and its members are in the process of rebuilding a fragmented organisation while they also tackle some existential questions. Many wonder whether or not the Brotherhood will be able to regain the popular support and base it once had, given the international repression against the movement and the perceived failure of the political project. Most importantly, they also ask what kind of organisation the Brotherhood aims to be moving forward, and what course it should pursue to exit its current crisis. Overall, these queries are driven by one fundamental question that remains central to the Brotherhood, that of why their experiment with power failed so prematurely. The different ways in which it is being answered offer a fascinating glimpse into the movement's current state of internal affairs.

During the first few years of my fieldwork, conducted in the wake of the military coup that changed everything, the most common answer I was met with was the categorical denial of any wrongdoing on the part of the Brotherhood. Leaders, members and ex-members alike almost unanimously pointed to the deep state and to intricate international conspiracies as the cause of Morsi's removal, lamenting their missed chance at finally governing after almost 80 years in opposition. Yet, with time, this answer started to change. As individual members began to settle into forced exile, the realisation that the current wave of repression is dramatically different from what the movement had experienced before started to drive processes of self-reflection. Removed from the Egyptian context and from the daily activities associated with the movement, some members saw the challenges posed by forced exile as an unprecedented opportunity to rethink the terms of their commitment to the Brotherhood. While this is not a unanimous process, I saw the change myself during repeated conversations and encounters with the same interlocutors. Members who previously had never questioned the Leadership's authority became gradually more critical; others who had always leaned towards more reformist approaches openly voiced their frustration towards the Brotherhood's immobility. Some of those who have been in the Brotherhood for their entire lives started questioning whether this was really the only way. Once, I was greeted by one of my recurrent participants in Istanbul with the news that he had left the movement, as he joked that I would not want to spend time talking to him anymore. Others went the other way, and took the brutality of al Sisi's crackdown against the movement as a sign that the Brotherhood is indeed fighting an existential battle against the regime, and that its message and aims are legitimised by the international campaign to suppress the organisation. Another group of members, who I only ever heard of, silently disengaged from the movement and its activities altogether, disappearing from the ranks but remaining in its periphery, becoming an incredible resource for whoever manages to eventually mobilise them again.

While all of these responses vary, they unanimously show that the coup and the experience of exile has deeply shaken the movement, dealing a heavy blow to the values and structures that previously allowed it to survive, and even thrive, under repression. As members take their new international dimension as an opportunity to rethink their belonging to the movement, other interpretations of the factors that led to the current crisis began to emerge. Rejecting the conception of the Brotherhood as merely a pawn in the hands of the Egyptian military and its international supporters, more and more voices now openly denounce the movement's own agency in bringing about the coup. The internal factors that are mentioned more often when talking about what went wrong with the FJP's rule are: the Brotherhood's unwillingness to reform its structure and message to adapt to its new position of power; the exclusionary process of the FJP's formation, which saw political positions appointed on the basis of loyalty rather than expertise; the lack of a clear vision for the implementation of the Islamic project; and the Brotherhood's miscalculation of how much legitimacy it actually had. There are current and former members who have started to extract from these factors some very clear lessons that should be learnt from the failed political experience, and that should inform the Brotherhood's strategies moving forward.

One of the most prominent lessons currently shaping internal debates is the need to remedy the movement's lack of professionalism, which meant that its members and leaders alike lacked the necessary skills and competences to successfully govern. This is an old grievance within the Brotherhood, but was brought back to the fore by the inconsistencies and contradictions in the FJP's rule. Prior to 2011, deviation from the Brotherhood's strict curriculum was punished with warnings and expulsion, often preventing members from seeking individual development. Yet, in the post-coup context, current and former members alike are enrolling back into education to study political and social sciences, are founding research centres, and are establishing dialogue with secular opposition actors in exile. While these activities are not condoned by the Historical Leadership, individuals are pursuing them regardless with the belief that, if they work on themselves, the movement with also benefit in the long term. Another key takeaway from the experiences of 2011 and 2013 is that the strict, hierarchical structures governing the *tanzim* need to be reformed in favour of more inclusive and democratic ones. This is also an old demand, but the need to renegotiate the relationship between the movement and its members has taken centre stage after 2013 and there are instances of transformations already being underway. While it is too early to speculate on whether or not these will lead to significant long-term organisational and ideological changes, members' reclamation of individual agency vis-à-vis the movement's strict structures is already evident in the proliferation of different strategies to respond to the current crackdown. Therefore, while the Brotherhood is no stranger to repression, what is uniquely new about the post-2013 context is the emergence of the belief that a single member has the ability and indeed the right to change the movement from within, imbuing the Brotherhood with the values, strategies and structures that they see most fit.

Analysing responses to repression by looking at individual experiences and strategies reveals that, in the aftermath of the coup, the Brotherhood is growing increasingly fragmented along ideological, strategical and organisational lines. Altogether, these dynamics highlight that while the *tanzim* partly survives, the Brotherhood is more divided than ever and that its collective identity and encompassing message are being challenged by its members themselves. The disintegration of established chains of command and the reshuffling of sources of power brought about by the dimension of exile mean that the biggest challenge facing the Brotherhood comes from within its own ranks. By presenting the voices and experiences of individual members, I have shown that the movement is now deeply fragmented and mostly split between two main trends: stagnation and adaptation. These are not fixed categories, but encompass the most evident strategies to tackle the current crisis. On one side are the Historical Leadership and those who remain faithful to them, whose response to the current crisis is treating it as yet another period of hardship in the history of the movement. They therefore call for unity and patience in the face of repression, and refuse to implement significant changes to adapt to the Brotherhood's new circumstances. On the other side there are a plethora of proactive and often competing strategies to exit repression, brought together by the belief that the Brotherhood needs to implement internal reforms to adapt to the dimension of exile. Overall, the main issue is that, eight years after the coup, the Brotherhood still lacks a unified, coherent message and plan of action bringing its members together. Even more importantly, another finding is that the very values and core principles that have been at the centre of the Brotherhood for decades are now being challenged. This is incredibly significant as, even though the adaptation camp encompasses a wide range of different strategies, these overarchingly share a call for the need of drastic, internal reforms and for greater pluralism, transparency and participation within the movement. Indeed, these processes have already begun to take place and the Brotherhood is in a unique position to undergo internal change and ideological renewal, as it faces its mistakes and attempts to learn from past experiences.

These dynamics are incredibly significant; however, they are still developing and it is too early to say whether or not they will lead to tangible transformations. After all, the Brotherhood has always relied on pragmatism in the face of hardship and the post-coup situation is no different. While tolerance for independent initiatives is growing, this does not necessarily signal a direct change in the movement's structures and ideology. Yet, one lesson from the scholarship on the Brotherhood and on Islamist movements more broadly is that repression of social movements, even of those as ideologically driven and internally structured as the Brotherhood, can lead to contradictory strategies to exit a situation of crisis. Collective responses are indeed important to analyse, but this focus often overlooks the significance of contradictory strategies, discourses and tactics that emerge out of a rupture of historical experiences of political participation. The case of the Brotherhood shows that, for some movements, the potential for real change and survival might lie in the responses that get dismissed or suppressed as they do not align with the official ones. Consequently, the scholarship on political Islam after 2013 needs to take into account the changed political, social and national contexts these movements operate within, approaching their study as different moving parts of a broader Islamist field that benefits from analyses going beyond established theoretical categories.

In the case of the Brotherhood, looking at individual strategies and responses to repression unveils the scale of the dissonance between collective and individual strategies. While the Historical Leadership and those who remain faithful to them are focused mostly on survival, members belonging to the adaptation camp have a more long-term vision and, crucially, they ask what kind of organisation the Brotherhood wants to be moving forward. Those who remain loyal to the movement's historical structures and hierarchies have undoubtedly been key to its survival so far, but the individuals who push for internal reforms, new values and internal dialogue are instrumental for the Brotherhood doing more than just surviving in the future, and starting to rebuild the prestige and popular base it once had. Overall, the divergence between stagnation and adaptation strategies shows that, in order to go beyond survival, the Brotherhood might need to rethink what its purpose and message are.

While it attempts to rebuild in exile, the Brotherhood and its members remain divided, but together. There are some fundamental ideological and organisational challenges ahead, but the movement has once again proven to be incredibly resilient in the face of repression. If anything, the regional and international campaign against the Brotherhood and political Islam more broadly further legitimises its message and existence, as demonstrated by signs of organisational continuity and even renewal. Ultimately, the one message getting louder and clearer is that the Brotherhood might need to engage in a deliberate process of self-reformation in order to rebuild and evolve. Yet, none of this can be achieved unless the movement restores the at least apparent unity that allowed it to survive through decades of illegality and repression. At the end of an emotional conversation with a senior member we got to the topic on what lies ahead, and I asked if he saw anything, rather than survival, bridging the divisions that emerged after the coup. After a short pause, he reminded me that the Brotherhood is first of all an emotional community, whose members are brought together by shared values, believes and experiences, in a complex ideological and social network that is built to maximise resilience:

> Slowly, things are slow, but we will never give up. If we die, if our generation dies, they [the younger generations] will continue. All of us, we are coming back to the mother organisation. So this is a time for re-gathering, for re-grouping.[1]

Notes

1 Author Interview. London, 2018.

Glossary

'amil	active or operating member, corresponding to the highest level of membership in the Brotherhood
bai'a	oath of allegiance, taken by an individual to become a member of the Brotherhood
da'wa	the act of preaching or proselytising (literally 'the call towards living an Islamic way of life')
fulul	the remnants of Hosni Mubarak's regime
Jamā'at al-Ikhwān al-Muslimīn	the Society of the Muslim Brothers
majlis al-shura al-'amm	the General Consultative Council, the Brotherhood legislative body
maktab Al-Irshad al-'amm	the General Guidance Office, the Brotherhood's executive body
maktab idari	the highest executive body within a governorate
mantiqa	region, corresponding to the second lowest administrative unit of the Brotherhood's field apparatus
mihna	ordeal, tribulation (i.e. period of trial, imprisonment and exile)
mu'ayyid	supporter, corresponding to the lowest level of membership in the Brotherhood
muhib	sympathiser, a fan of the Brotherhood and of its ideas, corresponding to pre-membership in the Brotherhood
muntasib	associate, corresponding to the second lowest level of membership in the Brotherhood

muntazim	organiser, corresponding to the second highest level of membership in the Brotherhood
al-murshid al-'am	the General Guide, the highest spiritual authority of the Brotherhood
shu'ba	division or branch, corresponding to the lowest administrative unit of the Brotherhood's field apparatus
tanzim	organisation, the organisation of the Muslim Brotherhood
tarbiyya	upbringing, education (literally 'cultivation')
usra	family or cell, corresponding to the smallest educational unit in the Brotherhood

Bibliography

Abdelkader, N., 'Islamist parties and social movements: cases of Egypt and Tunisia', *Review of Economics and Political Science*, 4:3 (July 2019), 224–241.
Abu Khalil, H., *The Reformist Brotherhood* (Cairo: Dawwin House, 2012).
Achen, C., Bartels, L., *Democracy for Realists: Why Elections Do Not Produce Responsive Government* (Princeton, N.J.: Princeton University Press, 2017).
Al-Anani, K., 'Egypt's Muslim Brotherhood faces a dilemma: religion or politics?' *The Washington Post* (20 June 2016) www.washingtonpost.com/news/monkey-cage/wp/2016/06/20/egypts-muslim-brotherhood-faces-a-dilemma-religion-or-politics/ (accessed 23 January 2021).
Al-Anani, K., 'Rethinking the repression-dissent nexus: assessing Egypt's Muslim Brotherhood's response to repression since the coup of 2013', *Democratization*, 26:8 (2019), 1329–1341.
Al-Anani, K., 'The young Brotherhood in search of a new path', *Hudson Institute* (October 2009) www.hudson.org/research/9900–the-young-brotherhood-in-search-of-a-new-path (accessed 16 April 2020).
Al-Anani, K., 'Upended path: the rise and fall of Egypt's Muslim Brotherhood', *The Middle East Journal*, 69:4 (2015), 527–543.
Al-Anani, K., *Inside the Muslim Brotherhood: Religion, Identity, and Politics* (Oxford: Oxford University Press, 2016).
Al-Arian, A., *Answering the Call: Popular Islamic Activism in Sadat's Egypt* (New York: Oxford University Press, 2014).
Al-Banna, H., *A Collection of Hasan Al-Banna Messages* (Cairo: Dar Al-Da'wa Publications, 2002).
Allatson, P., McCormack, J., 'Introduction: exile and social transformation', *Portal Journal of International Studies*, 2:1 (2005), 1–18.
Almeida, P., 'Multi-sectoral coalitions and popular movement participation', *Research in Social Movements, Conflicts and Change*, 26 (2005), 65–99.
Ardovini, L., 'Rethinking the *tanzim*: tensions between individual identities and organisational structures in the Muslim Brotherhood after 2013', *Middle East Law and Governance*, 13 (2021), 130–149.
Ardovini, L., 'Stagnation vs adaptation: tracking the Muslim Brotherhood trajectories after the 2013 *coup*', *British Journal of Middle Eastern Studies* (2020), www.tandfonline.com/doi/abs/10.1080/13530194.2020.1778443?needAccess=true&journalCode=cbjm20 (accessed 19 August 2021).
Ardovini, L., 'The Muslim Brotherhood in Turkey after the 2013 coup d'état: organizational renewal in the diaspora', in Dalia Abdelhady, Ramy Ali (eds.)

The Routledge Handbook of Middle East Diasporas (Abingdon: Routledge, forthcoming).

Ardovini, L., 'The politicisation of sectarianism in Egypt: "creating an enemy" the state vs. the Ikhwan', *Global Discourse*, 6:4 (2016), 585–595.

Ardovini, L., Biagini, E. (eds.) 'Assessing the Egyptian Muslim Brotherhood after the 2013 *coup*: tracing trajectories of continuity and change', *Middle East Law and Governance*, 13 (2021), 125–129.

Ardovini, L., Mabon, S., 'Egypt's unbreakable curse: tracing the state of exception from Mubarak to Al Sisi', *Mediterranean Politics*, 25:4 (2020), 456–475.

'Army warns it will not allow "dark tunnel"', *BBC News* (December 2012) www.bbc.com/news/world-middle-east-20651896 (accessed 16 April 2020).

Awad, M., Hashem, M., 'Egypt's escalating Islamist insurgency', *Carnegie Middle East Center* (October 2015), 1–31.

Ayoob, M., 'Muslim Brotherhood ripe for re-radicalization', *ISPU* (15 August 2013) www.ispu.org/muslim-brotherhood-ripe-for-re-radicalization-by-mohammed-ayoob/ (accessed 14 June 2020).

Ayoob, M., *The Many Faces of Political Islam: Religion and Politics in the Muslim World* (Ann Arbor, M.I.: University of Michigan Press, 2008).

Ayyash, A., 'The Turkish future of Egypt's Muslim Brotherhood', *The Century Foundation* (17 August 2020) https://tcf.org/content/report/turkish-future-egypts-muslim-brotherhood/?agreed=1 (accessed 2 September 2020).

Ayyash, B., 'Strong organisation, weak ideology: Muslim Brotherhood trajectories in Egyptian prisons since 2013', *The Arab Reform Initiative* (29 April 2019), 1–23.

Badawi, T., Al-Sayyad, O., 'Iran and the Egyptian Muslim Brotherhood: heading towards development or simply repair?' *Al Sharq Research Papers: Political Islam Movements* (September 2018), 1–62.

Badawi, T., Al-Sayyad, O., 'Mismatched expectations: Iran and the Muslim Brotherhood after the Arab uprisings', *Carnegie Middle East Center* (March 2019), 1–6.

Baser, B., Halperin, A., 'Diasporas from the Middle East: displacement, transnational identities and homeland politics', *British Journal of Middle Eastern Studies*, 46:2 (2019), 215–221.

Bauman, Z., 'Identity for identity's sake is a bit dodgy', *Soundings: A Journal of Politics and Culture*, 29 (2005), 12–20.

Bayat, A., *Post-Islamism: the changing faces of political Islam* (New York: Oxford University Press, 2013).

Bermeo, N., 'Democracy and the lessons of dictatorship', *Comparative Politics*, 29:3 (1992), 273–292.

Biagini, E., 'Islamist women's feminist subjectivities in (r)evolution: the Egyptian Muslim Sisterhood in the aftermath of the Arab uprisings', *International Feminist Journal of Politics* 22:3 (2020), 382–402.

Biagini, E., 'The Egyptian Muslim Sisterhood between violence, activism and leadership', *Mediterranean Politics*, 22:1 (2017), 35–53.

Boykoff, J., *The Suppression of Dissent: How the State and Mass Media Squelch US American Social Movements* (Abingdon: Routledge, 2006).

Brockett, C., 'A protest-cycle resolution of the repression/popular-protest paradox', *Social Science History*, 17:3 (1993), 457–484.

Brooke, S., 'Egypt', in S. Hamid, W. McCants (eds.) *Rethinking Political Islam* (Oxford: Oxford University Press, 2017).

Brown, N., 'The Muslim Brotherhood as a helicopter parent', *Carnegie* (May 2011) http://carnegieendowment.org/2011/05/27/muslim-brotherhood-as-helicopter-parent (accessed 16 April 2020).

Brown, N., Dunne, M., 'Unprecedented pressures, uncharted course for Egypt's Muslim Brotherhood', *Carnegie* (2015) https://carnegieendowment.org/2015/07/29/unprecedented-pressures-uncharted-course-for-egypt-s-muslim-brotherhood-pub-60875 (accessed 03 March 2020).

Brown, N., *When Victory is Not an Option: Islamist Movements in Arab Politics* (Ithaca, N.Y.: Cornell University Press, 2012).

Brubaker, R., 'The "diaspora" diaspora', *Ethnic and Racial Studies*, 28:1 (2005), 1–19.

Cesari, J., *What is Political Islam?* (Boulder: Lynne Rienner Publishers, 2018).

Checkel, J., 'Social construction and integration', *Journal of European Public Policy*, 6:4 (1999), 545–560.

Clark, J., 'The conditions of Islamist moderation: unpacking cross-ideological cooperation in Jordan', *International Journal of Middle East Studies*, 38:4 (2006), 539–560.

Clemens, E., 'Organizational repertoires and institutional change: women's groups and the transformation of U.S. politics, 1890–1920', *American Journal of Sociology*, 98 (1993), 755–798.

Darrag, A., Brooke, S., 'Politics or piety? Why the Muslim Brotherhood engages in social services provision: a conversation', *Brookings* (6 May 2016), www.brookings.edu/research/politics-or-piety-why-the-muslim-brotherhood-engages-in-social-service-provision-a-conversation/ (accessed 14 June 2020).

Darwich, M., 'Creating the enemy, constructing the threat: the diffusion of repression against the Muslim Brotherhood in the Middle East', *Democratization*, 24:7 (2017), 1289–1306.

'Egypt: New Constitution mixed on support of rights', *Human Rights Watch* (November 2012) www.hrw.org/news/2012/11/30/egypt-new-constitution-mixed-support-rights (accessed 16 April 2020).

'Egypt: Social programmes bolster the appeal of Muslim Brotherhood', *IRIN* (February 2006) www.irinnews.org/report/26150/egypt-social-programmes-bolster-appeal-of-muslim-brotherhood (accessed 16 April 2020).

'Egypt referendum strongly backs Constitution changes', *BBC News* (March 2011) www.bbc.co.uk/news/world-middle-east-12801125 (accessed 16 April 2020).

'Egypt sets presidential election rules', *BBC News* (January 2012) www.bbc.com/news/world-middle-east-16785829 (accessed 16 April 2020).

'Egypt to call March referendum this week: lawyer', *Reuters* (March 2011) www.reuters.com/article/us-egypt-referendum-idUSTRE71Q11620110227 (accessed 16 April 2020).

'Egypt's Muslim Brotherhood announce new board for members abroad', *Middle East Eye* (20 April 2015) www.middleeasteye.net/news/egypts-muslim-brotherhood-announce-new-board-members-abroad (accessed 12 September 2020).

Egyptian Muslim Brotherhood's post-2011 failure', *British Journal of Middle Eastern Studies*, 40:2 (2017), 211–226.

El Houdaiby, I., 'Islamism in and after Egypt's Revolution', in B. Korany, R. El-Mahdi (eds.) *Arab Spring in Egypt: Revolution and Beyond* (Cairo: American University of Cairo Press, 2012).

El Shahed, S., 'Freedom, bread, dignity: has Egypt answered January 25th demands?' *Al Arabiya* (January 2015) http://english.alarabiya.net/en/perspective/ (accessed 16 April 2020).

El-Errian, A., 'What the Muslim Brotherhood wants', *The New York Times* (February 2011) www.nytimes.com/2011/02/10/opinion/10erian.html (accessed 16 April 2020).
El-Ghobashy, M., 'The metamorphosis of the Egyptian Muslim Brothers', *International Journal of Middle East Studies*, 37:3 (2005), 373–395.
El-Hennawy, N., 'Commission announces proposed changes to Egyptian Constitution', *Egypt Independent* (February 2011) www.egyptindependent.com/news/commission-announces-proposed-changes-egyptian-constitution (accessed 16 April 2020).
El-Sherif, A., 'The Egyptian Muslim Brotherhood's failures', *Carnegie* (2014) https://carnegieendowment.org/2014/07/01/egyptian-muslim-brotherhood-s-failures-pub-56046 (accessed 03 March 2020).
El-Sherif, A., 'The Muslim Brotherhood and the future of political Islam in Egypt', *Carnegie Endowment for International Piece* (21 October 2014), 1–44.
Elyachar, J., 'History and anthropology upending infrastructure: Tamarod, resistance, and agency after the January 25th Revolution in Egypt', *History and Anthropology*, 25:4 (2014), 452–471.
Emirbayer, M., Mische A., 'What is agency?' *American Journal of Sociology*, 103 (1998), 962–1023.
Farag, M., 'Egypt's Muslim Brotherhood and the January 25 Revolution: new political party, new circumstances', *Contemporary Arab Affairs*, 5:2 (April 2012), 214–229.
Fathy, Y., 'From confrontation to division: the Muslim Brotherhood in Egypt from 2013–2016', *Al Sharq Research Papers: Political Islam Movements* (16 October 2019), 1–42.
Feldner, Y., 'Turkey-based Muslim Brotherhood TV channels – an emerging hotbed of extremism, jihadi ideology, and antisemitism', *MEMRI Inquiry & Analysis Series*, 1431 (8 January 2019), https://bit.ly/2mju4fm (accessed 12 September 2020).
Fhamy, G., 'How can religiously inspired ideas explain violent extremism in Egypt?' *Open Democracy* (November 2020) www.opendemocracy.net/en/global-extremes/how-can-religiously-inspired-ideas-explain-violent-extremism-egypt/ (accessed 30 December 2020).
Fhamy, G., 'Resilience against violent radicalization: why haven't more Islamists taken up arms in Egypt since 2013?' *EUI Working Papers* (March 2020), 1–27.
The Founding Statement of the Freedom and Justice Party (2011), www.fjponline.com/view.php?pid=1 (accessed 16 April 2020).
Francisco, R., 'The dictator's dilemma', in C. Davenport, H. Johnston and C. Mueller (eds.) *Repression and Mobilization* (Minneapolis: University of Minnesota Press, 2005).
Freedom and Justice Party's political platforms (2011), www.fjponline.com/articles.php?pid=80 (accessed 16 April 2020).
Gamson, W., 'Commitment and agency in social movements', *Sociological Forum*, 6:1 (1991), 27–50.
George, M., 'Emotions in politics', *Annual Review of Political Science*, 3:1 (2000), 221–250.
Gerring, J., 'Ideology: a definitional analysis', *Political Research Quarterly*, 50:4 (1997), 971–972.
Goodwin, J., Jasper, J. and Polletta, F., 'The return of the repressed: the fall and rise of emotions in Social Movement Theory', *Mobilization* 5:1 (2000), 65–84.
Goodwin, J., Jasper, J. and Polletta, F. (eds.) *Passionate Politics: Emotions and Social Movements* (Chicago: University of Chicago Press, 2001).
Gorman, A., Kasbarian, S. (eds.) *Diasporas of the Modern Middle East: Contextualising Community* (Edinburgh: Edinburgh University Press, 2015).

Grimm, J., Harders, C., 'Unpacking the effects of repression: the evolution of Islamist repertoires of contention in Egypt after the fall of President Morsi', *Social Movement Studies*, 17:1 (2018), 1–18.

Hall, S., 'Cultural identity and diaspora', in Jonathan Rutherford (ed.) *Identity: Community, Culture, Difference* (London: Lawrence and Wishart Ltd, 1990).

Hamid, S., McCants, W. and Dar, R., 'Islamism after the Arab Springs: between the Islamic State and the Nation State', *Brookings* (January 2017).

Hatina, M., 'The "other Islam": the Egyptian Wasat Party', *Critique: Critical Middle Eastern Studies*, 14:2 (2005), 171–184.

Hellyer, A., 'Egypt after the Arab Spring: revolt and reaction', *Adelphi Series*, 55 (2015), 453–454, 35.

Hinnebusch, R., 'Egypt under Sadat: elites, power structure, and political change in a post-populist state', *Social Problems*, 28:4 (April 1981), 442–464.

Honari, A., 'From "the effect of repression" toward "the response to repression"', *Current Sociology*, 66:6 (2018), 950–972.

House of Commons Foreign Affairs Committee, 'Muslim Brotherhood review: main findings' (17 December 2016), https://assets.publishing.service.gov.uk/government/uploads/system/uploads/attachment_data/file/486948/53163_Muslim_Brotherhood_Review_-_PRINT.pdf (accessed 30 December 2020).

House of Commons Foreign Affairs Committee, '"Political Islam", and the Muslim Brotherhood Review. Sixth Report of Session 2016–17' (1 November 2016), https://publications.parliament.uk/pa/cm201617/cmselect/cmfaff/118/118.pdf (accessed 30 December 2020).

Jasper, J., 'Emotions and social movements: twenty years of theory and research', *Annual Review of Sociology*, 37 (2011), 285–303.

Jasper, J., Polletta, F. (eds.) *Passionate Politics: Emotions and Social Movements* (Chicago: University of Chicago Press, 2001), 267–281.

Kaminsky, A., *After Exile: Writing the Latin American Diaspora* (Minneapolis: University of Minnesota Press, 1999).

Kandil, H., *Inside the Brotherhood* (Cambridge: Polity Press, 2015).

Khan, M., 'Islam, democracy and Islamism after the counterrevolution in Egypt', *Middle East Policy*, 21:1 (2014), 75–86.

Kirkpatrick, D., Fahim, K., 'Morsi faces ultimatum as allies speak of military "coup"', *The New York Times* (1 July 2013) www.nytimes.com/2013/07/02/world/middleeast/egypt-protests.html (accessed 14 June 2020).

Kotan, B., 'An overview of Turkish-Egyptian relations since the Arab Uprising', *TRT World* (27 November 2017), www.trtworld.com/mea/an-overview-of-turkish-egyptian-relations-since-the-arab-uprising-12658 (accessed 14 June 2020).

Kraetzschmar, H., Rivetti, P. (eds.) *Islamists and the Politics of the Arab Uprisings. Governance, Pluralization and Contention* (Edinburgh: Edinburgh University Press, 2018).

Laub, Z., 'Egypt's Muslim Brotherhood', *Council on Foreign Relations* (3 December 2012) www.cfr.org/africa/egypts-muslim-brotherhood/p23991 (accessed 16 April 2020).

Lia, B., *The Society of the Muslim Brothers in Egypt: The Rise of an Islamic Mass Movement 1928–1942* (Reading: Ithaca Press, 1999).

Lichbach, M., 'Deterrence or escalation? The puzzle of aggregate studies of repression and dissent', *Journal of Conflict Resolution*, 31:2 (1987), 266–297.

Lynch, M., Schwedler, J., 'Introduction to the special issue on Islamist politics after the Arab uprisings', *Middle East Law and Governance*, 12:1 (2020), 3–13.

Mabrouk, M., 'The view from a distance: Egypt's contentious new Constitution', *Brookings: Middle East Memo* (January 2013).
Magued, S., 'The Egyptian Muslim Brotherhood's transnational advocacy in Turkey: a new means of political participation', *British Journal of Middle Eastern Studies*, 45:3 (2018), 480–497.
'MB Chairman: we seek to participate not to dominate', *Ikhwan Web* (April 2011) www.ikhwanweb.com/article.php?id=28432 (accessed 16 April 2020).
McAdam, D., *Freedom Summer* (New York: Oxford University Press, 1990).
McAdam, D., McCarthy, J. and Zald, M. (eds.) *Comparative Perspectives on Social Movements* (New York: Cambridge University Press, 1996).
McCarthy, R., *Inside Tunisia's al-Nahda: Between Politics and Preaching* (Cambridge: Cambridge University Press, 2018).
Meijer, R., Bakker, E., *The Muslim Brotherhood in Europe* (London: Hurst, 2012).
Mellor, N., *Voice of the Muslim Brotherhood* (London: Routledge, 2016).
Melucci, A., *Challenging Codes: Collective Action in the Informative Age* (Cambridge: Cambridge University Press, 1996).
Menshawy, M., *Leaving the Brotherhood: Self, Society and the State* (London: Palgrave Macmillan, 2020).
Meringolo, A., 'Egypt: Rafiq Habib and Muslim Brotherhood-Coptic relations', *Reset Dialogues* (August 2011) www.resetdoc.org/story/egypt-rafiq-habib-and-muslim-brotherhood-coptic-relations/ (accessed 16 April 2020).
Michel, R., *Political Parties: A Sociological Study of the Oligarchical Tendencies of Modern Democracy* (New York: Collier Books, 1962).
Mitchell, R., *The Society of the Muslim Brothers* (New York: Oxford University Press, 1969).
Moore, W., 'Repression and dissent: substitution, context, and timing', *American Journal of Political Science*, 42:3 (1998), 851–873.
Moss, D., 'Repression, response, and contained escalation under "Liberalized" authoritarianism in Jordan', *Mobilization*, 19:3 (2014), 261–286.
'Muslim Brotherhood tops Egyptian poll result', *Al Jazeera* (January 2012) www.aljazeera.com/news/middleeast/2012/01/2012121125958580264.html (accessed 16 April 2020).
'Muslim Brotherhood: Khairat al Shater', *Islamic Human Rights Commission* (May 2007).
'Muslim Brotherhood's Mursi declared Egypt's President', *BBC News* (June 2012) www.bbc.com/news/world-18571580 (accessed 16 April 2020).
Nugent, E., 'The psychology of repression and polarization', *World Politics*, 72:2 (April 2020), 1–44.
O'Brien, K., Deng, Y., 'Repression backfires: tactical radicalization and protest spectacle in rural China', *Journal of Contemporary China*, 24:93 (2014), 457–470.
Osman, T., *Egypt on the Brink: From Nasser to the Muslim Brotherhood* (London: Yale University Press, 2013).
Osterman, P., 'Overcoming oligarchy: culture and agency in social movement organisations', *Administrative Science Quarterly*, 51:4 (2006), 622–649.
Pahwa, S., 'Pathways of Islamist adaptation: the Egyptian Muslim Brothers' lessons for inclusion moderation theory', *Democratization*, 24: 6 (2017), 1066–1084.
Pargeter, A., *Return to the Shadows: The Muslim Brotherhood and An-Nahda since the Arab Spring* (London: Saqi Books, 2016).
Philbrick Yadav, S., 'Roundtable: future of political Islam in the MENA under the changing regional order', *Maydan* (2018) www.themaydan.com/2018/08/

roundtable-future-political-islam-mena-changing-regional-order/#journal2 (accessed 3 March 2020).

Polletta, F., Jasper, J., 'Collective Identity and social movements', *Annual Review of Sociology*, 27 (August 2001), 283–305.

'Profile: Egypt's Mohammed Morsi', *BBC News* (April 2015) www.bbc.com/news/world-middle-east-18371427 (accessed 16 April 2020).

'Profile: Egypt's Tamarod protest movement', *BBC News* (July 2013) www.bbc.co.uk/news/world-middle-east-23131953 (accessed 16 April 2020).

'Rabaa: the massacre that ended the Arab Spring', *Middle East Eye* (2018) www.middleeasteye.net/news/what-is-rabaa-egypt-massacre-ended-arab-spring-1041665049 (accessed 03 March 2020).

Roy, O. 'Political Islam After the Arab Spring', *Foreign Affairs* (2017) www.foreignaffairs.com/reviews/review-essay/2017-10-16/political-islam-after-arab-spring (accessed 03 March 2020).

Rubin, B. (ed.) *The Muslim Brotherhood in Focus: The Organisation and Politics of a Global Islamic Movement* (London: Palgrave Macmillan, 2010).

Rubin, B., *Islamic Fundamentalism in Egyptian Politics* (New York: St. Martins Press, 1990).

Said, E., *Reflections on Exile and Other Essays* (Cambridge, MA: Harvard University Press, 2001).

Samir, D., 'The Muslim Brotherhood's generational gap: politics in the post-revolutionary era', *AlMuntaqa*, 1:2 (2018), 32–52.

Sanin, F., Wood, E., 'Ideology in civil war: instrumental adoption and beyond', *Journal of Peace Research*, Anniversary Special Issue, 51:2 (March 2014), 213–226.

Schwedler, J., 'Can Islamists become moderates? Rethinking the inclusion-moderation hypothesis', *World Politics*, 63:2 (2011), 347–376.

Schwedler, J., 'Conclusions: new directions in the study of Islamist politics', in Hendrik Kraetzschmar, Paola Rivetti (eds.) *Islamists and the Politics of the Arab Uprisings: Governance Pluralisation and Contention* (Edinburgh: Edinburgh University Press, 2018).

Soage, A., Fuentelsaz Franganillo, J., 'The Muslim Brothers in Egypt', in B. Rubin (ed.) *The Muslim Brotherhood in Focus: The Organization and Politics of a Global Islamic Movement* (London: Palgrave Macmillan, 2010).

Stryker, S., Owens, T. and White, R. W. (eds.) *Self, Identity, and Social Movements* (Minneapolis: University of Minnesota Press, 2000).

Sullivan, D., Abed-Kotob, S., *Islam in Contemporary Egypt: Civil Society vs. the State* (Boulder: Lynne Rienner Publishers, 1999).

Tabaar, M., 'Assessing in(security) after the Arab Spring: the case of Egypt', *American Political Science Association* (2013), 727–735.

Trager, E. 'The unbreakable Muslim Brotherhood' (Sept/Oct 2011) www.foreignaffairs.com/articles/north-africa/2011-09-01/unbreakable-muslim-brotherhood (accessed 16 April 2020).

Trager, E., 'Think again: the Muslim Brotherhood', *Foreign Policy* (2013) http://foreignpolicy.com/2013/01/28/think-again-the-muslim-brotherhood/ (accessed 03 March 2020).

Vannetzel, M., 'The party, the *Gama'a* and the *Tanzim*: the organisational dynamics of the Egyptian Muslim Brotherhood's post-2011 failure', *British Journal of Middle Eastern Studies*, 40:2 (2017), 211–266.

Vasquez, M., 'Diasporas and religion', in Kim Knott, Sean McLoughlin (eds.) *Diasporas: Concepts, Intersections, Identities* (London: Zed Books Ltd, 2010).

'Why the Egyptian Muslim Brotherhood needs to transform in order to survive', *World Politics Review* (20 February 2018), www.worldpoliticsreview.com/articles/24221/why-egypt-s-muslim-brotherhood-needs-to-transform-to-survive (accessed 14 June 2020).

Wickham, C. R., 'The path to moderation: strategy and learning in the formation of Egypt's Wasat Party', *Comparative Politics*, 36:2 (January 2004), 205–228.

Wickham, C. R., *The Muslim Brotherhood: Evolution of an Islamist Movement* (Princeton: Princeton University Press, 2013).

Willi, V., *The Fourth Ordeal: A History of the Muslim Brotherhood in Egypt* (Cambridge: Cambridge University Press, 2021).

Willi, V., Ayyash, A., 'The Egyptian Muslim Brotherhood in 2016: scenarios and recommendations', *German Council on Foreign Relations* (15 March 2016) https://dgap.org/en/think-tank/publications/dgapanalyse-compact/egyptian-muslim-brotherhood-2016 (accessed 19 July 2020).

Wood, E., 'The emotional benefits of insurgency in El Salvador', in J. Goodwin, J. Jasper and F. Polletta (eds.) *Passionate Politics: Emotions and Social Movements* (Chicago: University of Chicago Press, 2001).

Wright, R., *Secret Rage: The Wrath of Militant Islam* (New York: Simon & Schuster, 2001).

Zaid, M., 'El Erian to political parties: win votes then discuss power', *Ikhwan Web* (June 2011) www.ikhwanweb.com/article.php?id=28713 (accessed 16 April 2020).

Zollner, B., 'Does participation lead to moderation? Understanding changes in the Egyptian Islamist parties post-Arab Spring', in Hendrik Kraetzschmar, Paola Rivetti (eds.) *Islamists and the Politics of the Arab Uprisings: Governance Pluralisation and Contention* (Edinburgh: Edinburgh University Press, 2018).

Zollner, B., 'Surviving repression: how Egypt's Muslim Brotherhood has carried on', *Carnegie Papers* (2019) https://carnegie-mec.org/2019/03/11/surviving-repression-how-egypt-s-muslim-brotherhood-has-carried-on-pub-78552 (accessed 3 March 2020).

Index

accountability 27–28, 64, 84, 107, 112, 129
activism 29, 78, 119, 124
  political 2, 105
  transnational 56, 106, 112
adaptation 15, 57, 61, 77, 85, 101–102, 105, 107–111, 113–114, 118, 121, 127, 143–144
agency 3, 5, 7–8, 14–15, 20, 23–24, 27–28, 56–57, 64, 66, 70, 72, 77, 82–83, 85–91, 96–98, 107, 111, 127, 129, 133, 142
al Azhar 119
al Banna, Hassan 14, 21–22, 78, 81, 85, 113, 122–123, 128, 124
  Brotherhood's 5th Conference 22
  ideology 21
  tarbiyya 81
al-Hudaybi, Hassan 102
al-Shater, Khairat 26, 31, 33, 35–37, 39, 43–44, 64, 74, 123
al Sisi, Abdel Fattah 1, 22, 41, 51–52, 54–56, 70, 74–75, 99, 113
al-Tilmisani, Umar 25
alienation 59, 77
approach
  gradualist 21
  revolutionary 31, 74, 135
Arab uprisings 1, 3, 10–13
  2011 uprisings 4, 20–21, 25–26, 29, 38–39, 41, 44, 52, 55, 61–62, 64, 65, 70, 79, 89, 96, 106, 119, 124
authoritarianism 1, 4, 22, 53, 79, 103

Badie, Mohamed 37, 74

change
  ideological change 121
  internal change 8–9, 15, 58, 60, 64, 66, 72, 89, 109–110, 114, 117, 130, 143
  value-change 87, 120, 125, 127, 131, 136
civil society 4, 11–12, 20, 56, 90, 103, 124
Conservative 24, 26, 29, 31, 35, 37, 39, 43, 71, 123
Constitution 32, 41, 42, 50
  'Brotherhood Constitution' 40, 51
  1971 Constitution 33
Crisis Management Committee 73–76, 100, 128
cultivation 77–78, 80–81, 83–84, 85

da'wa 4, 21, 76, 106, 113, 121–124, 127, 130, 133
  faction 26, 74, 122
deep state 13, 19, 29, 36, 38, 41–43, 49–50, 53, 71, 141
diaspora 56, 87–88, 96
discontent 11, 65, 97
  internal 13, 35, 54, 72, 83, 107, 130
  popular 13, 40–41, 51, 71, 72
disengagement 55, 57, 61–64, 84, 87–88, 110, 130, 134–135
divisions 14–15, 21, 25–28, 33, 39, 55, 57, 70, 73, 76, 91–92, 101, 113, 121, 123, 130–131, 137
  fragmentation 5, 7, 10, 14–15, 24, 27, 42, 54–55, 57, 59, 60–61, 70, 73, 77, 85, 92, 96,

99–101, 108, 119, 128, 131, 137
Wasat Party 27, 70, 72, 83, 89, 121

Egyptian Current Party 27, 35, 43, 60, 90
elections 4, 11, 22–23, 32–33, 36–37, 41, 49–51, 74–75, 82, 129
El-Fotouh, Abu 26, 28, 32, 36–37
exile 1–3, 7, 9, 12, 15, 69, 72, 74–75, 77, 92, 96–97, 99–101, 106, 117–119, 125, 127, 129–130, 135, 137, 140, 142–144
  forced 5, 14, 24, 56–58, 65, 70, 86–87, 89, 91, 103, 105, 107–109, 132–134, 141
expertise 37, 40, 43, 52, 64, 71–72, 83, 111–112, 125–126, 142
Ezzat, Mahmoud 74, 100

Freedom and Justice Party (FJP) 6, 13, 19–21, 23, 26–28, 30, 32–37, 39–41, 43, 50, 54, 56, 62–64, 71, 74–75, 85, 90–91, 108, 110–111, 124–125, 132–133, 135, 137

gender equality 40
General Guide 5, 25, 27, 32, 65, 73, 74, 81–82, 100, 102
Guidance Bureau 5, 28–32, 35, 40, 65, 82, 105, 128–129
  Guidance Office 5–6, 33, 73–74, 76, 99, 105, 118

hierarchical 3, 43, 54, 102, 120
  structure 3, 7, 20, 23–25, 28, 30, 44, 53, 57–58, 60, 65, 70, 72, 77–79, 81–83, 87–89, 99, 110, 128, 133, 136, 142
High Administrative Committee (New MB) 73–76, 99, 102, 108, 128, 133–135, 137
Historical Leadership 7, 15, 27–28, 55, 57, 65, 69, 73–77, 82, 86, 89–90, 99–100, 102–105, 107–108, 112, 118, 122–123, 126, 128–132, 134, 136–137, 142–144
human rights 29, 40

identity 1, 3, 5, 23, 122
  collective 2–4, 14, 22, 53–54, 58, 63–64, 69–70, 78–79, 81, 83, 87–89, 92, 96, 98, 102, 108, 121–123, 133, 135–136, 143
  individual 9, 81, 87, 98, 102, 134
  organisational 3–4, 6, 53, 78
ideology 2–3, 6, 9, 21, 28, 35, 72, 78, 81, 83, 85–88, 98, 105, 112–113, 119–123, 127, 130, 134–136, 143
  renewal 111, 113–114, 120, 123, 143
Ikhwan 25, 27–28, 40, 58, 63, 71, 75, 80, 91–92, 98, 103–104, 106, 109, 111, 113, 119–120, 122–129, 132, 134–135, 137
'Ikhwanization' 39
individualism 14, 23, 53, 88, 92, 108, 110
indoctrination 54, 79, 122, 124
International Organization 73–76, 135, 137
Islamic state 36, 39, 50
isolationism 44, 50, 52, 55, 72, 119–120
Istanbul 7, 10, 27, 58–59, 66, 69–70, 73–74, 90, 100, 104–106, 109, 112, 119, 124, 126, 128, 131, 133, 141
Itthihadiya 40–41

Kamal, Mohammed 74–76, 99, 137
Kefaya 40

legitimacy 40, 57, 65, 71, 75, 104
  electoral 51
  Islamic 42
London 7, 69, 71, 74–75, 100, 105–106, 119, 130, 132
loyalty 7, 37, 39, 43, 54, 64, 71–72, 79–81, 83, 89, 92, 111, 113, 117, 128–131, 137, 142

Malaysia 2, 56, 75, 123
media channels 56, 58, 103, 106–107
  Al Sharc 106
  Al-Watan 106
  Ikhwanweb 106
  Mekammelyn 106

Misr al'n 106
Rabea TV 106
mihna 4, 22, 53, 69, 79, 103, 107, 132
mobilisation 7, 56, 77, 97, 124
　political 106–107, 132
Morsi, Mohammed 1, 26, 31–32, 34, 36–38, 41–42, 49–51, 53–54, 57, 61, 69, 71, 85, 90, 99, 101, 103, 140
Mounir, Ibrahim 74, 76, 100, 106
Mubarak, Hosni 19, 21–23, 25–26, 29, 31, 33, 37, 42, 53, 55, 62–63, 71, 82, 102, 111, 132
Muslim Sisterhood 9, 137

Nasser, Gamal Abdel 22, 25, 53–54, 102

obedience 28, 54, 60–61, 66, 79, 81, 85, 108, 112, 120, 129, 133
　listen and obey 5, 24, 53, 63, 65, 79, 89, 102

participation 4, 23, 29, 31, 114, 143
　political 7, 12, 33, 97, 144
pluralism 5, 40, 54, 56, 61, 66, 114, 132, 136, 143
political Islam 5, 11–12, 71, 144
　Islamism 10–11
　　Islamist movements 1, 7, 10–11, 13, 38, 42, 70, 123, 144
professionalism 27, 39, 43, 54, 72, 84–85, 111–112, 124, 126, 130, 133, 142

Qatar 2, 56, 75, 105, 107, 123
Qutb, Sayyd 102

Raba'a 1, 24, 73, 128
　massacre 2, 12, 25, 52–53, 65, 72
Reformist 26, 29, 32–33, 35, 40, 103, 124–125, 127
reforms 2, 14, 15, 20, 24, 26, 39, 72, 75, 104, 114, 118, 122, 127, 129–130, 133, 136–137, 140, 143–144
renewal 3, 7, 9–11, 90, 100, 111, 113–114, 117, 120–124, 131, 138, 143–144

resistance 4–5, 21, 23–24, 53–54, 56, 66, 69, 102–103, 106, 118, 132, 141
revolution 19, 28–30, 32–35, 37, 39–41, 50, 63, 71–72, 90, 92, 109, 111, 119, 127, 137

Sadat, Anwar 22, 53, 102
self-reflection 6, 9–10, 14, 61, 64, 71, 87, 108–111, 125, 128–129, 131, 133, 141
Shura Council 32, 36–37, 65, 82, 99
social movements 3, 5, 7–8, 10–11, 53, 60, 76–78, 97, 118, 120–121, 144
socialisation 8, 58, 80–82, 86, 122
stagnation 1, 6, 7, 24, 30, 41–42, 57, 61, 63, 75, 82, 85, 101–102, 104–105, 107, 109, 118, 143–144
subjectivity 64, 87–88, 98
Sudan 56, 75, 131
Sudan, Mohammed 30, 36, 43, 103, 129
Supreme Council of Armed Forces (SCAF) 19, 31–33, 36, 51

Tahrir Square 31, 33, 52
Tamarod 41, 51
tanzim 6, 53, 61, 66, 70, 72, 73, 76–79, 80, 82–83, 111–112, 129, 142
　disintegration 14, 89, 127
tarbiyya 78, 81, 84, 122
trauma 8, 53, 69, 91, 97–98, 101, 108
Turkey 2, 9, 24, 56, 70, 105, 106–107, 122–123, 129, 131

university 25, 28, 85, 89, 92, 111, 119
　Cairo University 90

'wait and see' strategy 104–105, 132–133
women 25, 34, 75, 127, 130

youth 20, 24, 26–27, 29, 31–33, 35–36, 40–41, 49, 55, 73, 89, 91, 100, 104, 124–125, 127, 130, 137

EU authorised representative for GPSR:
Easy Access System Europe, Mustamäe tee 50,
10621 Tallinn, Estonia
gpsr.requests@easproject.com

www.ingramcontent.com/pod-product-compliance
Lightning Source LLC
Chambersburg PA
CBHW051615230426
43668CB00013B/2109